Men's Ways of Being

New Directions in Theory and Psychology

Series Editors
Rachel T. Hare-Mustin and Jeanne Marecek

Focusing on emerging theory in psychology and related fields, this scholarly/trade series examines contemporary ideas broadly associated with postmodernism, social contructionism, feminist theory, and other critical reformulations of psychology. We seek manuscripts that propose or exemplify new ways of doing psychology, that reconsider foundational assumptions of psychological inquiry and practice, and that offer new approaches to therapy theory and practice. Among the topics considered are the social construction of such categories of difference/hierarchy as gender, race and ethnicity, class, and sexuality; and the politics of knowledge. Of interest as well are works that examine ways in which psychology—as a body of knowledge and a cultural institution—replicates or challenges arrangements of power and privilege in society.

Rachel T. Hare-Mustin, Villanova University, and **Jeanne Marecek,** Swarthmore College, coauthored *Making a Difference: Psychology and the Construction of Gender.*

BOOKS IN THIS SERIES

Men's Ways of Being, edited by Christopher McLean,
Maggie Carey, and Cheryl White

Sex Is Not a Natural Act and Other Essays, Leonore Tiefer

Celebrating the Other: A Dialogic Account of Human Nature,
Edward E. Sampson

Seldom Seen, Rarely Heard: Women's Place in Psychology,
edited by Janis S. Bohan

Men's Ways of Being

EDITED BY
Christopher McLean,
Maggie Carey,
and Cheryl White

with a foreword by
Rachel T. Hare-Mustin

WestviewPress
A Division of HarperCollins*Publishers*

New Directions in Theory and Psychology

Copyright © 1996 by Westview Press, Inc., A Division of HarperCollins Publishers, Inc.

Published in 1996 in the United States of America by Westview Press, Inc., 5500 Central Avenue, Boulder, Colorado 80301-2877, and in the United Kingdom by Westview Press, 12 Hid's Copse Road, Cumnor Hill, Oxford OX2 9JJ

Library of Congress Cataloging-in-Publication Data
Men's ways of being / edited by Christopher McLean, Maggie Carey, and
Cheryl White.
       p. cm.
   Includes bibliographical references and index.
   ISBN 0-8133-2652-4 (hardcover).—0-8133-2653-2 (pbk.)
   1. Men. I. McLean, Christopher. II. Carey, Maggie. III. White,
Cheryl.
HQ1090.M475 1996
305.31—dc20   95-52166
                                                                            CIP

10   9   8   7   6   5   4   3   2   1

Contents

Acknowledgments

The following papers in this book have been published previously, and have been included with permission from the relevant publisher/s:

Carey, M. 1992. "Healing the Mother Wound." *Dulwich Centre Newsletter*, 3&4.

_____ . 1992. "Perspectives on the Men's Movement." *Dulwich Centre Newsletter*, 3&4.

Hall, R. 1992. "Partnership Accountability." *Dulwich Centre Newsletter*, 3&4.

Law, I. 1992. "Adopting the Principle of Pro-Feminism." *Dulwich Centre Newsletter*, 3&4.

Lee, P. 1991. "Growing Up as a Man." *Dulwich Centre Newsletter*, 1.

Smith, G. 1992. "Dichotomies in the Making of Men." *Dulwich Centre Newsletter*, 3&4.

Tamasese, K. & Waldegrave, C. 1993. "Cultural and Gender Accountability in the 'Just Therapy' Approach." *Journal of Feminist Family Therapy*, 5(2):29-45. Republished 1994 in *Dulwich Centre Newsletter*, 2&3:55-67.

Ward, B. 1992. "A Feminist Journeying in Relation to Men." *Dulwich Centre Newsletter*, 3&4.

White, M. 1992. "Men's Culture, the Men's Movement, and the Constitution of Men's Lives." *Dulwich Centre Newsletter*, 3&4.

Foreword

Men's Ways of Being represents a dramatic turning point in the debate on what it is to be a man, an insightful rethinking of the questions of men and masculinity. These brilliant and thoughtful essays do not stop with men's fears and pain, but show how men can take action to change the very demands of masculinity.

The common belief is that nature defines what it is to be a man. The prescriptions for masculinity and the restraints on men at deviating from the standards for masculinity are seldom questioned. Men do not typically ask: "In what way does my being a man influence or distort what I am doing?" Men have been regarded as true representatives of society. Being a "real man's man" means being superior to women and other lesser men, being a warrior, a hero. Since maleness has provided the standard, to aspire to its opposite is meaningless. What would "a real woman's woman" be? "A woman can only be as good as a man, there is no point in being as good as a woman", was the way Dale Spender put it some years ago. At various points in history, women have questioned the implications of the male standard and asked what it is to be a woman. Only recently, in response to the contemporary feminist movement, have men begun to question what it is to be a man.

Men's Ways of Being calls for an examination of how men maintain patriarchy by fiercely disciplining each other to be "real men", and to uphold the standard of dominant masculinity. Nothing cuts closer to the bone than men's fears about being seen as womanly, and the contempt and condescension of a patriarchal system towards traits deemed feminine. The sanctions for deviating from traditional masculinity are indeed harsh, as Laurence Carter relates in experiencing discrimination against homosexuals, and Peter Lee describes in a moving personal account of struggling with problems in school, in "manly" sports, and marriage.

As the authors in this book observe, the term "men's movement" encompasses a diverse range of orientations and activities. One orientation emphasises personal growth "men's rights", and "men's liberation", purportedly achieved by rejecting the "soft man" and the influence of women. Mothers, especially, have traditionally been regarded as having malevolent power that weakens and contaminates men. Some of men's actions in this segment of the men's movement have been troubling, not only to women, but to other men.

Many analysts have also questioned the backlash from angry white males who see themselves as victims of women and minorities who are presumably benefitting unfairly at men's expense. Others have criticised the self-preoccupation of some men's groups. As *Business Week* (a leading business magazine in the United States) observed, there's no question that navigating the shoals of masculinity today is a difficult and dangerous business. But ... "forever questing for fulfillment is one big bellyful of narcissistic nonsense" (Sept.13, 1993). In contrast to those men's groups emphasising self-enhancement, personal growth, or men's rights, other men have organised in groups that are anti-sexist and pro-feminist. These groups have challenged the oppression of women and children by men, and engaged in activities directed at countering the sexual abuse and battering of women and girls by men.

This book presents a third way for men. It acknowledges men's confusion and pain without denying men's privilege and dominance. It clarifies the issues of oppression and patriarchal power. It recognises that the notion of men's and women's parallel struggles often conceals anti-feminism. It anchors theory in personal action and the lived experiences of boys and men. It calls for men's co-operation with women and subordinated groups. And ultimately it focusses on change - the ways individuals and institutions can change that will lead to new forms of masculinity and equality among men and women. The relevance of this new framework extends far beyond merely balancing gender tasks or sex roles to include concern for those in marginalised social groups.

The social construction view underlying the analyses in this collection sees masculinity as having multiple and contradictory meanings and different significance in different social contexts. The constructionist view makes apparent the connections between the world we live in - this time and place - and the meanings we use and that use us. Ideas of masculinity are not "truths" about men's nature independent of the culture and politics of society. Dominant masculinity has maintained its power and the illusion of universality by being unexamined. It is a disguised ideology whose workings have been concealed by asserting the essential naturalness of gender differences and gender requirements. The close examination of the meaning of masculinity provided in this book offers the possibility of moving beyond the usual categories in which we think. For example, through an examination of the dichotomies in the making of men, Gregory Smith demonstrates how the idea of the "true nature" of men loses sight of the ways we impose prescriptions on what men can be. His analysis of the demands of masculinity reveals how men's sense of entitlement and men's sense of inadequacy are linked to violence in society.

The deconstruction of masculinity is a central project of this volume. Deconstruction reveals the hidden assumptions and values that underlie the meanings of masculinity. But the authors do not stop there. They go beyond deconstruction to provide alternative ideas of masculinity and the pathways to achieve them. Thus, in an outstanding analysis drawing on the work of Foucault,

Michael White shows that essentialist notions of human nature are actually ruses that disguise what is taking place. By challenging the essentialist project, he demonstrates how men can resist the pursuit of "authentic" masculinity and expose the myths that support and glorify patriarchal culture. He illustrates some processes that can be used to draw on neglected aspects of experience to develop alternative narratives of the self. David Denborough reports a similar project on alternatives for boys in his work directed at reducing violence in the schools. He elicits from boys their ideas of masculinity as "being tough" as opposed to "being yourself". Boys' understanding of their need to "be some-body" emerges through his work. That working-class boys experience school as humiliating and disempowering and turn to violence to express "being somebody" foreshadows the experiences of adult men who are not in privileged groups, described in other chapters. Another alternative narrative for being a man is provided by Rob Hall in a partnership accountability model that exemplifies the work on social justice in the "just therapy" project in New Zealand.

The fresh view of masculinity provided here will be welcomed by men who have felt uncomfortable with the demands and costs of male privilege and the brutality of institutional violence. It will also be welcomed by women who have felt bewildered by men's refusal to acknowledge men's advantaged position. It is not a men's movement in opposition to feminism. Nor is it a distancing from issues of gender that some men have used to maintain the status quo. The nuanced view of masculinity is one that is grounded in social justice and community. Christopher McLean expresses this ideal when he points out that what is problematic about male social development is not simply the restraints on men's ability to express feelings about their own experiences, but rather the restrictions on their capacity to connect with the experiences of others.

What is so different about this book is the authors' ability both to respect men and boys caught in traditional patterns of masculinity and, at the same time, address masculine experience in the context of gender inequality and dominance. They recognise that men are stressed by the competition and work patterns that traditional masculinity demands, that men feel isolated and lonely, that men are frightened by failure, that men resort to violence to solve problems. In a moving essay relating how she has come to appreciate the degree of alienation men have from others, Elizabeth Biff Ward, a leading feminist thinker and activist, calls for a shared struggle to change the dominant paradigm of masculinity.

In a collaborative effort that recursively links theory to practice and ideas to action and personal experiences, this group of gifted thinkers and practitioners provide a model for the future. Their origins are in Australia and New Zealand, but many are well known in the United States and Canada, as well as Europe, through their publications and through workshops and teaching institutes at universities and training centres. These authors push the boundaries of theories of masculinity by being self-reflexive about their own experiences, thereby demonstrating how private experience is related to public issues. Rather than reproducing problematic aspects of the dominant men's culture, such as erecting a new standard of what it is to be a white, middle class, heterosexual male, a standard that will generate its own set of exclusions, they provide a range of alternative narratives for men's ways of being. Their new ways of thinking and working provide an extraordinary vision for those who are concerned about the experiences of men and women, boys and girls.

Rachel T. Hare-Mustin
Haverford, Pennsylvania

Introduction

Christopher McLean, Maggie Carey and Cheryl White

This book is part of a process and part of a journey. It has a history, which is still continuing. We have great hopes for where the journey will lead us, but there is a sense that it has only just begun. This book is part of an invitation and a challenge extended by a group of Adelaide (South Australia) women to the men around them; a challenge to look at the effects of their ways of being as men; an invitation to care enough about these effects to want to do something about them; and an invitation to join in partnership with women, so that we can move together towards challenging injustice and building a truly humane community.

Even though it is made up of separate chapters, each bearing the name of an individual author, it is very much a collective endeavour. The ideas and understandings have emerged from the lived experience of a community of people, as they attempted to make sense of some difficult questions about our understandings of masculinity and how we can construct an understanding of gender that is a co-production between men and women.

Most of the chapters were originally presented as public seminars, dealing with issues that were very much alive in the wider community at that time. The book does not attempt to provide a comprehensive, theoretical coverage of issues relating to masculinity. Some chapters are quite theoretical, and some are more personal; the overall position of the book, however, is that theory is useful only in so far as it emerges from reflection on lived experience, and is helpful in taking action. Of course, reading other people's writing and engaging with their ideas is part of lived experience, but it should not be privileged above everything else.

Because this collection has emerged from a particular time and place, there a number of very important questions that are not covered. Indeed, the importance of these questions has become much clearer to us as a result of the processes which produced the book. Starting to grapple with issues of partnership between men and women has led us towards a clearer sense of the importance of dealing with issues of race and sexuality. These are touched on in a number of papers, and Laurence Carter deals specifically with heterosexual dominance. These issues are very much alive in our community at the present time and, if we were starting the book now, rather than finishing it, a great deal more space would be devoted to them.

One of the major understandings reflected throughout these papers is the importance of historical context. For this reason we believe it will be useful to the reader to know something about how the book came to be written.

The story begins in 1991, when "men's issues" began to make their presence felt in the relationships and discussions of a number of Adelaide friendship networks. While the men's interest in these ideas seemed to be a welcome development, many women felt distinctly uneasy, without being quite sure of the reasons for their disquiet. At this time a group was formed, bringing together people interested in looking at issues of gender and social justice as a co-production between men and women. Though loosely structured, this group became an important forum for the exploration of ideas around gender, and a reference group for issues as they arose over the next twelve months or so. As the group talked together, it became increasingly apparent that the participants all shared a sense of unease at the representations of a "new" masculinity being propounded by the men's movement at that time.

Debates over power and men's alleged oppression became widespread at this time, and these discussions sometimes turned into heated arguments which seemed to have no possibility of resolution. Women, and an increasing number of men, became increasingly concerned by the views that were being put forward and published in the name of gender justice. Couples and friends found themselves divided in ways that had never occurred before, and women have since expressed how hard those times were for them. It was hard to discuss the impact of these views and writings with men they knew and trusted, and who now seemed unwilling to consider or enter into women's experience of what was happening. There was a sense of betrayal and a real bewilderment at the men's inability to see what was so clear to the women. But, above all, there was a fear that the divide could not be bridged and that they would reach no shared ground; that if it were not possible to do this with men with whom the women felt a heart connection, how much harder would it be to do with others?

Throughout this time in Australia, media attention was being given to a couple of issues that directly highlighted some of the oppressive practices and biases against women that pervade our culture. One of these centred on comments made by an Adelaide judge in a "rape-in-marriage" court case. In summing up the case, the judge had commented: "There is, of course, nothing wrong with a husband faced with his wife's initial refusal to engage in intercourse, in attempting, in an acceptable way, to persuade her to change her mind, and that may involve a measure of rougher than usual handling." *(The Advertiser,* 12 January 1993, p.5) The other involved a series of television advertisements for beer in which "beer-men" (i.e. real men) were depicted and defined in grossly stereotyped and sexist ways, such as having a dog that pulls off a young woman's jeans with its teeth as she lies on a beach ("now that's a beer-man's dog"!). In contrast, male hairdressers, obviously stereotyped as gay, were ridiculed and portrayed as being the opposite of "beer-men".

The response by many men involved in men's movement activities was to declaim and protest about both of these issues. Letters were written and petitions signed. Public comment was made. Though clearly lauding these actions, it became difficult at times for the women who had voiced concerns at issues of sexism and misogyny appearing within the men's movement, to feel comfortable with this level of self-righteous protest, when their own concerns had not been addressed.

In order to gain some appreciation of the larger context of these issues, several of the group travelled to North America to interview various people about the men's movement there. This experience was very useful, and, after they returned, it was decided to present a series of public meetings. The intention was to present a framework for understanding issues of masculinity that addressed issues of patriarchal power and gender injustice, while providing avenues for co-operation between men and women. These presentations and workshops took place throughout 1992, and then on through 1993 and 1994.

That first series of talks was titled "Men and Social Justice", and many of them are reprinted in this book. It began with a presentation on "Gender Accountability", an issue that generated an enormous amount of interest and intense debate. The series was extremely popular, with each workshop being booked out well in advance, and many people having to be turned away. In 1993, a group of women co-ordinated a series on "Women & Social Justice", covering topics such as reproduction, disability, mental health, Aboriginality, young feminists, survivors of domestic violence groups, and heterosexual dominance. Another series, "Men's Ways of Being", was also presented, further exploring and workshopping ideas based on understandings of the socially-constructed nature of gender.

The issue of accountability, and the absolute importance of a process of engaging in respectful listening and responsiveness in this dialogue between men and women, became more and more apparent the further we entered into the conversations generated by these presentations and workshops. The availability of such a process, as well as a group of people who were willing to attempt to put it into practice, has opened the way to new possibilities of understanding between men and women. This process is really just starting. It is not only about coming to some shared understandings or appreciating the nature and extent of our different gendered experience; it is about challenging oppressive practices, and hopefully about righting some injustice.

The new understandings and heightened awareness of the complex issues involved in looking at masculinity have come out of a range of experiences that were often very painful for many people, and we want to acknowledge that pain. To challenge dominant culture is never going to be an easy task, and to challenge it within one's own community is perhaps the hardest task of all. However, that is where the challenge must take place if the need arises, for how else can we move forward with a lived understanding of new ways of being as both men and women, unless we have grappled with these understandings together.

The pain and frustration of the time outlined above has not been without its costs for everyone involved, particularly for the women. The men are just starting to realise how blind they have been to the consequences experienced by women who continually raise issues in the hope of being met half way, only to be disappointed yet again. Part of the privilege of being male is that gender issues are something that men can choose to take up or put down, depending on their other commitments or priorities - for women, however, their very lives, or those of their daughters, may depend on the struggle for gender justice.

One of the great unanswered dilemmas for men, which this book in part seeks to address, is how they can step away from positions of power and dominance, and enter into relationships of equity, both on an individual and collective level. If men are in a position of power, why would they want to give it up? If there are good reasons, how can more men be convinced of these? This book does not seek to provide any definitive answers, but hopes to contribute to the ongoing process of finding new ways of being. If one thing has become clear from the learning we have done so far, it is the crucial importance of accountability processes in forming partnerships between dominant and marginalised groups. Change needs to happen in partnership, and this partnership must recognise the realities of power differences, and find ways of addressing them.

Modern Western culture, however, finds it extremely difficult to come to grips with issues of power, accountability, and the importance of structured power differences in forming the contexts of people's lives. This society is deeply committed to the idea of individual, equal and independent agents interacting freely in pursuit of their own highest good. In this context, injustice, violence, poverty, racism, and sexism can only be understood as individual aberrations that should be rectifiable with better education and communication skills. "Culture" is seen as vaguely equivalent to "lifestyle", and concepts such as "the culture of poverty" imply that people basically choose their life situations and are responsible for the consequences.

Where our society does recognise the realities of power, it does so on an individual and hierarchical level. Individuals can be more or less powerful within organisations, for example, and can exert this power over other individuals. We have great difficulty, however, in accepting that our society is fundamentally structured by collective power differences, formed along such lines as class, race, gender, ethnicity, and sexual preference. If we are to facilitate real changes in people's lives, we need to recognise that individuals can only be understood in the context of the structured power relations that operate both within and between cultures.

Once we understand how deeply implicated our individual ideas and understandings are within our own particular cultural position, and realise how our own personal practices participate in the collective exercise of power over other groups (if we happen to belong to a dominant group), it can be very difficult to see any way forward. The realisation of our own complicity can easily lead to a paralysing sense of guilt that benefits no-one. Some theorists argue that there is in fact no way out of this dilemma. Human beings, they say, are formed and bound by culture, and there is no way of standing outside of it. Personal agency is an illusion, and liberation is an unrealisable fantasy.

Accountability structures, as presented in various chapters in this book, offer a practical way forward. They start from the recognition of the centrality of structured power differences in our society, and develop means of addressing them, so that groups that have been marginalised and oppressed can have their voices heard. It is important to recognise that this concept of accountability is primarily concerned with addressing injustice. It provides members of the dominant group with the information necessary for them to stand against the oppressive practices implicit within their own culture, of which they will often be totally unaware.

This clearly has many benefits for members of the dominant group, which are spelt out in some of the articles. In particular, working collectively, rather than as individuals, is often experienced as liberating and transformative. However, there is a real danger that this can be seen as the main reason for accountability structures. Members of any dominant group are used to being the centre of meaning. Everything is seen in terms of their needs, and processes for rectifying injustice can easily re-read as ways of helping members of the dominant group to become better people, or to deal with the distress they feel on realising their participation in injustice. While this may be an important and admirable effect, it does not do anything to shift the balance of attention away from the dominant group.

The other danger is that accountability structures may be simply seen as ways of improving "communication". They clearly provide effective ways of enabling different groups to tell their stories, and to have their stories listened to. However, they work on a fundamentally different set of assumptions than those which characterise most current attempts to improve communication. Firstly, in accountability structures, different groups are definitely not equal. A recognition of the differences in power between them is central to the process. Secondly, the existence of injustices inflicted by one group upon others is not some sort of mistake or aberration that can be fixed by listening better. Injustice is an integral characteristic of the relations between the groups, and dealing with it requires a commitment on the part of the dominant group to take action to change the basic structures that produce it. And thirdly, there is no notion of compromise. This notion of accountability is based upon the recognition that the best judges of when an injustice has occurred are those who have experienced it. For members of a dominant group to participate in accountability structures requires a clear commitment to doing whatever is necessary in order to understand the perspective of the marginalised group. There is no room for concepts of balancing competing "interests" in order to reach a compromise position.

One of the obvious concerns about such ideas is the notion that they involve a simple reversal of positions of power. Notions of "power over" are so central to our understandings that it is very difficult to envisage any other way of being. If we are giving up power over others, then this must involve them exercising it over us! The articles in this book demonstrate clearly that this is not necessarily the case. Rob Hall's paper uses the term "partnership accountability" to emphasise this point, and explores the differences between this process and the hierarchical, upwardly focussed concepts of accountability currently practised in most organisational settings.

Rob writes of his own struggle with the question of how to act, as a man, in response to gender issues raised by women, and explores men's reluctance to accept feedback about how they work. Inspired by The Family Centre model of accountability, he outlines his attempts to use these ideas in his work with violent and abusive men, in group training processes, and in examining his own work practices and relationships with colleagues. He provides a detailed outline of a number of specific instances in which experiments with accountability processes have led to very positive outcomes.

The paper by Kiwi Tamasese and Charles Waldegrave, "Cultural and Gender Accountability in the 'Just Therapy' Approach", describes the work done at The Family Centre in New Zealand, where these concepts of accountability were pioneered. It explores the question of how workers from different cultural and gender positions can protect against gender and cultural bias in their work on a day-to-day basis. The inadequacy of dominant social science models in dealing with these issues is raised, as well as the possibility that more liberative structures may be found in the practices of other, less hierarchically organised cultures.

Kiwi and Charles note the slowness of therapists to address issues of conflict amongst themselves while being very concerned to facilitate resolution in the conflicts of others. Their experience suggests that one of the benefits of instituting accountability structures is that therapeutic organisations begin to reflect and model the sorts of relationships which workers strive to facilitate in families. They also stress that the prime purpose of these structures is to address the needs of the marginalised. They are not offering some utopian vision that promises easy answers, but a process that recognises the difficulties involved, and provides a direction for dealing with them.

The understanding that emerges from these chapters is that accountability is essentially an ethical process. It brings together groups of people who speak from positions of unequal power and who have diverging experiences. It enables dialogue to occur where it has frequently been impossible, and it enables trust to be built where it has previously been broken. The collective nature of discrimination in our society is recognised, and members of the dominant group are challenged to address it collectively rather than individually. Most importantly, it allows the voices of marginalised groups to be heard when they have so often been silenced or ignored. This is not an easy process, and it involves considerable levels of vulnerability and trust on both sides. As Kiwi and Charles say: *Our concern springs from the pain of our colleagues who feel we have failed them. We trust their pain and their ability to discern the significant obstacles, and they trust us to take them seriously and act honourably. The process is a vulnerable one for both sides.*

What this process offers us is the possibility of building genuine partnerships across the deep divides of our society, and the hope that we can work effectively together to promote social justice. The editors and authors hope that this book will contribute to this process.

Postscript

Since writing this introduction, the editors of this book have become increasingly aware of the importance of racism as a pervasive factor in our own ways of thinking and working. We tried to rethink the gender aspect of our work, without confronting our own racism. As editors, we did not recognise this in our own thinking when inviting authors to write on specific topics. And it is our responsibility that the only chapter specifically dealing with issues of race and culture is written by a Samoan woman and a New Zealand man - Kiwi Tamasese and Charles Waldegrave.

We deeply regret our failure to address the issue of racism in the lives of Australian men. In Australia there is no aspect of our lives as white people which is not fundamentally based on the dispossession of indigenous people, and this certainly applies to our notions of what it means to be men.

In the time since this book was written, we have begun an attempt to engage in a number of discussions and projects in order to start looking at our part in these issues. If any readers are interested in hearing more about our struggles in exploring the issues of race and cultural differences, they can contact us direct.

PART ONE

Theory

1

The Politics of Men's Pain

Christopher McLean

The "discovery" and articulation of men's[1] pain has been one of the central, motivating forces of the men's movement since the 1970s. Men are said to be suffering under the strictures of a male culture which is allegedly as dehumanising for them as it is for women. This claim has been the cause of a great deal of controversy among men. Is it legitimate for us to even think about our own pain while women continue to experience such horrific levels of violence? Are we simply continuing an age-old pattern of male self-centredness? Or is a denial of pain one of the building blocks of masculine oppression of women which desperately needs attention if men's behaviour is to be changed?

I believe that a theoretical understanding of men's pain is of crucial importance to the current men's movement. I would also argue that a lack of such understanding is one of the main factors causing it to move in such worrying directions. The subjective experience of personal suffering is very real to many men, and the way that this pain is explained - the stories that men tell themselves about it - will largely determine the action they take in an attempt to improve their lives. For example, the claim that "men are oppressed too" places men and women on an equal footing, and removes the need to face up to fundamental power differences structured along gender lines.

A denial of male pain, on the other hand, conflicts totally with men's actual experience of themselves. For this reason, a validation of that experience is an essential part of any attempt to get men to change. This is *not*, I must emphasise, another appeal to women to "understand their men". It is a call for *men* to reach a more sophisticated understanding of subjective masculine experience, that places it firmly in the context of gender inequality, domination and exploitation. Until this happens women will continue, quite legitimately, to view any men's movement with suspicion.

The idea that a theoretical examination of masculinity has something practical to offer men and women is unlikely to be greeted with much enthusiasm. In our society, theory is regularly criticised as useless, irrelevant, or downright dangerous. Geoffrey Elton, a prominent, conservative historian, has described theory as the "intellectual equivalent of crack", which always overrides facts, and which is always wrong (Stone 1992, p.3). On the other hand, some radical critics have claimed that theory is incompatible with a truly liberative practice, which should be drawn exclusively from experience (Gatens 1986, p.14).

I believe that theory, is in fact, inescapable. Theories are basically stories we construct to make sense of our lives and to justify our actions. "Common sense", for example, is a theory which is so deeply embedded in our ways of thinking that we cease to be aware of it at all. If we want to make sense of a particular theory, we have to ask ourselves who is using it, in what context, and to what uses it is being put. Theory gives the ability to define meaning and is a source of power over people's lives. We only have to think of the effects of economic rationalism to recognise the power of theory.

I am not at all interested in theory for its own sake - but I am interested in its role in facilitating change. In this paper I argue that there are significant costs to men in participating in the structures of gender injustice, and that a theoretical understanding of these costs can play a part in convincing men of the need to dismantle these structures. To change the definition of masculinity is to change what men understand themselves to be and what they can become. There are, of course, a whole range of theories about masculinity, ranging from "common sense" notions, through biological determinism focusing on hormonal and genetic differences, to the internal, psychological theories of the self-help movement, the archetypal dualities of Jungian psychology, and the neo-Freudian theories of Lacan and company. I do not claim to be an expert on these theories, and am not going to spend any time analysing them and explaining why I do not believe that they are particularly useful to the political project of changing men's ways of being. However, I will stress again that all of these theories need to be seen in the light of who is using them, why they are being used, and what real effects they are producing on people's lives. My experience suggests that all of these theories, no matter what the intention of their proponents, tend to strengthen the notion that divisions between men and women are somehow natural, and in doing so direct attention away from structural power differences between men and women.

The theoretical approach that I find most exciting, and which is producing much of the work on masculinity emerging from universities in recent times, is strongly influenced by feminist scholarship - particularly feminist post-structuralism and socialist feminism. Very baldly put, this approach argues that human beings are social products, and that who they are is not determined by innate, universal characteristics. This is not to say that human beings are not shaped to some extent by biological factors, or that we can simply and easily change who we are, simply by deciding to. It is to say, however, that human possibilities are far more open-ended than our culture accepts, and that we cannot justify our prejudices by hiding behind biological or psychological determinism.

From this perspective, if we want to understand gender relations, we have to look at the dominant and competing stories that a particular society tells itself about men and women, the meanings and values that are given to these concepts, and how these meanings are embedded in the network of power-relations within that society. Very interesting work is now being produced by men and women from a variety of disciplines, approaching masculinity in this way - from film theory, literary studies, linguistics, cultural studies, sociology, history and women's studies. A common thread is, I think, the insight that the very act of looking at masculinity as the product of a specific cultural context is, in itself, a potentially revolutionary act. Dominant Masculinity - with a capital M - maintains its power by not being examined, and by creating the illusion of universality.

Historically, masculinity has been taken for granted, and has not been the target of intellectual examination (Middleton 1992, p.153). Men have generally addressed issues of power and identity in general terms. Philosophy, politics, history and sociology have talked about men's experience as if it was human experience. When particular values are regarded as universally valid, those who do not conform to them - women, and people from different cultures and classes - come to be regarded as inferior, which in turn justifies exploitation, oppression and exclusion.

An important aspect of being a "real man" is not thinking or talking about being a man - being completely at ease with one's masculinity, and getting on with the job of dealing with practical matters. Recent studies seem to indicate that men are largely unconscious "not only of their own motivations and the roots of their prejudices, but also of the range and variety of attitudes within their own sex". This internal blindness also results in them remaining "oblivious of the force of their united pressure on women" (Roberts 1992, p.116).

This blindness is painfully clear in universities, where male academics remain oblivious to the gender bias that is fundamental, not only to the subject matter that they look at, but to the analytical concepts that they use and the research methods they employ. These insights have clearly emerged from work done by feminist scholars over the last twenty years, and the recent work done by men on masculinity would have been impossible without the theoretical framework provided by feminist theory.

What has sometimes been called the "New Men's Studies" seeks to locate itself firmly within a feminist framework, and sees its role as challenging masculine universalism by investigating the specific nature of masculinity in particular historical and cultural contexts (Brod 1987; Kimmel 1987b). This work demonstrates that it is clearly impossible to continue talking about masculinity as if it were the same for all men. Investigations inevitably lead us to differences - between white men, black men, middle-class and working-class, country and city, gay and straight, young and old. Detailed examination of these differences allows the inaccuracies of dominant images to be exposed, as well as demonstrating their function in systems of power and oppression.

In this paper, and in my research generally, I am focusing on white, middle-class, heterosexual masculinity. This is precisely the masculinity which has sought to construct itself as the universal norm, and which is expressed in all sorts of ways throughout our culture. It is a norm which is intensely prescriptive, rather than descriptive, and it does not necessarily describe the reality of those men who belong within its cultural fold, let alone those men who are excluded. However, it does provide the standards against which men measure themselves and construct themselves, and whether they respond to this by embracing it, rejecting it, or remaining unconscious of it, they are all inescapably affected by it.

My intention in focusing on this area is personal and general. It is my own culture that I am looking at - and in a sense I am not qualified to look at any other. It is a journey of self-discovery, as I attempt to understand the forces at work in creating my own sense of self, my place in the world, and the conflicts and difficulties I experience. It is also, hopefully, a political project, in that it is men like me who hold the power in this society, and who need to change if major social improvements are to be achieved.

However, there are also dangers involved in only focusing on difference. It is important not to lose sight of what experiences are held in common. When I talk about "men" in this paper, I would like it to be quite clear that I am referring basically to dominant masculinity - but I am also not assuming that the experiences I talk about are necessarily exclusive to this group. Men and women share many experiences, as do men from different cultural and class backgrounds. However, what is different, even when there are similarities, are the contexts within which these experiences take place, and the meanings which are given to them.

For any man working in this sort of area, one of the questions that has to be dealt with is the political implications of engagement with feminism. There are very real concerns, expressed by both men and women, that men's involvement in this area is simply an attempt to maintain a position of power and to keep the focus of attention where it has always been - on men. As feminist theory has established a very important position within intellectual circles, access to it provides a potential power base. It also can seem to allow a few men to feel different from and superior to the "unreconstructed" mass of their biological brothers.

I think that these questions have to be taken seriously. It is not such an easy thing to be entirely sure about one's motives in such situations. However, it is also clear that no serious examination of masculinity is possible without engaging with feminist theory. Feminist scholars have been looking at issues of gender for a long time, and grappling with issues of sexual preference and differences between cultures and classes. Any attempt by men to study masculinity without recognising this debt and learning from the accumulated wisdom would be an act of extreme arrogance and a repetition of men's traditional rejection of women's knowledge.

Feminist theory has an enormous amount to offer men who are trying to come to terms with some very difficult problems. For example, is it possible for men, who are thoroughly enmeshed within a masculine culture, to deconstruct or dismantle their own culturally determined masculinity? Feminism offers men a very different view of themselves. A view which may be extremely confronting, but which, none-the-less, provides the opportunity to see ourselves as others see us. To get feedback about the way our attitudes and activities affect others, and to gain an insight into a very different vision of human possibilities. This is a very considerable gift that men are frequently rejecting simply because they feel threatened and afraid - and I don't think that it is necessary. Much of what I read by feminist authors continues to amaze me with its sense of deep compassion for the predicament in which men find themselves (Segal 1990; French 1991; Miles 1991).

At the moment, the "Men's Movement" seems to be defining itself largely in opposition to feminism. There is a growth industry that uses the undoubted facts of men's health problems, teenage male suicide, high rates of drug "problems", and soaring male unemployment to "prove" that men are just as badly off as women - perhaps even worse - and that they are, as the title of one recent book proclaims - *Not Guilty*. The "Men's Rights Movement", led by men like Warren Farrell, argues that men are oppressed and that feminism has gone too far. One only has to listen to any talk-back radio show to hear how receptive many men are to these ideas. Men are only too keen to see themselves as victims, and the so-called "insight" that men are suffering has been embraced by many women as well as men.

I believe that it is vitally important that an alternative theoretical understanding of men's pain and frustration is produced that allows men to understand their own experiences within a context that leads to productive changes for both men and women. Once men become aware of the realities of male violence, abuse and oppression, it is often difficult to know where to move next. If my sense of identity is deeply tied up with being a man, and men are oppressors, where does that leave me? In seeking change, am I in effect wishing myself out of existence? What does it mean to say that men are in a position of power, when I personally feel powerless? And how do I understand the pain, suffering and sense of injustice that I also experience?

Whenever the question of men's pain comes up, it is important to stress that it is not a question of **explaining** men's actions, let alone **excusing** them. According to Lynne Segal, an important part of changing dominant masculinity is to understand its contradictions and strains, and to identify where men are most vulnerable to pressure for change (1990, p.xi). My experience suggests that men are most vulnerable in the area of their inner pain - but that the way that it is understood will determine the actions that follow.

I would like to suggest that three factors are central to producing a productive analysis that validates men's subjective experience while placing it firmly within the context of structured masculine oppression. These factors are: the central role of power relationships in our society as a whole, and in masculine values in particular; secondly, the gendered nature of emotion, and its role in maintaining power differences; and thirdly, an understanding of what is actually meant by "oppression".

Numerous scholars have identified the pursuit of power for its own sake as the supreme value of patriarchal culture (French 1991, p.354; Miles 1991, pp.200-205; Middleton 1992, p.213), and it is certainly a regular theme among philosophers. According to Nietzsche, "joy is only a symptom of the feeling of attained power. The essence of joy is a plus-feeling of power" (Miles 1991, p.200). Hegel attributes the emergence of human consciousness to the "fear of annihilation by other men. To know yourself as a man is to know that other men may enslave and destroy you" (Middleton 1992, p.215).

Thus, for men, two things go inextricably together - the desire for power and the fear of failure. No alternative exists. The authors of one study in Britain concluded that "to be a loser is to suffer a terrible fate. In the course of therapy with men, we find that no matter how great their success, they are haunted by the spectre of failure. Indeed it is our impression that men are driven much more by fear of failure than by the desire to succeed" (Miles 1991, p.205).

According to Rosalind Miles, "to be a man it is not enough simply to be: A man must do, display, prove, in order to establish unchallenged manhood" (1991, p.205). All of the major sources of manhood are continually under threat or intrinsically transitory - money, political power, physical strength, sexual performance. Lynne Segal notes that men's oppressiveness comes from their "wretched fear of not being male-enough" (1990, p.317). "Making a man out of a boy" means teaching him that the human sacrifices of the power struggle are essential to the process of becoming a man. Institutions that make men out of boys involve brutalisation, physical and emotional abuse, emphasis on hardness and strength, contempt for sensitivity, delicacy and emotional intimacy. Not all boys experience such treatment, but they are all aware of its existence. Marilyn French notes that "no boy escapes the knowledge of the severities of "manliness" in our society, and those who feel they have not achieved it live with lingering self-doubt, self-diminishment" (1991, p.578).

Masculinity is often most clearly defined in terms of what it is not - what it is afraid of being - and what men most definitely are *not* is *women*. Men are men because they don't cry, don't feel, don't need, and contempt for women is a deeply ingrained characteristic of our culture. Ever since the story of Eve and the Apple, we have been extremely good at blaming women for all our problems. There is the ever-present blaming of women in cases of domestic violence and rape, blaming mothers for their sons' "hypermasculinity", blaming unemployment on working wives, and the ultimate absurdity of a member of President Nixon's cabinet blaming the 1970s energy crisis on women using too many household appliances (French 1991, p.355).

This fuels a basic masculine inner conflict, because boys' mothers have generally been the source of all the love and security in their lives. The pain of separation, as boys realise that they have to reject this nurturing female world if they are to survive as men, is, I believe, deeply scarring (Silverstein 1994). The female world remains both intensely desirable and repulsive. It offers pleasure, love and security, but also threatens to undermine the masculine facade.

The way in which this deeply dehumanising split is maintained is by dividing men amongst themselves as well as against women. Men are defined as competitors, rather than as allies. A "real man" stands alone - alone from women and from other men. He is independent and self-sufficient. Above all, he copes without complaint. We even celebrate the fact that achievement never comes without personal pain and sacrifice. We are expected to admire our leaders for their willingness to sacrifice the pleasures of personal relationships with their families, and we admire our sports stars for their willingness to train so hard and so long that they never have a moment to develop intimate friendships.

The inner split within the male psyche is enforced largely by other men. Fathers brutalise sons, in the interest of toughening them up to survive in a harsh world. Groups of boys turn on those who are different, and instil a fervent desire not to stand out from the crowd. Team sports and military service continue to be widely valued as ways of turning boys into men. They provide the essential ingredients of violent competition, the willingness to inflict pain on others in order to win, and obedience to the "captain". They are both about toughening men so that they learn to ignore pain and emotions, and both use being "like a girl" as the ultimately humiliating reprimand.

This toughening plays a direct social function. Peter Lewis, discussing his time in the army argues: "Under that regime women stood for emotions and feelings that might, unless they were outlawed, impede discipline. In the end, a trigger had to be pulled, a button pressed and it took 'men' to do it because only men were capable of surrendering all compassion." (1991, pp.185-6)

Male camaraderie or "mateship"[2] is founded on sharing the rituals of masculine identity. The exclusion of women is an integral aspect, and many of these rituals turn out to be destructive or oppressive. Binge drinking, gambling and violent sports are obvious examples. Men become close through the experience of battle, through conquering the wilderness, hunting, and even through the ritual of pack rape. This kind of male friendship, however, is extremely fragile. If unspoken limits are transgressed or rules broken, then the full fury of male condemnation rapidly descends upon the head of the guilty party.

I remember, at the age of five, in my first year of primary school, observing a large group of boys running between the classrooms. One broke off and called out to me to "come and chase the crewcut!" Being somewhat naive, I remonstrated with him, explaining that it was not right to chase someone just because they had a funny haircut - and the whole group stopped, turned around and started chasing me. In absolute terror, I took refuge in the big girls' classroom with my older sister. But I lived with the humiliation of having to resort to such measures, and a lasting realisation that it is dangerous to speak out against injustice

The contempt for women implicit in masculinity is demonstrated in all sorts of ways. Where men are ridiculed in cartoons and on television, it is usually because they are under the control of women. To diminish a man, it is only necessary to draw him doing the dishes, sewing, or wearing an apron; and most of the worst forms of ridicule and abuse applied to men involve comparison with women. If we, as men, want to question the hostility to women implicit in masculinity, we only need ask ourselves how we would feel being required to wear women's clothing to work or to the local pub (French 1991, p.580).

The acceptability of women wearing men's clothes is often held up to demonstrate that women are freer than men. I think that it is more accurate to say that women can wear men's clothes because of the high status of masculinity, while men cannot wear women's clothes because of the inferiority they imply. In addition to this, it is generally expected that women wear men's clothes in such a way as to accentuate their sexual attractiveness in men's eyes. When women are considered to actually look like men, it often results in ridicule or abuse.

Probably the most crucial way of dividing men amongst themselves is through the taboo against homosexuality. Homophobia is a powerful weapon for preventing challenge to masculine ways of being. Theorists of masculinity have shown how: "The homosexual - heterosexual dichotomy acts as a central symbol in all rankings of masculinity. Any kind of powerlessness, or refusal to compete, among men readily becomes involved with the imagery of homosexuality." (Carrigan et al, 1987 p.86) Most men know full well the fear of being labelled a "poofter"[3] at any sign of difference, particularly in the expression of affection or weakness.

This problem is of direct relevance to the "men's movement". The existence of another "men's movement" - gay liberation - has often been seen as an embarrassment and a threat. For a long time, it was feared that any identification of the two in the public mind could discourage the participation of heterosexual men, and provide ammunition for a hostile press. Consciously or unconsciously, the presence and contribution of the gay liberation movement were largely ignored. Parts of the men's movement today include "challenging homophobia" as one of their goals, and aim to be "gay affirmative" in their activities. However, I do not believe that anything like full recognition is given to the fact that: "Gay activists were the first contemporary group of men to address the problem of hegemonic masculinity ... [and] were the first group of men to apply the political techniques of women's liberation, and to align themselves with feminists on issues of sexual politics." (Carrigan *et al* 1987, p.83) Heterosexual men have, as yet, scarcely begun to address the issues of heterosexual dominance and their own homophobia that would enable them to enter into a productive dialogue with gay men and gay organisations.

One of the central paradoxes of masculinity is that while men, as a group, clearly hold the reins of power, the majority of men experience themselves as powerless. During the twentieth century there has been an increasing centralisation of all aspects of life, and men have experienced a loss of autonomy and control over their lives totally at odds with traditional masculinity (French 1991, pp.305-6; Kimmel 1987a, p.148-9; Pleck 1987, p.28; Roper & Tosh 1991, pp.18-19). Most men, if they are lucky enough to have a job, work in some sort of institution, which is hierarchically structured and which generally allows them little sense of personal agency. According to Marilyn French, "institutions are created to centralise, harness and manifest power over others" (1991, p.323). They appeal to individuals by promising personal power - but these promises are largely illusory. The power is lodged in the institution, not in any particular person.

It is obvious that many men experience significant amounts of suffering in their lives - through poverty, class and racial oppression and homophobia. The important question here, however, is whether even those men who appear to be most privileged within patriarchy also suffer as a result of dominant definitions of masculinity. This is a strategic question, as much as anything else, because it determines whether these men are simply the enemy who are having a wonderful time at everyone else's expense, or whether they too have something definite to gain by relinquishing their power and changing their ways.

According to Marilyn French, who looks at this question in some detail, "the ironic truth is that a religion of power is a religion of fear, and that those who worship power most are the most terrified creatures on earth" (1991, p.357). Power is personally costly in that it narrows the experience of life into the pursuit of something that can never be achieved. No-one ever has enough power because no-one is ever secure from threat - particularly from one's closest associates.

The pursuit of power and control denies men love and sensuality, and leaves only desire and the excitement of conquest. Men are generally distant from their children and partners, and their working lives are dominated by competition and mistrust. The higher men go on the ladder of success, the harder it is for them to trust other men and to make real friendships. "The pleasures of relaxed, anonymous movement through the world, of easy conversation with others, of trust and love as part of a community, are impossible for them" (French 1991, p.339). The world's most powerful men, like Stalin and Hitler, lived in constant terror of assassination; we can all observe our elected leaders aging rapidly in office, as they look over their shoulders for the next challenger. Many large corporations are ruled by overt confrontation and humiliation, right up to the highest levels. One American executive has written about how the top managers of ITT were subjected to monthly interrogation sessions, where they had to submit to public humiliation, and act as if it were a joke (French 1991, p.334).

All of the institutions within which men lead their lives are implicitly or explicitly hierarchical. From the family, with the father as the (at least nominal) head, through schools and sporting teams, the church, business, industry, trade unions, politics, law, crime, prisons, hospitals, medicine - they all encourage striving for success, which may involve stepping on the shoulders of one's friends and associates. The struggle and the structure tend to become all absorbing, and men are encouraged to regard all other parts of life as secondary.

Men's working lives are a permanent battlefield, with countless casualties, whose failure only serves to increase the prestige of those who succeed. The myth is maintained that everyone can be winners if only they try hard enough, and every man who fails believes it is because he is not good enough, rather than because the system is inherently wrong. Clearly, not every man is a winner, and most men's lives are ruled, not so much by an active desire for power and success, but by the inner knowledge of having failed as a man, and the fear of being discovered.

It's well known in all sorts of areas - including universities - that it is not always advisable to do one's best, for fear of threatening one's superiors. Good work may result in punishment rather than reward, and institutions are full of men, "disappointed over lack of advancement, and resigned to half-hearted, half-minded work that seems to be all that is wanted from them" (French 1991, p.334). Attempts to improve procedures or introduce something new are often met with suspicion, and loyalty to an institution is likely to be met with betrayal, as employees are abruptly dismissed with a note in the pay packet.

One of the real problems of dominant masculinity is that it is riddled with contradictions. It is made up of a host of stories and expectations, many of them quite incompatible. On the one hand, we are taught to regard power and success as the supreme value, but on the other hand, when we leave work, we are expected to be able to go home and enter into happy, equitable relationships with our partners and children. We are taught to despise women and to desire them. We are taught to fear other men as competitors, but to worship the idea of mateship[2]. The attempt to integrate these contradictions requires men to perform bizarre operations on their lives, and to develop a form of splitting that has high personal costs.

It is, in fact, this process of splitting which forms one of the fundamental characteristics of dominant masculinity. That is, the ability to maintain discrete islands of consciousness that are mutually incompatible, while being completely unaware of the contradictions involved (Middleton 1992, p.152). We can see this around us all the time. Men who insist that they love their wives and children, but continue to abuse them. At an extreme level we can see it in Nazi concentration camp commandants who went home each evening, with a clear conscience, to apparently happy family situations (Koontz in Middleton 1992, p.114).

This question of "splitting" brings us to the problem of emotion. Much of the men's movement literature on masculinity focuses on men's emotional illiteracy. We are, apparently, out of touch with our feelings, which we need to reclaim and celebrate (Mason in Middleton 1992, p.119). Men are not allowed to express their vulnerable and nurturing emotions, and are consequently psychologically and socially deformed. This is often viewed as the mirror image of women's experience - which is characterised by a prohibition on the emotions associated with personal power and assertiveness. This model actually allows men to be defined as worse off than women, as the "feminine" emotions are defined as most conducive to the experience of fulfilling human relationships, which are themselves assigned the highest possible value.

There is, I think, some truth in this picture, and it may seem very close to what I have just been talking about. However, there are some serious problems associated with it. In particular, there generally seems to be little awareness of the gendered power structures within which emotions are constructed and expressed; and this model also lends itself to the belief that all that is needed is personal, internal change by individuals, probably through some form of individual or group therapy.

It is certainly true that the public display by men of emotions, other than anger, is generally judged very negatively in our culture. The process of turning boys into men, has, historically, been one of systematic abuse, both physical and emotional, designed to teach boys not to show most emotions, except in certain ritually prescribed circumstances, and if possible not to feel them. Boys are taught to fear intimacy and self-revelation, as the consequences are generally pain and humiliation at the hands of other boys, and to hate whatever causes them to experience fear (French 1991, pp.292-3).

However, it is crucial to recognise the function that this emotional brutality has in the maintenance of power structures - whether based on gender, class or race. We come from an incredibly violent and expansionist culture, and warfare has played a central role in the history of our society. War continues to be a favourite metaphor, in business, sport and politics, and the media loves to talk of the "war of the sexes". Some in the men's movement want to insist on the value of the "warrior archetype" - something which I believe, in our culture, with our history, is entirely misplaced. It may be perfectly legitimate for people from other cultures - Maori, Samoan, Aboriginal or Native American - to celebrate their warrior heritage, but for us to use these traditions to justify our own obsession with "warrior energy" is inappropriate and smacks of cultural appropriation.

Emotional numbness or indifference is a powerful weapon - it allows a person to inflict pain on others without being affected or swayed. Some important studies have shown how the power wielded by soldiers stems from their lack of self-reflection and empathy, while their training involves dehumanising and demonising the enemy. It is important to recognise that this is only an extreme form of general masculinity (Holloway in Middleton 1992, p.190). Our culture encourages men to see women as "the enemy" - always seeking to control us and emasculate us. Women generally either don't understand that "a man's gotta do what a man's gotta do", or actively conspire to prevent him from doing it.

Men are not simply victims of distorted emotional roles. Their pain and suffering are real, but they also hide feelings in order to withhold information which might give others power over them. The absence of intimacy serves two important purposes: it allows participation in the struggle for power, which is associated with success in life, and it protects men from the feedback that might reveal their inadequacies (Middleton 1992, p.121). While women are taught to desire emotional intimacy, and men to withhold it, men are actually in a position of power - they have something women want, and certainly won't give it away for nothing. In a culture that values power above all, and fears powerlessness, this is in itself a source of contempt for women - men believe that women can't help themselves; they give themselves away emotionally and can therefore be exploited. As Henry James writes of such a relationship in *The Golden Bowl*: "It was her nature, it was her life, and the man could always expect it without lifting a finger" (Middleton 1992, p.196).

The role of men's pain and emotional silence in the perpetuation of dominant masculinity is clearly shown in the area of aging and sexuality. Medically, we know that from the age of 40 the production of testosterone falls steadily, and that by the age of 55 a third of all men are incapable of strong and regular erections. More men consult their doctors about impotence than about anything else, but each suffers in silence and alone (Miles 1991, p.252). Sexual performance is such a fundamental part of masculine identity that when it starts to fade men feel themselves literally unmanned (Tiefer 1987, pp.165-184). Age inevitably destroys the rock-hard erection which figures so powerfully in the metaphors of phallic power, yet we are not taught to expect it or to talk about it. Open discussion of the realities of male sexuality threatens the maintenance of the ideology of masculine invincibility. As Rosalind Miles says: "The insistence that impotence must be cured by medical or surgical treatment absolves [men] from having to contemplate the problem of what identity [they] might have outside [their] genital reality." (1991, p.253)

It is simply not true that men are not intensely emotional, nor that they do not desire love, nurturing and affection. However, the values and power relationships inherent in dominant masculinity make it difficult for such feelings ever to be expressed in clear, open and equal ways. Men are taught to hide their emotions from themselves, and not to admit to their needs. Olga Silverstein (1994) has written movingly about the process of separation between mothers and sons, which plays such an important part in separating men from a direct and uncomplicated relationship with their feelings. However, here again we meet the complexity and contradiction of masculinity. Men's emotional distance does not mean that they do not have feelings, nor that they do not have them catered to. It is one of the bitter ironies of patriarchy that men, who now see themselves as so emotionally deprived, actually have their emotional needs continually catered to by women.

In our culture, girls are raised from a very early age to be aware of, and take care of, the emotional business of life. Boys come to experience emotional nurturing as an unquestioned part of life, without even recognising that it is there (Middleton 1992, p.181). Mothers, wives, sisters and daughters continuously orient themselves around fulfilling the needs of their fathers, husbands and sons *in advance* - without having to be asked, allowing the appearance of manly independence and control that would be shattered if men had to admit their needs and ask for what they were actually being given. An example of women's efforts to prop up the male ego is provided by sexuality research. A number of studies show that, when women fake orgasm, they are almost invariably doing it to save their partner's (rather than their own) feelings of adequacy (Berg 1990, p.168). The fact that men may not *feel* nurtured says more about their awareness of what is happening than about the activities of the women in their lives.

A note of caution here: this is one area where it is clearly dangerous to talk simply about "men". The emotional constitution of white, Western men, brought up in a highly competitive, individualist culture, cannot be extrapolated to other cultures with different values. There are also some interesting studies that indicate that the stereotypes held by middle-class culture of working-class men - that they are even more emotionally brutalised than nice middle-class boys - may be far from accurate (Walker 1994). And of course there is the example of gay male culture which, in dealing with the suffering associated with HIV-AIDS, has demonstrated that intimacy, nurturing and emotional supportiveness is far from impossible for biological males.

Stereotypes of men's emotional lives can also contribute to women's invisibility. The flip-side of men's supposed emotional isolation is the idealised picture of the wonderfully close and supportive friendships that women apparently experience, simply by virtue of being women. In actual fact, much of the memory-work done by feminist scholars suggests that women have often experienced extreme feelings of isolation (Crawford *et al.* 1992, p.189). Girls are kept isolated - and "safe" from male violence - at home, as are adult women in the suburban nightmare of the nuclear family. It is not so long ago that the dominant stereotype of women was that they were incapable of having real friendships with each other, because they would always be competing for men's attention. Women's connections are something that they have struggled for, against the pressures of masculine control, and the women's movement has played a vital role in this. To regard women's relationships as somehow "natural" is to deny the importance of their struggle to achieve them, and to deny the possibility of men doing the same.

It is also important to recognise that emotions are not unequivocally good and liberating. They are not automatically an expression of some inner, authentic being - in fact, they are highly manipulable. In our own society politics is very much about emotions, and talking about issues in a reasoned manner is recognised as spelling electoral death. Recently, a visiting American guru of "power selling" announced that advertising is not about selling products, but about selling emotions (The Business Report, *Radio National*, 21/7/93). Highly sophisticated techniques are now used to test advertisements. Audiences are linked up to a battery of machines which measure galvanic skin responses, and laser beams are focused on each person's pupil to see exactly what images are being watched, millisecond by millisecond, and to register pupil dilation as an indication of emotional reactions to particular images.

I am not trying to downplay the importance of emotion, or the reality of men's subjective sense of emotional deprivation and suffering. I think that these experiences are real and of enormous significance. The point I am trying to make is that they do, however, need to be put in context. The simplest way of expressing this is to say that men's pain is not the *cause* of their abuse of power, but that the structured abuse of power, *requires* men to be emotionally abused and desensitised. Masculinity consists of those personality traits that are necessary for the preservation and perpetuation of an unjust and oppressive system. It creates the emotional splitting and illiteracy that then allows men to abuse others, as well as being susceptible to emotional manipulation by those in positions of power. While not all men benefit equally from the system, they do provide its shock troops and rank-and-file enforcers. They provide cannon fodder for the factories, offices and unemployment lines, and without their participation and compliance the system could not continue.

If this analysis is accepted, then it is clearly not enough to try to change the problems associated with dominant masculinity through personal, emotional change. Personal work is clearly necessary to enable men to recognise what is happening in their lives - to own the pain they feel and are inflicting on others. However, without a recognition of the ways in which many of our fundamental cultural values and institutional structures are perpetuating this pain, and that particular social groups are profiting from it, then the potential for truly productive change is very limited.

This, finally, brings me to the problem of "oppression". It is clear - at least to me - that men suffer as a consequence of conforming to the values of dominant masculinity. Even those who seem to benefit most do so at enormous personal cost. To argue otherwise is to accept patriarchy's lies - that the pursuit of power, to the exclusion of all else, can lead to happiness and a sense of personal fulfilment. I don't believe it, and all the studies I have seen indicate the opposite. But does the recognition of this fact entitle men to regard themselves as "oppressed"? My answer is a definite "No"!

Peter Middleton has defined power "as the possibility of affecting others, effects that can be bodily, emotional, or cognitive ... Power is a network of possibilities into which any individual may be able to place him or herself, but the entry restrictions are complex and exclusive" (1992, p.151). In this context, "oppression" is the occupation of strategic points in this network of power by a particular group, which then uses its position of dominance to exclude, exploit and demean people who do not conform to its entrance requirements.

"Oppression" refers to a relationship between groups, and institutions are those bodies that structure and control the crucial points in the networks of power, where people meet and interact with each other. There is no doubt that the most powerful institutions in our society are occupied, at the highest levels, almost exclusively by men. Where women are included, it is only after demonstrating allegiance to the institution's values, and it is generally true to say that the more women there are in an institution, the lower its status in the overall hierarchical structure of society (French 1991, p.316).

If "oppression" refers to a relationship between groups, and men are oppressed, where is the group that is oppressing them? One favoured answer is that men are oppressed by institutions - but institutions are simply the means of organising relationships between people, in the interests of a dominant group. So, the argument is circular - men are oppressed by institutions, which represent the interests of men - so men are oppressing themselves. I want to make it quite clear that I am talking of *gender based* oppression. Men clearly oppress other men on the grounds of class, race and sexuality. However, it is meaningless to argue that men are oppressed on the grounds of their gender. As I have already said, it is perfectly legitimate to argue that men *suffer* as a result of conforming to gender stereotypes, as long as it is also recognised that this suffering contributes to the maintenance of systems that actually oppress others. This is particularly important as the claim that men are oppressed seems mainly to be used to disqualify women's claims of oppression, and to justify men not taking responsibility for their own actions.

The reason that this question arouses such strong feelings is that it involves questions of identity and moral value. The ability to claim membership of an oppressed group gives moral weight to one's claims, and confers an identity and history of which one can be proud. At conferences dealing with social change, people generally seek to identify themselves in terms of their oppression - and it is this that confers the right to a voice in such forums (Middleton 1992, p.145). It is difficult, as a white, middle-class, heterosexual man from a developed country that is oppressing its indigenous population, to feel that I have a right even to be heard - unless it's because I'm unemployed, or a single parent. But I don't think that this is the way to go. Men don't *need* to see themselves as oppressed to have their experiences validated.

I would argue that there is a powerful and just position where men from the dominant culture can stand, and from which action can be taken - and that position is the willingness to listen! To enter into relationship with those who have suffered at the hands of male oppression, to listen and to find out how one's actions have affected, and are affecting them, and then to act from this understanding. To me, it is the beginning of reestablishing community - breaking down the isolation that comes from our collective insistence on independence, superiority and control.

It does not mean *handing over* "control" - it means forming relationships which are *not based on control*, but on a desire for mutuality and understanding. Men's fears in this area are very real - we have been taught that we are either winners or losers - if we are not in charge, we are under the thumb, and the result is humiliation and abuse. Letting go of this can be a very scary business.

But my experience has been that when one demonstrates a willingness to listen, then the response is usually favourable. I don't believe that women are out to turn the tables and replace one oppression with another, just as I don't believe Aboriginal people are out to take our back yards. In actual fact, a preparedness to listen generally results in a being listened to as well!

The final thing I would like to say goes right back to the beginning, and the question "why study masculinity?" I believe that gender is a much more radically destabilising concept than men have generally realised. We are not really aware of the extent to which our concepts of ourselves, of others, of the entire world, are constituted by our concepts of masculinity.

When we take seriously the project of deconstructing masculinity, it can be profoundly disturbing. We have to start questioning our most dearly held attitudes - about relationships, love, sexuality, desire, success and strength - everything that goes to make up our sense of identity. Men's groups have a role to play in this - to subvert the competition and distrust that is fundamental to patriarchy, and to collectively examine the construction of our gender identity. However, without an active commitment to seeking connection with, and feedback from, those groups who have traditionally suffered at the hands of dominant masculinity, there is a very real danger that we will rest on the laurels of our own good intentions, and replay old patterns of which we are simply not aware.

The general conviction that men have to achieve their liberation on their own, without reference to women, is, I believe, potentially disastrous. Men argue that women had to form their own women's groups and that men need to do the same. This fails to recognise that men have *always* been separate from women, and that this separation is fundamental to traditional masculinity. Male bonding has always involved the exclusion of women, and this exclusion has been based on superiority, exploitation and a deep, unspoken fear of women's difference.

My experience suggests that many men come to the men's movement suffering deeply from the effects of broken relationships. Often they believe they have been unjustly treated by their partners and are grieving for the loss of their children. The separation from probably the only source of emotional closeness they have known as adult men is subjectively experienced as an act of violation. I sense that at least some of the desire that men experience to bond in all-male groups is a desire to form a collective defence against the emotional power of women.

Women are still being defined as the enemy, though using different language. It is important for men, if they are to make sense of their pain, to recognise that it is quite different from that of women *in terms of its social context*. Men have been brutalised, desensitised and pitted against each other in order to turn them into oppressors - and women have been the target of much of that oppression. Men need to seek reconciliation not only with their brothers, but above all with their sisters, who have been abused for so long.

The greatest possible threat to patriarchy would consist of men being willing to truly listen to women, learn from them and follow in their footsteps. This does not mean running to them for nurturing and consolation. Men have always done that, and it is there that men's groups can fulfil their most important function. In cutting themselves off from women, however, men are isolating themselves from a wealth of wisdom and experience in a way that is deeply impoverishing to men personally, and destructive to the world at large.

The current wave of the women's movement has been engaged in the struggle against sexism for the last twenty or more years. Women have been exploring the meanings of masculinity and femininity and thinking deeply about a whole range of associated issues. For a men's movement to think that it should start the process right from the beginning, rather than being willing to follow women's lead, is an act of arrogance or blindness. The men's movement needs to address questions of accountability to women as a matter of urgency. A failure to do this can only be interpreted as maintaining two of the fundamental planks of patriarchy - the denial of women's knowledge and authority, and the maintenance of "separate spheres".

It is also crucial to recognise that masculinity is not only contained within individuals - it is deeply entrenched in the most powerful institutions of our society. The police, the military, political parties, the legal system and the media, all exhibit and enforce the characteristics of patriarchal masculinity. Big Business, universities, schools and sporting clubs all inculcate the masculine value of survival of the fittest, and select for success those who conform. As we see how culturally specific and collective our precious "individuality" is, it becomes clear that personal problems need social as well as personal solutions. Our relationship difficulties cannot be separated from the way that men collectively act in the world at large, and the problems of the world at large cannot be separated from men's internalised values.

Any fundamental change in men's thinking will inevitably involve confrontation with these institutions. Refusal by a business executive to focus exclusively on profit could lead to loss of promotion or dismissal. Refusal by a soldier to follow orders could lead to his death. Refusal by a student or employee to conform to expectations could lead to economic marginalisation and poverty. These are realities which all men involved in the struggle against patriarchy will have to face - but if we do so in solidarity with women, rather than seeking to recreate and celebrate some "ideal" masculinity, then we all stand to gain.

Notes

1. When I talk about "men" in this paper I want to make it clear that I am not excluding myself from the issues I discuss. At times I shift into talking about "we", when I want to emphasise that I am including myself in the collectivity of dominant masculinity. The use of "we" does not imply that I am assuming that only men are reading this piece - it refers to the subject of the book, not to its readership.

2. Australian colloquialism for male friendship (i.e. buddy) with a connotation of excluding women. The concept of mateship has particular references to men's friendships developed during war and other situations of hardship.

3. Australian colloquialism for a gay male, i.e. faggot.

2

Dichotomies in the Making of Men
Gregory Smith

Throughout Western history, there have been a number of dichotomies which have been very powerful in shaping our images of masculinity. These dichotomies are neither inevitable nor intrinsic, but are constructs which have become pervasive and compelling. They operate both as restraints against changes men might make, and as an implicit knowledge base to the way men construct themselves. These dichotomies or 'splits' in men's shaping of themselves can be seen to have informed many of the injustices which have occurred through the centuries and much of the sense of alienation and confusion which many men experience today. They also act to perpetuate many of the destructive and unfulfilling ways of operating which are so characteristic of men in our times. They tend to be so pervasive as to be often unquestioned and almost unnoticed as guiding principles. Instead, they often are taken as part of the 'nature' of men.

The implicit assumptions we hold tend to guide our view of what is 'natural'. Recently, the idea of a 'true' nature of men or finding a 'true masculine' has been widely considered in the so-called men's movement. This idea also seems to lose sight of how we construct masculinity, and would seem to impose another prescriptive dichotomy, of 'true' and 'false' men, to carry on a long history of such prescriptions. All such dichotomies can be called into question.

In raising any dichotomy or any distinction, it can often seem, after a while, that the distinction is compelling and 'natural' rather than one of many possible distinctions or combinations of ideas. Making any dichotomy involves the making of two categories, and the making of these categories will involve highlighting some distinctions and disattending to others. To distinguish between two people we could use many dichotomies as a guide (male/female, short/tall, rich/poor, member of dominant culture/marginalised culture, etc.). Each category draws our attention to a different way of thinking of them. The whole dichotomy of masculine and feminine, or even men and women, can be called into question in this light. This may seem an inevitable and compelling distinction, but it can hide more than it highlights. Who could imagine drawing up a list of adjectives which described male qualities and a separate list for female qualities and hope in any way that it was definitive? To consider any quality (e.g. strength, openness, aggression, caring) as exclusively male or female is clearly a social or cultural judgement. John Stoltenberg (1989) talks about how even biologically there are blurred lines dividing men and women, that in fact there can be seen to be something of a biological continuum and what he suggests should be celebrated is each person's uniqueness rather than a strict categorising into male and female. Clearly there are some physical differences and biological differences which do lead to unquestionably different experiences for men and women, such as the experience of childbirth. However, these differences do not necessarily dictate social and behavioural differences. So, while speaking of men and women as separate categories may be helpful around some issues, I think it is important to hold in mind that even this is not always a helpful categorisation.

Each of the following dichotomies has been, I believe, very powerful in the shaping of men and masculinity in Western society. Each has tended to construct men's thought and action in ways which often feel normative and compelling, rather than being simply one of a potential myriad of choices.

Rational versus Emotional

The dichotomy between rational and emotional is the first to be discussed. Rationality has always been seen in Western culture as being more important and more valuable and as being more male. Emotions and emotional qualities have generally been seen as being 'lower', less valuable and as associated with being female. (While this has been often commented upon, I have been particularly informed here by Winnie Tomm's outline of a history of these ideas in relation to women [1987], and James Nelson's [1992] analysis in relation to male sexuality and spirituality.) Men are seen as being above emotions, and it is considered that they **should** be above emotions. Emotions in many ways have been written out of men's life in much of the philosophy of Western culture. This proceeds from Greek thought in which male consciousness was usually associated with the transcendent and female consciousness was associated with nature, with the body, or with matter. Men were seen as having a capacity for transcendence, via rationality. Men in this view should be above matter, above nature, and above the world, which was more associated with women.

Indeed, rationality was seen as being the essence of human nature. It was the rational that lifted people above the animals, and this was seen as being essentially male; women were seen as rationally deficient. This continued through the Middle Ages where, for example, Aquinas agreed with Aristotle in emphasising rationality, but said that the main reason for using rationality was for God's purposes and that men were more capable of this and women much less so. Obviously these viewpoints are misogynistic and have very real negative effects for women, but the focus here will be on the impact on men and men's views.

This focus on the rational was strongly reinforced by Descartes. His central saying *cogito ergo sum*, or "I think therefore I am", identified rationality as being the highest value, implicitly in relation to men. The body was seen as being a complicated mechanism; the emotions were largely disregarded. Even Kant continued this dualism. Kant's influence can be seen in some ways to have laid groundwork for later constructivist thought, as he saw the world as being projected from internal constructs rather than being externally objective. He spoke of the 'fair sex' and the 'noble sex' where virtue for women was founded on beauty, and virtue for men was founded on reason. In this view, women are essentially identified with diversion and men with the capacity to be noble by reason and the transcendence connected with this.

Universal versus Particular

These ideas lead to a second dichotomy: the universal versus the particular. Many of the ideas associated with rationality link the rational with a transcendent position, suggesting one can stand above the particularities of interaction to see some universal truths. Much Western religion focuses on the eternal rather than the temporal. Generally speaking, there has been a powerful hierarchy constructed, with God at the top of the hierarchy, and then men, followed by women, nature and the rest of creation. In this view, there is an all-seeing, all-powerful, all-knowledgeable God, able to have an overview of universalities and having power over men. Men are next in the order, having some capacity to connect with universal truths and universal principles, and being in a position of power and control over women. Women, in turn, are seen as less able to connect with these universalities and consequently less powerful. These ideas have been a common thread through most Christian and Western history. In more recent times, they have been espoused by scientific and positivist world views, where the emphasis has been upon uncovering universal truths. The scientific or positivist view would postulate that there are universal laws or universal rules, and that the scientist discovers these universals.

The knowledge of this universality has generally been associated with men. Our language has described it in terms of men, who generally have been designated as the rational ones able to pursue this. Our language has historically rendered women invisible, as several feminist authors have described (e.g. Spender 1980). In contrast to these universals, particular thoughts and experiences have been seen as less significant. The particular thoughts or experiences which support the universal are subordinate; in a sense, those which do not fit in with the universal should not be held up as challenging the overview. Taken from a religious viewpoint, to challenge a particular point can challenge the total position. One can imagine almost humorously that if someone said: "God made the world and all is good", and they then add: "except for cane toads, He made a bit of a mistake there", it implicitly challenges the entire position. One begins to add other things ("what about blowflies?") where He may have made a bit of a mistake, and the entire assumption of a universal truth begins to crumble. So, to maintain a universal truth can mean to ignore the particularities except where they can be made to fit in with that universal truth. An anecdote related more to a scientific viewpoint apparently occurred when the steam engine was first invented. A scientist who saw the steam engine working said: "It's all very well that it works in practice, but does it work in theory?"

This emphasis on having universal truths, and having a position in a hierarchy based on that, has a profound impact on men who then, I believe, feel some urge or pressure to assume that they can speak of universal truths. This leads to a disregarding of much particular experience; women's experience has been almost continually disregarded by men over the centuries. Even to hear other men's experience becomes a challenge or threat, as each particular is either bolstering or attacking the position of knowledge which it is implied men should have.

Mind versus Body

The third dichotomy, which overlaps somewhat with the preceding two, is the dichotomy of mind versus body. Again, to look at Descartes: if we have the idea that 'I think therefore I am', there is a disregard of the body in that; and again following Descartes, if the body is seen as just a machine, there is no sense of saying 'I feel therefore I am' or 'I move therefore I am'. In a way this contradicts some of our day-to-day experience. I am certain that when I go to a restaurant I am much more inclined to think "I eat therefore I am" than to be caught too much in the rational world, but we see the 'mind' as significant and the body as subordinate.

There are powerful images in our society, and in many others (although, significantly, not in all societies); images of warriors and images of men as 'fighting machines'. This reinforces the entire idea of men's bodies being instruments or mechanisms under their control. Much army training is about the 'toughening' of men, so that they learn to ignore pain and to ignore body feelings (and emotions). Their bodies should be treated as things which are instrumental so that if they are given orders they can follow them out, regardless of what their body feelings may be. Disattending to pain is seen as being a higher virtue. This is to a point where it is not only enduring pain that counts, but the highest status is given to one who doesn't feel pain, doesn't feel fear, doesn't feel tiredness, someone who is completely cut off from his body. These warrior and militaristic images are very powerful in our daily lives, as well as in their specific contexts.

Metaphors around this are very pervasive, both in direct form and related forms such as the metaphors used for sport. Many of the metaphors which are widely used regarding sport are reflective essentially of combat, and these are intricately interwoven. For example, during the Gulf War one very disturbing aspect of reporting in many newspapers was the way that the conflict became so readily described using "Bush versus Hussein" metaphors, using sporting metaphors about 'showdowns', and speaking in a sporting way. In fact it seemed as though there was a blurring between the sports pages and the front pages. On the first page was "Bush versus Hussein in showdown", or "Bush scores" or "first points to Bush". On the sports pages were things like "Desert Storm comes to Football Park".

Militaristic metaphors pervade our lives. Business, for example, is perceived in terms of 'hostile takeovers', of 'bolstering positions', of 'attacks and counterattacks'. When people organise some sort of negotiation this is often described in terms of battle, where someone 'pulls out their big guns', or another 'fires the first salvo' against the opposition. The language of these militaristic images becomes part of our accepted way of viewing interaction, particularly male interaction, and pervades not only business, but much of daily life and relationships. Bodies become merely objects or mechanisms in the broader scheme of battle and of life.

In Australia there is a particular tradition of Australian men being stoic (rather than necessarily being as aggressive as men seem to be in the American tradition). The 'Aussie male' is enduring: the boundary rider, the swagman, the shearer, the drover. Someone who gains ennoblement by enduring, by very much ignoring their body sensations and their bodily needs.

Body enjoyment and sensuality get written out when looking from these viewpoints, and a mechanical or even hostile view of bodies becomes normative. Men's hostile view of their bodies can take many forms. For example, many of the terms young men use regarding enjoyment become linked with a destructive element: young men go out drinking and 'get blind', 'get paralytic', 'get wasted', and enjoy speaking about it in those terms the next day. If this seems extreme, one might consider how many men could speak comfortably of nurturing aspects of their body, say nurturing their skin with moisturiser. Men responding to hugs, responding to any sort of physical contact with other men, not only get linked to a sort of homophobia, but the whole idea of having any sort of physical enjoyment in that way becomes associated with being unmanly. Also, at times of defining male identity, there is an ethos that men should not care about themselves, and that strength is defined as turning off to body sensation. In many cultures rites of passage involve pain and humiliation, either more formally through pain such as some of the scarification or circumcision rituals in tribes, or through some of the fazing and 'bastardisation' that occurs so often in institutions. Informal activities that teenage boys engage in (often referred to as types of rites of passage) involve acts which are quite destructive, such as drinking to extreme excess, dangerous driving, for some even physical fighting.

Some cultures allow more sensuality. By looking at these cultures there seems to be an inverse relation between sensuality and violence. James Nelson (1988) elaborates on the research of James W. Prescott:

> To recover the body is to recover our capacity for pleasure, an important issue in violence. Considerable data now reveal the connections between these, and the extensive cross-cultural research of neurophysiologist James W. Prescott is a case in point. In society after society he discovered the close correlations between peacefulness and the experience of body pleasure, and between violence and the suppression of body pleasure. The positive connections were impressive: societies that are sex-positive and body-positive, and convey this to children through touch and physical nurturance, are demonstrably much more cooperative, peaceful societies. The same is true of individuals. The negative correlations also hold: pleasure-deprived youngsters are much more likely to become violent adults, and body-negative societies are predictably violent. (p.81)

Another cross-cultural example comes from David Gilmore's *Manhood in the Making* (1990), which describes traditional Tahitian cultures as allowing more sensuality. There is much less emphasis on the destructive element of manhood and maleness and more on the ability for men to be in touch with their feelings and their body sensations.

If we take this idea that the warrior or militaristic idea of bodies is pervasive, then the body is not only denied but almost needs to be seen as being punished. The body becomes an instrument of other values which are predominantly values of power and domination. Rather than the body being part of ourselves or being a means of pleasure, awareness of pleasure is denied, and power and performance are the only things which remain. Perhaps the 'softest' element that remains is having some reassurance that the instrument is functioning.

Furthermore, if the body is viewed as an instrument to be disciplined and controlled, as something irrational and to be mastered, then whatever may evoke a response in this body, whether body feeling or emotion, will have a half-known confusing quality. It will be seen as needing to be disciplined and controlled, even as being absolutely bad and needing to be punished. In fact, anything that makes the man feel at all can be seen as negative and requiring a controlling response, or, in the extreme, a response of violence. This has obvious implications for men's attitudes toward sexual violence, which I shall discuss later. Emotion is part of this too. The earlier dichotomies also are involved as both emotion and body feeling are 'particulars' which lower the 'transcendence' of rational, universal direction.

James Nelson (1988) also makes the point that this sense of needing the body utterly controlled and turning off to it also leads to wanting simple clear answers without ambiguities because the body feelings may be viewed as ambiguous, and therefore threatening to the image of being in control. This then encourages a world view which seeks clear and absolute categories. In turn this leads to a world of more dichotomies which are taken as absolute.

Higher versus Lower

Another dichotomy which is perhaps implicit in some of the others is a more general dichotomy of higher versus lower. As mentioned earlier, there has been a traditional hierarchy with God at the top and then man, and then the rest. Similarly, there has been a traditional hierarchy of pure spirit of God, and then men who have been associated with reason, and then women who have been linked with body and emotions. Implicit within this is the idea, not only of knowledge, but of control, as knowledge and power are inevitably interlinked. Foucault (1979, 1980) clarified how any body of knowledge will include and co-exist with ways of operating upon the knowledge, and any power will have a body of knowledge to inform its action.

Implicit within this is the linking of men's identity with competition and "success"; that men must compete and they must do better than the others, men must move "up the ladder", men must overcome someone else in order to be men themselves.1 As hierarchy and control are linked, men may feel pressure to 'control' the women with whom they live. In another context, they as adults control children rather than being able to find other metaphors or other more egalitarian approaches to this (such as helping them develop responsibility). This is a pressure which ties in with the idea of reason being higher than emotion, the mind being higher than the body and men needing to take a position of being hierarchically superior to women. "The head of the household" is a common phrase which seems to link these ideas. For men to be men they also need to take a position of being higher or hierarchically superior to other men. So this sense of being 'one up' or being more in control becomes very powerful and driving for men.

Separateness versus Connectedness

While the above dichotomies would seem to cluster together and overlap, a different theme is found in the dichotomy of separateness versus connectedness. Men's identity is also seen as being in terms of separateness, that men should 'stand alone'. The idea that men should stand alone is very prominent throughout most Western cultures. Thus boys become men largely by being able to stand alone and not be affected by relationships; particularly they should 'cut the apron strings'. One could consider day-to-day expressions such as 'not being a mummy's boy' and 'standing on your own two feet'; being able to 'look the world straight in the eye'; being able to 'stand tall'; 'stand against the tide', etc., as reflections of this.

We also have the ideas popularised through most of modern psychology that the highest form of person is an 'individuated' person or a 'self-actualised' person, and that this is a person who is essentially separate. This is so pervasive it almost gets difficult to see, but one could consider a 'community-actualised' person as an alternative to a self-actualised one. Even in family therapy 'differentiation' (Bowen 1978) of self from others is often the more emphasised dimension.[2]

Moral development has also been seen as having its highest levels characterised by the capacity for the application of a universal and consistent set of values from a position of reflection (thus implying rationality, universality and separateness as essential) (Kohlberg 1963).[3] While there have been critiques of these views (e.g. Gilligan 1982), they remain extremely pervasive. They are also very male views, as women in our culture may be seen to give greater value to relationship and connectedness, and to define identity through relationship in a way men do not.

Nancy Chodorow (1978) suggested that growing girls come to define and experience themselves as continuous with others; their experience of self contains more flexible or more permeable ego boundaries. Boys come to define themselves as more separate and distinct with a greater sense of rigid ego boundaries and differentiation. The basic feminine sense of self is connected to the world, the basic masculine sense of self is separate. This would seem to be an important and accurate distinction. It is interesting that this basic difference in itself is being recognised more as people begin to acknowledge that the earlier models of self were essentially based upon male authors and male viewpoints which assumed the more separate the better. Chodorow suggested the fundamental reason for this could be that infants and young children receive their primary nurturing from a woman and so girls can retain their primary identification with the woman as they grow older. The boy must stand aside from that as he discovers he is different from the mother and experiences separateness.

However, there is still a predominant theme that this separation from the mother is primary and separation generally is central to maleness.[4] Most significant in our day-to-day approach is the assumption that separateness and connectedness are seen as mutually exclusive. If, on the other hand, we value healthy autonomy rather than just being cut off in an extreme manner, then I would argue that connectedness can help to create autonomy. As someone feels more healthily connected and more of a sense of belongingness, then one can easily see a development of more confidence, more sense of self, rather than a denial of self. There is more of a capacity to be close, and with that goes a capacity to constructively separate. This sense of self through belongingness is in contrast to the overall view of men as simply standing alone, being separate, or being 'cut off'.

It can also be questioned how much of this separateness is based on the primary identification, and how much of it may be based instead on social roles and the manners of acting toward people based on those social roles. There is much evidence to suggest that boys and girls are treated differently almost from birth. Indeed, where very young babies have been wrapped up so that one cannot immediately tell whether they are boys or girls, those children described as being boys and described as being girls have been handled quite differently by both men and women. The boys are treated much more roughly and the girls are held more gently. Even in relatively 'progressive' households it seems that there are many residual differentiating ways of acting toward children. In any case, where people have taken some of this mother/son split as being primary and as leading to male separation, the belief can act to generate that way of being. On the other hand, if boys can feel a sense of allowing themselves to be more connected with their mothers as well as with their fathers, this can produce a sense of a solid base to be going forward as an individual. This is in contrast to a sense of always having to be watching for signs of being too connected and, at the extreme, proving themselves not connected (proving themselves not a 'sissy' or a 'mummy's boy', and so on).

One important implication of this sense of separateness is that, in having a mentality of standing alone, it becomes very difficult for men to ask for help. Men should, by these traditional standards, be people who know the answers. This is further reinforced by the idea of men needing to be rational and being higher in the hierarchy. This leads to a situation whereby it becomes a sign of growing up to not listen. If one is meant to be cut off and separate then not listening becomes a virtue, and to actually listen, whether it is to women's experience or the experience of others, can be seen as a sign of not being separate enough; the ability to not listen becomes a sign of being a man. The implication is that the less a man listens the more of a man he is.

Individual versus Collective

Another dichotomy which links closely with this one is the dichotomy of individual versus collective. I heard a recent address by Kiwi Tamasese (Waldegrave & Tamasese 1992) speaking of differences in therapy approaches when working with white (Western or European descended), Samoan and Maori groups. Tamasese said how very difficult it was for whites to be able to think collectively, and I think this is very true, particularly as it applies to white men (white women seem much more able to think in terms of group decisions and group process). Western men generally think 'individually', which follows from being separate or being individuated. This means that to be able to think in terms of what men-as-a-collective do, or what we as a group of particular men do (e.g. 'middle class', 'working class', 'professional' men, etc.) becomes very difficult for men. It involves a way of thinking that is almost foreign to our culture.

When men do in fact discuss issues related to men, or very often when they hear women talking about what men do to women, they very often respond to this on a personal basis. It then links them with a sense of shame and inadequacy. This feeds an avoidance of the issues as these are links with a sense of personal shame and personal inadequacy, rather than a sense of collective guilt, collective shame, or collective movement toward re-addressing what men have done as a group. My understanding is that in Samoan or Maori cultures (and probably many others) the thinking is collective; decisions, shames, and triumphs exist in the group more than the individual. This is very different to our culture, where things are seen in terms of the individual.

In speaking of things which men do wrong, it is then enormously difficult for most men to identify how all of us have, in subtle ways as men, encouraged attitudes of violence or refused to stand up against attitudes of violence. When men perpetrate acts of violence they should of course take individual responsibility. However, many men's responses to them is either to excuse them or to see it only as an individual issue. Men find it enormously difficult to look at the social issues which affect all of us as men and which create a social backdrop of subtle condoning of violence. By recognising that we can think in a collective way, it becomes much easier.

Inadequacy versus Development

Another significant dichotomy is one which I might call learning versus insufficiency. Alternatively, this might be thought of as development versus nature. A very powerful image in our culture is that men do not learn to be men, or men do not develop their manhood in our culture, but that men just are; manhood is just something which is there. One has it or one doesn't. There is no general recognition of people training to be men, of one becoming a man. There is no general way to speak of someone developing degrees of manliness or degrees of identity as a man. What happens instead is that there is a continuous sense of a threat of insufficiency. This is linked with the ideas of manhood generally being described negatively rather than positively, being focussed on the things which are signs of not being a man. Much of the language about this therefore centres around the flaws to be uncovered and what one shouldn't do. The schoolyard sayings: "boy's don't cry", "don't be a sissy", "don't be a girl", are reflective of this. All of those sayings reflect signs of not being competitive enough, not being tough enough, or not being unfeeling enough, which are flaws to be uncovered. The prescription is that men should keep the "armour" against the threat of this insufficiency being exposed, rather than in any way looking at a sense of development or learning, and becoming more of something. Indeed, if we compare this with the idea of personal growth, to even think of personal development we have to really stand aside from any masculine ideas and enter a different realm. The two languages of what is meant to be 'manly' and of personal development or personal growth stand very separately. "Masculine growth" sounds almost bizarre or becomes a strictly physical reference. Buried within these different ideas lurks the idea of the "true masculine"; that somewhere underneath all of this there is a true masculine that should be the true essence of what is a man. In the light of these dichotomies, the "true" masculine can be seen as another yardstick for insufficiency.

Person versus Self

A broader and subtle dichotomy, which at first may seem trivial or distracting from the preceding ones, is a dichotomy which stems from our cultural use of language and the way our language defines our reality. This is a dichotomy I might refer to as 'me versus myself'.

In Western language we often speak very much of our 'selves' as a way of referring to what is happening for us, but in fact that speaking tends to almost define "self" as a separate entity so that we can have in a sense a relationship with ourselves. At times speaking of a relationship with ourselves can be quite a helpful way of discussing what is happening for us or developments we are making. Taken to its extreme, and when examined closely, it is a strange concept. If we ask someone, "How are you getting on with yourself now?", it doesn't sound too bizarre, but if someone answers, "Well, myself and I had a falling-out but we appear to be patching it up and we're getting on a bit better now", it sounds a little less sensible. Or, if someone says, "Well, I had to ask myself a question", it sounds quite commonplace, but if you follow it by asking, "Well, what did yourself say back?" and "What did you say back to yourself's response to what you first asked yourself?", it begins to assume a nonsensical nature. One could imagine someone who has been caught for doing something wrong saying, "Myself made me do it".

In a sense these are just language traps and philosophically this distinction can be resolved by recognising that the problem arises from losing sight of how we use our language. Following Wittgenstein (1953), language is not referring to fixed objects, but operates more in the sense of 'language games', whereby we can interact with other people and co-ordinate between ourselves. While these differences arise in language rather than in reality, they become very important because the language structures our reality. Real effects are experienced in relation to how our language structures our reality - in this case, how we have a relationship with ourselves. In this regard, and following on from the points above, there is generally an assumption, when speaking of men, of a negative self. Furthermore, a man must consciously watch his self, in the sense that a man and his self are two separate things. The self may be exposed, showing the insufficiency of not being male enough, by being associated with emotions, body feelings, or other elements which are considered to not be sufficiently male. Or, alternatively, it may be that the self is seen as something violent, explosive, something that is like an untamed force, or an animal. So, there is a sense of men needing to control themselves, and this can be seen to connect with the encouraged lack of awareness about body feelings. There is often a sense that, no matter how deeply the self is contained, something may slip through, or that it may build up until it became explosive. Control of the self becomes very important, and the self is supposedly not developed but can only be contained. People can 'let off steam' to help control this, but this letting off steam doesn't actually develop or change the self. This self remains like some sort of dark mass, dark force or untamed animal which lurks underneath.

Linking with the previous dichotomy, there is a sense of men needing to prove their manhood which is uniquely male in our culture. There is almost a burden of proof on men, and if their selves have slipped through to be shown as not living up to that, there is a sense of shame and inadequacy. This is a scarcely acknowledged but ever-present shadow to men's experience. Generally this sense of proof can come through things like competition, or performance being hierarchically superior, as mentioned before. The terms used around this are the terms which often relate to war or to hierarchy; someone being higher or someone winning (the terms of winning and losing being very powerful). Other terms relate to being bigger or being stronger, generally to being more of anything. In our culture the phrase 'what he is worth' is widely used and generally refers to money, the number of dollars (more dollars equal more worth). Even when men do win, say, a final in a sports event, what is often spoken of is a sense of relief at not being proved insufficient. Many everyday sayings also relate to this proof, e.g. "is he a man or a mouse?", "he really proved himself", that someone "should be manly", that "he is a real man's man" or "he's a real man". These terms do not have much at all in the way of female equivalence. One doesn't hear, "is she a woman or a mouse?", or a description of a woman being a real woman's woman. In fact, those terms can begin to sound almost bizarre.

A Table of Dichotomies

The dichotomies in this paper are by no means an exhaustive list, but are possibly the most compelling of the dichotomies which have been implicit in men's construction of themselves over time. They can each be seen to tie one with another and, taken as a whole, can be seen to inform many of the difficulties men experience, and to inform many of the wrongs men continue to do. Listed as a table, these main dichotomies [5] are:

Rational vs Emotional
Universal vs Particular

Mind vs Body
Higher vs Lower
Separate vs Connected
Individual vs Collective
Inadequacy vs Development

Controlling Metaphors & Metaphors of Control

Having looked at some of these dichotomies, I think it is helpful to touch on some of the powerful metaphors which go hand-in-hand with these dichotomies and which both inform and are informed by them. Many have already been touched upon, such as the idea of proof and combat, sporting and battle metaphors. These metaphors become very powerful in shaping our understanding of men, and very powerful in men's ways of thinking about how they should act as men. They are very powerful in influencing men's relationship with themselves. As Lakoff & Johnson (1980) point out, we cannot stand apart from metaphor, and the metaphors that we use help to constitute the reality we live in. Also, any metaphors will tend to highlight some aspects of experience and to hide others and, by this, tend to be compelling toward certain ways of acting and thinking.

Some metaphors which are powerful are the ideas of men standing alone, of success being linked with hierarchy. In line with this, many men are encouraged to gain their esteem through success and performance, and this is defined through competition and draws heavily on metaphors of war and sport (e.g. that a man wins contracts, wins a position, wins status, wins a woman, or that men conquer, conquer the environment, conquer their opponents, etc.). Other metaphors that are related to leadership and can relate at times to animal metaphors, someone is the top-dog, the leader of the pack, or, in terms of hierarchy, that he moves up the ladder, that he is "on top of" the situation.

Particularly, however, I would like to focus on the metaphor of being in control. As mentioned, there is a sense of men needing to control themselves, as if the self is some dark force or wild animal. Men should also be in control of the situation. This can come out in terms of competition where the men need to take charge of their opponents, be in control, or be a "step ahead". Men also need to be in control of their emotions, and need to be in control of their bodies. In line with this, men are encouraged to have all the answers; to not have the answers is a sign of weakness. This can be seen to link with earlier metaphors of being rational, of being higher, and of being separate. Hence men in a relationship should have the answers, and the way for men to display caring is by problem-solving. Men who just listen to their wives in their relationships can feel that just listening is an admission of inadequacy; 'real' men should in fact not listen but should know what to do and should have the answers.

Just sharing an experience or simply relating or connecting, which is often what women ask for in relationships, can be seen by men, or felt by men unconsciously, as a sign of inadequacy or weakness, leading to a felt need to respond harder by saying what has to happen and how the problem can be solved by action. Following this, if a man has tried everything and it hasn't worked, then it must be someone else's fault. There is a need then to actively demonstrate that it is someone else's fault, otherwise it would be an admission of inadequacy, and an attack upon this sense of maleness. One could raise questions about the implications of this for male therapists, who often experience pressure to have the answers. Also in line with this, it is clear that being emotional and having the answers are often in direct contradiction, therefore men often experience themselves as being placed in a relationship bind in relationships.

This notion of control and the associated ideas of hierarchy and power suggest that if someone is to be a man in these terms and assert control, they should be hierarchically superior. If that is not immediately acknowledged, then in fact they have almost an obligation, if one follows these dichotomies closely, to exert power, or to assert their position. This idea of control is a central metaphor which strikes in many ways to the core of maleness, informed by the various dichotomies discussed above, being linked with 'rationality', the need to hold a universal truth, to be hierarchically superior and not to be connected.

All of this, in many ways, links with the core of what maleness is in our society, and this control is an essential guiding metaphor that also links with two aspects particularly related to violence in our society. These two elements are a sense of entitlement, and a sense of inadequacy. Many feminist authors have commented on men's sense of entitlement, entitlement to have power over women, in a sense of being affronted if their 'rights' are breached, and enforcing that through violence. The other side of it is the sense of inadequacy that many men experience or try desperately to avoid. By implicitly following the prescriptions for maleness when difficulties arise, particularly in relationships, men can have a feeling of great inadequacy and powerlessness. In attempts to respond to that, notions of control and of power arise because these are very much linked with maleness in our society.

Sex & Violence

If men are unaware of their body and unaware of their emotions, they are more likely to attribute any feelings that arise to other people as they become unused to attributing to their own process and taking responsibility for it personally. There is a sense then, that they are impacted upon by others (rather than having their own feelings), and, because of the notion of control, they must respond to this impact. This can arise in a sense of competition and dominance, and particularly in terms of sexual aggression. This thinking helps to make sense of an abhorrent logic that, in a way, if a man feels impacted upon by a woman - such as feeling attracted to her in a sexual sense, or feeling hurt by her in an emotional sense, then he would feel a certain urgency to respond, or to feel himself lessened or degraded as a man - she has impacted upon him and he must respond. I think this can be seen to feed into how "justifications" for rape are used - not only by rapists, but by men and women who look on. For example, saying not just that a woman was attacked, but that awful phrase of her having "asked for it". This ties in with the idea of her having an "impact" on the man or the man feeling an "impact" of some arousal, and then acting upon that by wanting to reassert power. In this regard it's worth specifying that, in relation to sex, if we follow through these dichotomies which are so pervasive in forming our attitudes toward maleness, the whole notion of sex as being sensual, as being intimate, as being connected, even as just simply being physically pleasurable, becomes denied.

Logically following from the above dichotomies whereby men are out of touch with their bodies and linked in with power, hierarchy, and separation, sex becomes a mechanism of power and male bodies become mechanisms of power and domination. Indeed, if the culture allows no sensuality but only values power, aggression or control, then sex itself becomes viewed as an act of power, aggression or control.

An extreme example of this was in a recent ABC television documentary, "Without Consent", in which rapists and women who had been raped were interviewed. The rapists repeatedly talked about a sense of power, a sense of control. Some spoke of enjoyment of the humiliation of the women which was linked very little with a sexual element but with a language of power, of control, and of violence. Sex in this extreme becomes an act which is utterly unsensual and utterly devoid of emotions linked with intimacy. The informing values, however, are not extreme, but are commonplace in our culture. If the society values individualism and power, then sex also becomes seen as a demonstration of individualism and power.

Following these prescriptions, it may be that in sex there may be a brief moment of intimacy for men: they can allow that sense of intimacy and connectedness to arise at that moment (almost furtively) but not allow it to arise at other times. On the other hand, sex itself can be seen as an act of separateness. Some men have commented on sex being almost a defense against intimacy; by being able to move back toward performance, they can use their body in a performance mode, rather than becoming emotionally intimate.

Also of relevance here is that the language we have for sex is often linked with male aggression. Many slang terms are also terms of destruction. For example, 'fucking' and something being 'fucked' - as in destroyed. Similarly, terms for genitalia are also terms of insult. As Spender (1980) points out, while there are many terms for male sexual assertion, there are no terms for healthy female sexual assertion. Recently, a number of gender neutral terms would seem to be emerging, such as 'bonking'. (In this regard, I have always been taken by the Asian term 'jig-a-jig'. While this no doubt relates to sexual movements, it also sounds bizarrely like an image of the penis as a teabag.)

Anger

Linked with this we can view anger as a special case of emotion. Following on from the earlier statements, one might expect men to deny all emotion, but it can be seen quite broadly that anger is an emotion which men are capable of commenting on without shame in our society. Anger seems to be the one emotion about which men can speak. This can be seen to follow the dichotomies that have been mentioned, for two reasons - the first less significant, and the second more so. Firstly, if men are out of touch with emotion and bodily experience, if their feelings are ignored, not noticed, or denied, then they are likely to be not attended to until they feel extremely strong, or reach the point that they are impossible to be put aside. So at that point it may be that, if they're feeling very emotionally aroused, this is the point at which they can acknowledge emotion. As their emotions are meant to be "other", then anger at this intrusion of emotion and body feeling makes more sense than, say, fear or sadness. The anger is in part at having to feel, being forced to show a 'weakness' in the machine.

Secondly, the relation anger has to men's role and interpersonal definition is what can make this feeling seem overwhelming. The anger often flares when control and status is threatened, so it takes its place in interpersonal politics. Other feelings of hurt, powerlessness, and so on, may have been present but, as they build, what can be noticed, and what can be allowed to come forward, is anger. Anger in this sense is 'politically correct' and is an allowable expression of emotion because it is linked with enforcing the higher status for men. Anger links with exerting control or power. In this sense, anger is traditionally prohibited for women as they are prohibited from exerting power or control. For women, on the other hand, the 'politically correct' emotions are non-aggressive: vulnerability, sadness, pain, distress, tearfulness. These emotions can elicit higher status responses from men (i.e. men can act in ways which are nurturing and reassuring, men can provide answers, men can take charge).

I think that other powerful emotions which men occasionally express are stereotypically seen as anomalous and causing discomfort in those around. Where men are seen as breaking down (and this metaphor is significant: the machine breaking down for a while before the mind pulls it back together), or when men have 'lost control' and cry, express hurt, sorrow, powerlessness, etc., it seems anomalous. Often other men turn away from this and experience discomfort in its presence. Again, all of these actions can be seen to be linked with the twin elements that feed men's violence - that of entitlement and an easily triggered sense of inadequacy.

Touching upon this sense of inadequacy and recognising the restraints, dichotomies and pressures which unconsciously form some of men's responses is very important, I believe, in finding ways of discussing these issues between the genders, and in moving toward overcoming some of the inequities. I think it is important to bear in mind that often when women feel powerless it is not the case that men feel powerful - it may be that men are acting in ways which women interpret as being acts of power, but they may at times be driven, for men, by a sense of inadequacy or of being shamed as a man. Also one can understand the impossibility of men asking for help within this context, as men are meant to be rational, have the universal truths, and stand alone. To ask for help would be an acknowledgement of standing aside from all of those positions, and would touch on a sense of powerlessness. It is worth re-emphasising that the powerlessness is not just the feeling itself which is uncomfortable, as it is for anyone, but it is a feeling which is compounded by striking at the heart of what a man often feels he must be.

Having spoken of many of these issues, I think it is important to emphasise that these are stereotypical restraints operating upon men in our culture. It is important also to acknowledge the very negative ways in which these restraints have impacted upon women, although that has not been the central focus of this particular paper. It is important to acknowledge that not all men follow these dichotomies and the prescription which follows them, and there are many different ways of challenging and standing apart from them.

Alternatives & Directions

I would like to mention a few constructive ideas which follow from the above discussion. Firstly, I think that, by being aware of these dichotomies, we can begin to speak in terms of "both-and", not "either-or", so that people can begin to incorporate the emotional with the rational, the body with the mind, etc. In many cases, it would be better to focus more on the 'other' half, so as to value connectedness over separateness, and the particular over the universal. There can be many models which avoid the dichotomy and generate other categories and distinctions.

A helpful example of how the rational/emotional dichotomy can be avoided can be found in the work of Belenky *et al.* (1986). In a study entitled "Women's Ways of Knowing: The development of self, voice and mind", a study was undertaken of the epistemological basis of women's self-regard. Five different ways of knowing were described. The first category was a category of silence, in which women were so oppressed or so underconfident that they felt no security in their ability to know anything - even if they directly experienced something. If later that experience was contradicted by someone else, they would doubt or deny their former experience. The second category was received knowledge. Knowledge is received from someone else as a student may learn at school, accepting information given with little or no evaluation. For women it may be repeating the views of their husbands in a dependent way. The third category was subjective knowledge which was based on personal experience, particularly emotional experience and 'gut' responses. The fourth category was procedural knowledge which relates to knowing analytically. This would link with the traditionally more 'rational' thinking whereby one applies rules of analysis to situations, events, or data, and draws conclusions based on those rules of analysis. The fifth category is constructed knowledge, whereby an awareness of received, subjective, and procedural knowledge is combined within a general understanding that the object of knowledge is in part determined by the receiver. There is no access to an entirely objective knowledge or an absolute position.

This model of knowing is relevant to the current discussion in that it provides a helpful alternative to a rational/emotional split and, rather than 'rational' approaches being taken as higher, the 'higher' form of knowledge is one which combines awareness of received, subjective, and procedural knowledge. This has particular relevance for men in valuing received knowledge - to accept the experiences of others and provide space for their stories, rather than denying other experiences or feeling a 'universal' position should be imposed. It provides a model which can view listening to women, and to members of different cultural groups, as enriching. The model also values a focus on emotional experience, as well as the best aspects of 'rational' thinking, without needing to be caught in an either/or bind.

Secondly, implicit within all the above is the recognition of how constructed our identities are. Many people in the 'men's movement' speak of finding a 'true masculine'. When these dichotomies are explicated it seems incongruent to look for the 'true masculine'. Would one rebalance the list of dichotomies? Would 'trueness' arise from the integration of all of them? If we removed these dichotomies, would 'trueness' be what is left? I would suggest that these dichotomies are implicitly based on the idea of a 'true masculine', and the search for a 'true masculine' will only perpetuate the restraints which are there. At best, looking for a 'true masculine' may provide a more egalitarian and open set of specifications for maleness. The question needs to be not "what is the 'true' masculine?", but "what effects do our beliefs have - how do our prescriptions for maleness affect ourselves, women, and the world?", so that we can remain ethically and creatively alive.

Even if it was ever possible to find a 'true masculine', it is certainly not discoverable in the ongoing context of our society where women are being repressed, because so much of the idea of true masculinity leads back only to having these dichotomies which separate women from men, and which continue the oppression of women, and the self-repressive shaping of men.

Thirdly, it should be clear from the above discussion that men's position has generally been valued and women's voice ignored. Where men have claimed a privileged right to rationality and universal truths, the particulars of women's experience have been denied, ignored or actively suppressed. In this context the search for a 'true masculine' becomes another way of continuing male privilege by valuing men's voice over women's. Many in the 'men's movement' have said men need to find themselves in the company of men. It is enormously important that men meet with other men, particularly where it facilitates the breaking down of isolation, the sharing of emotional experience, and a development of intimacy with other men. However, men cannot redefine themselves in isolation. Women at the beginnings of the 'women's movement', I suspect, needed to meet separately to find a voice, because women's voice had so long been silenced in our patriarchal culture. Men are in a context of men's voice traditionally being heard, and women's suppressed. In this context, men need to listen to women as well as to each other. To work on issues of men and maleness, only in isolation, would be to perpetuate the problems with which we are grappling - it would be to assume male issues as universal and ignore the particulars of women's experience, to continue to privilege men as 'higher', to perpetuate separateness, etc. Learning to listen and **not** have the answers, and to not take control, are steps in the process. Acknowledging and responding to women's experience becomes a crucial step in overcoming the restraints operating upon men. It becomes central in men's freedom, as the idea of freedom itself can be loosened from the old dichotomies.

Generally, recognising these dichotomies can help in a range of areas where men are 'stuck' or alienated. For instance: where blocks occur in communication, one could draw out some of the other feelings or assumptions which feed into the block, such as taking on personally the sense of a collective issue and then feeling personally inadequate in relation to a collective issue.

It can be helpful also to look at encouraging body awareness and sensuality, and encouraging nurturance, rather than body denial. For example, sport can be seen less in terms of competition and more in a sense of being in "flow" with the body; we can focus on process rather than result.

There can be an encouragement for men to start to think collectively.

Also, to be able to allow feelings of powerlessness or inadequacy in relationships without tying that to identity and an urgency to do something, can, in itself, be very freeing for men, and prevent an escalation of control and alienation.

Furthermore, given that these prescriptions for men are social constructs, they can be changed socially. Just having names for these ideas can, at times, be helpful in interaction. There can be an ability to use terms in a social context which challenge the restraints and the beliefs which underpin much of this behaviour, without attacking or challenging the person. Metaphors can also be used which encourage models other than those based on dichotomies (for example, to speak of strength coming through connectedness rather than "control", or development through allowing our vulnerability rather than through isolation).

The various implications of models of manhood based on these dichotomies are perhaps especially salient for counsellors and therapists working with men. An awareness of such prescriptions can be used in helping men to challenge the unquestioned beliefs which so often constrain all of us.

Finally, one very important aspect of all of this is that, unlike the struggle of feminism which had to struggle with many political structures, social structures, and bureaucracies (to gain equal pay for equal work, capacity for women to gain promotion, child care practices, and so on), most of the things which have been so oppressive of men and have contributed so powerfully to the ongoing oppression of women, can be changed by changing a way of thinking.

If men can challenge the prescriptive ideas which they have operated under, they can begin to throw off oppressive ways of acting towards themselves and others.

Conclusion

In this paper I have discussed a number of dichotomies which prescribe a way of being for men in Western culture. The combination of these dichotomies generates a powerful prescription for men's identity - a prescription which, in turn, generates much of men's alienation and often oppressive practices. Such dichotomies are not inevitable or intrinsic, but are constructs which have become pervasive and compelling.

To search, as many people suggest, for the 'true' nature of men would seem only to perpetuate such dichotomies and, in turn, support men's often self-destructive and oppressive practices.

On the other hand, if we are clearer on how our identities are constituted by conforming to specifications such as those above, then we can choose to be free from these specifications and begin to redevelop our relationships and redefine ourselves.

Notes

1. A somewhat different emphasis could be provided by choosing 'dominant vs. submissive' as a category, instead of 'higher vs. lower'.

2. While this differentiation is linked with an increased capacity for making emotional connections in the present, it is the separating which is emphasised rather than the reconnecting in Bowen's scheme.

3. James Nelson's analysis of separation and moral development has drawn this moral position and critique to my attention, although his conclusions are very different to

mine, placing far more emphasis on biologically determined factors.

4. This challenging of the idea of separating from the mother has been influenced by Johnella Bird's explanation of the impact of gender socialisation upon therapy with men (1992). An element of Bird's presentation included re-emphasising the mother/son relationship in contrast to the recent trend to emphasise the father/son relationship.

5. I have not included 'person vs self' as this relates more to the broader question of language which informs these dichotomies.

3

Cultural and Gender Accountability in the "Just Therapy" Approach
Kiwi Tamasese & Charles Waldegrave

This paper addresses the issues of cultural and gender accountability within therapeutic organisations. It is written from the perspective of a Samoan woman and a Pakeha (white) man in an agency that is structured into three cultural sections. The paper discusses the issues and agency experience around two critical questions: How do workers, women and men and people of different cultures in an agency or institution, protect against gender and culture bias in their work on a day-to-day basis? Furthermore, how do they do this in societies where sexist and racist assumptions are an integral part of the upbringing and way of life, as they are in most modern industrial states?

The authors draw deeply from their agency experience as they outline the possibility of responsible partnerships between the genders and cultures. In doing so, they address issues of pain, vulnerability, cultural caucusing, institutional space, and the convergence of meanings that were previously conflictual.

There is an increasing awareness these days of insensitivity and injustice in therapy experienced by women and cultural groups different from the dominant one. In the family therapy field, feminist writers and theoreticians (Goldner 1985, 1992; Harre Hindmarsh 1987; Kamsler 1990; Luepnitz 1988; McKinnon & Miller 1987; Walters, Carter, Papp & Silverstein 1988; among many others) have identified both the patriarchal determinants of family life and their infusion in therapy in modern Western societies.

To date, much less has been written concerning cultural bias in therapy (Boyd-Franklin 1989; Durie 1986; Gurnoe & Nelson 1989; McGoldrick, Pearce & Giordano 1982; Waldegrave 1986, 1990). There is, nevertheless, an emerging consciousness of the inadequacy of social science models that grow out of ideas from one culture being applied to another.

Social science theories, models and practices, for example, were largely formulated in one general cultural context - that of Western Europe and white North America. We have learned that social science is not a neutral gathering of information, as many have claimed. Rather, we have come to view it as one cultural way of describing events. When these descriptions are imposed on families of subjugated cultures, where understandings of behaviour and healing are quite different, the opposite of healing often occurs. This is because their places of belonging - their cultures - are displaced in the process.

Literature on these subjects identifies the biases in mainstream theory and practice, and offers alternative processes and personnel to overcome gender and cultural bias. By personnel, we refer to women therapists being more appropriate to address many of the problems women come with to therapy. Likewise, therapists of the same culture as the clients are much more likely to understand and facilitate the strengths of families of those cultures as they attend to the stresses that bring them into therapy.

The aspect that is not addressed in the writings on this subject, apart from our own (Waldegrave 1990), is the issue of "accountability". How do workers, women and men and people of different cultures in an agency or institution, protect against gender and cultural bias in their work on a day-to-day basis? Furthermore, how do they do this in societies where sexist and racist assumptions are an integral part of the upbringing and way of life, as they are in most modern industrial states?

It is surprising that so little has been written on this aspect around which so many organisations experience conflict. Most therapists have experienced the situation where a group that has been unjustly treated in society begins to raise subtle and not so subtle experiences of discrimination which they discern among their colleagues and in their workplace. When such discussions centre on issues of culture and gender, feelings can run very high.

In our experience, therapists, who are usually very concerned to facilitate resolution in the conflicts of others, tend to be very slow to address these issues among themselves. Instead, people on both sides of the conflict retire hurt, and are left to carry a mixture of feelings of fear, outrage and distrust. This does not inspire in the organisation an atmosphere of co-operation and respect. These are two of the values that are necessary for both a just institution and a just therapy.

Naming the Injustice

When an individual or a group articulates concerns about gender or cultural bias within an organisation, relationships can quickly become precarious. The naming of this problem conflicts with the status quo, and feelings of comfort immediately dissipate, especially among therapists whom one can expect to have acute sensitivity to the pain of others. The experience can be disturbing, upsetting, guilt-inducing, and polarising and generally creates disharmony.

This article is not written to address situations where outright hostility or total rejection of such claims occur. Our concern is with the liberal therapeutic environment where such claims are often acknowledged, but subtly avoided. In our experience three common outcomes of such naming strengthen the resistance to change. These we identify as "paralysing", "individualising" and "patronising" responses.

Naming an injustice is an essential early step in the process of overcoming it. It usually highlights the issue, and relieves some tension in the person or group that considers they have been unjustly treated. Likewise, it often encourages a self-conscious reflection in the person or group that is considered to have acted unjustly. This too, is an essential part of any process of change.

Obstructions to this process occur when there is a recognition of some substance to the claim, but terrible fears about its implications. Men, in particular, though not exclusively, are susceptible to this in conversations on gender. So too are white people, women and men, in conversations on culture. They are often too nice to fight it; they just become paralysed.

Paralysis is a guilt response that takes in the criticism and deeply experiences the shame associated with it. The problem with it is that many people can't move beyond it. They note the complaint, agree with it, and offer sympathetic responses. Many people in this situation feel overwhelmed with the enormous process of changing the institution they work in, afraid of the bewildering implications for their own future and the possibility they might cause the same offence some time in the future. To avoid these risks and open conflict, they do nothing and feel impotent. Unfortunately, the passivity functions as a form of control because it further entrenches the status quo.

Individualising is a closely associated response when threatened with criticisms of cultural or gender oppression. "Liberal" white people and "sensitive" guys, somehow, separate themselves from their cultural and gender histories, and claim they can only be responsible for their personal behaviour. They then attempt to be individual paragons of cultural or gender equality.

The problem with this approach is that it cleverly sidesteps the institutional and collective reality of the problem of discrimination. It is the collective of men and the history of patriarchy which has created the environment that privileges the decisions and actions of men over women. No matter how committed to women a man may be, he may still continue to benefit at every level in a patriarchal society, at their expense.

Individualising the problem avoids both the sense of belonging and the responsibility to change the fundamental problem. I, a white person (one of the authors), was not alive when my ancestors and others colonised New Zealand. As a result of it, however, I have grown up with access to resources and other privileges denied to many Maori people. I now have the choice of working with my own to stop this collusion, or to continue benefitting from it. Individualising does not address this basic issue.

54   *Kiwi Tamasese & Charles Waldegrave*

The *patronising* response is more crude, but no less common than the other two. It refers to people from the discriminating group who U-turn to such an extent that they become self-appointed spokespeople for the group their culture or gender oppresses. Men start speaking for women, and white people become the articulators for discriminated cultures. Not only is this sort of response quite inappropriate, it is likely to be inaccurate and resented.

Responsible Partnerships Between the Genders and the Cultures

In the "Just Therapy" approach, we have endeavoured to discover a way that responsibly addresses the institutional and individual modes of cultural and gender discrimination. The approach attempts to reverse the societal bias against women and the dominated cultural groups.

Cultural Sections and Gender Caucuses

Within our overall collective at The Family Centre, the Maori and Pacific Island sections are self-determining. The Pakeha (white) section, because it is the dominant culture, runs its own affairs, but is accountable to the other two sections. Although all staff are committed to developed concepts of equality, unintentional impositions are still likely to occur because of our cultural histories. This accountability ensures an ongoing process of monitoring against intrusion into the processes of the groups that are dominated in the wider society.

Likewise, the women and the men caucus separately at times to address their own issues. As with the cultural work, we have found it helpful to agree to creative forms of accountability and monitoring that address our gendered histories and consequent biases. The women's work is self-determining. The men manage their affairs and responsibilities, but are accountable to the women. The point of such caucuses is to highlight the particular concerns of key groups so that their needs are not lost in a compromised partnership.

Cultural caucuses have now been institutionalised as cultural sections. With regard to gender, we have formalised groupings of men and groupings of women into separate caucuses. The women's caucus call the men's caucus to a meeting when an issue of injustice is felt in staff relationships, models or practice.

Issues are laid out, and a convergence of meanings is sought about the incidence. This may take one or several meetings depending on the complexity of the issues. Policy decisions emanate from these discussions. Meetings can also be called where a group wishes to put forward innovative ideas for discussion. We set clear boundaries to ensure the caucuses carry out their responsibilities. For those associated with injustice, the primary responsibility is to collectively transform attitudes, values, structures and forms of relationships that dominate. The responsibility of the subjugated groups is to identify their pain, recover their untold stories, and articulate their direction in relation to others who share the same pain.

Caucusing enables a collective of voices to speak as one. It is particularly helpful where a gender or cultural grouping has fewer numbers and lower status positions in an organisation. Their collective voice can be heard in a more equal manner. We value the voice of each individual in many discussions. On other occasions, it is important to hear the collective voice of women, of men, or of different cultural groups. Having met together previously, each caucus can share both their concerns and responsibilities. This sets up a different dynamic and focus in discussion.

Radicalising Modes of Accountability

The unique aspect of this approach is the reversal of usual modes of accountability. Because management and decision-making is commonly exercised primarily by men or white people, the patriarchal and racist assumptions in society simply permeate the therapeutic community. Our reversal consists of full recognition of dominated groups to be self-determining, and a requirement of the dominant groups to check out key aspects of their orientation and projects with the other groups.

This process has been very effective, because it enables a genuine monitoring of discriminatory behaviours and processes. In our view, the best judges of injustice are the groups that have been unjustly treated. Thus, the women are accorded the role of guardians of gender equity, and the Maori and Pacific Island sections the guardians of cultural equity at The Family Centre.

They have the right at any time to call the agency, or parts of it, to address equity issues. When they do, the agency is absolutely committed to seeking a solution that satisfies the guardians to whom the rest of the agency is accountable. This is not an authoritarian process. We endeavour to seek a consensus that we can practice with integrity, that satisfies those to whom we are accountable.

Sometimes an issue can be satisfactorily resolved in one meeting. On other occasions, where the issues require a lot of discussion and fundamental shifts in thinking, resolution may take a number of meetings over months. We persist until those to whom we are accountable consider their concerns have been adequately dealt with. The commitment not to give up has enhanced trust and facilitated creative solutions.

In practice, when the Maori or Pacific Island sections or the women have a grievance, we usually move through the following process:

1. *Institutional Space*. Time is set aside to hear the cause of concern. The group that considers they or their people have been unjustly treated, or an agency practice needs to be changed, are accorded uninterrupted space to tell their story. We refer to this as institutional space, because so many agencies do not set time aside for such a process and, if they do, they often don't allow uninterrupted space. Only after all the aggrieved people have articulated their concerns can discussion ensue, initially around points of clarification on both sides. This first step involves hearing the story, and the meanings the group is giving to events that have occurred.

2. *Converging of Meaning*. The group associated with the injustice is then committed to listen as openly as possible and authenticate the complaint in whichever aspects they can, with integrity, agree. This is not an empty-headed agreement. After clarification of any misunderstandings and points of fact, we usually discover substance in the concerns that have been brought forward.

Most white therapists and most male therapists, for example, would avow anti-racist and anti-sexist practices. The difficulty they have in practice is that they seldom experience what discriminated people experience. Furthermore, they are seldom in situations where they are required to respond to the issues raised by a caucus of colleagues with stories that are very different from their own. They are usually aware of the stories of at least some discriminated people, however, and, if invited to authenticate a complaint, they usually can.

The authentication from the group associated with the injustice enables a converging of meaning between the two parties. Where this occurs authentically it is very painful, but anti-sexist and anti-racist learnings take root in an organisation. Furthermore, an analysis has taken place and the substantive issues have been agreed on, which enables some practice goals to be set towards resolution.

It is important to note that this process does not occur cheaply. We are not interested in "politically-correct guilt" or "white and male flagellation". Our concern springs from the pain of our colleagues who feel we have failed them. We trust their pain and their ability to discern the significant obstacles, and they trust us to take them seriously and act honourably. The process is a vulnerable one for both sides.

3. *Addressing Our Own*. Having reached considerable agreement about the problem, and having shared the emotional pain of the hurt that has come between us, we begin to carve out a better future together. Sometimes the problems centre directly around our own actions. On other occasions they centre around sexist and racist practices that impinge on the agency from outside, which we could have done more to prevent.

Male therapists, for example, are often insensitive to the feelings of violation female therapists may experience when working with a family in which abuse has occurred. Likewise, a narrow clinical focus can completely overlook the constant strain and pressure therapists from dominated cultures experience, when working with their own people. The people they work with usually have so few of society's resources allocated to them. These experiences can raise broader contextual and social policy priorities for an organisation.

We endeavour to talk together with the same sensitivity and skill that we practice in our best therapy. Where we have directly hurt another, we apologise. When the pain is very deep we are sometimes "unprofessional" enough to cry, just like the families that come to see us. After all, we tell them it is healing to cry, don't we?

We endeavour to discern the colonising and patriarchal influences around the problem, and try not to separate ourselves, our cultures, and our genders from our histories and current contexts. We deeply analyse the different meanings we give the same events, and try to understand and value marginalised meanings.

We then agree to new practices that deepen the respect and sensitivity among us. These new practices take on a collective, as well as an individual dimension. Men in the agency, for example, are seen to be responsible, not just for themselves but for each other. The unenviable task of honing new sensitivities among men is not just left to women. Likewise, Pakeha (white) people are expected to develop responsible anti-racist perspectives among their own. These new strengths are not driven by reaction but by the deep commitment to honour each other.

Our agency often chooses to go a step further in this direction. We frequently take responsibility to address these issues in the wider therapeutic community, and even beyond that in society as a whole. It forms a central part of our writing, teaching, media work, research, and work in the community. As with the work in the agency, the dominating groups are seen to have a major role in developing cultural and gender sensitivities among their own.

4. *New Perspectives.* In our experience, this approach has inspired trust between the cultural groups and the genders. Because the agenda of the dominating group was jointly agreed to by the dominated groups, and because the latter have the powerful right to both monitor and call to account, a genuine partnership has the possibility to emerge. The quality of that partnership depends on the spirit in which it is carried out.

Though the processes are often painful, new relationships, new therapies, and a greater sense of wholeness is spawned. Probably most important of all, the therapeutic organisation begins to reflect and model the sorts of relationships we strive for among families. In our experience, most agencies fail to address the issues among themselves that they expect the families they see to work on.

We recognise that the creativity that has emanated from The Family Centre over the last decade has its origins in this process. The partnerships encourage us to consider different meanings and different processes. The rightness often gives birth to new ideas.

The trust that develops between groups, who in any other organisation nurse resentments, enables creative and equitable arrangements between the cultures and the genders. Stories and practices from groups that have been dominated become central to the life of the organisation. These include, for example, women's stories, cultural practices around greeting and food, processes during meetings, and spirituality in the broadest sense.

Over the years this process has helped us negotiate a path through many conflictual situations. The details of those discussions are obviously confidential as staff members have approached each other vulnerably. From a cultural perspective, we have addressed such issues as: the silence some cultures prefer to Western verbalisation; respect and time given to elders in some cultures that is comparable with the respect and time given to influential achievers and people of status in the white world; opportunities for expressions of spirituality in situations where Europeans often feel a little uncomfortable; and the setting aside of a greater proportion of the financial budget and other resources for hospitality and gifting which involves audit justification within the institution.

These discussions between caucuses require a lot of sensitivity. They are discussions that most institutions do not make time for, and so the dominating culture simply holds sway in that structure. People from dominated cultures usually politely co-operate with the status quo, and so the therapeutic institution mirrors the power difference that frequently occurs in the therapeutic relationship as well.

From a gender perspective, we have addressed such issues as respect for women workers' knowledge of the complexities, vulnerabilities, and potential dangers in family life. This has required men to stand aside and listen to quite different meanings given to events in family life from those which they were taught or experienced personally; changing every structure of our organisation to reflect gender equity and participation at all decision-making levels, from workshop presentations to the structure of our Trust Board; and the development of non-patriarchal policy guidelines as, for example, in work with men who abuse, that are overseen by the women in the agency. An example of this is outlined in another paper (Waldegrave 1990).

These examples are not an exhaustive list of the issues we have worked together on, to discover equitable partnerships. They simply indicate some areas that point to the types of discussions and dialogue we have become involved in. Interestingly, they do not only benefit the women and Maori and Samoan workers. Men, for example, have gained a greater sense of identity and co-operation as they have learned to recognise their vulnerability together. Pakeha (white) workers have also benefitted significantly. One example is reflected in the new-found openness to the wisdom of their own elders. This has led to their direct help and input on specific projects.

Pain as a Preferred Meaning

The pain carried by many women and people from subjugated cultures who seek therapy from us is not unfamiliar. We know its touch, its feel, its many, many faces. We link into it intuitively. For those of us from histories of colonisation and subjugation (one of the authors), the pain of loss is immense. As the Samoan novelist Albert Wendt has put it: "we are what we have lost" (Wendt 1991).

Consider this usual scenario: a country is colonised; her indigenous people made to live on the periphery and are enforced to ape the "civilisation" of the dominant culture. They are then told that they will never make the grade anyway. Their histories, distorted/erased/dismissed, are left untold.

These are the faces of pain that we see daily as families seek therapy from us. This is also the pain that we as therapists from these cultures carry in so many institutions in which we work. We as women have a long history of being unnamed, cancelled, made extra, and having our contribution to humanity taken for granted. These are the faces of pain. It is also the pain of many women therapists.

"We are what we have lost." Though the pain is immense, we, as women and peoples of subjugated cultures, can vouch for its potentialities for change. Such pain is not only directly inflicted, it can also be just as piercing through subtle passivity, non-action, and even silence.

Remember the instances when that pain became so immense that we refused to be allocated the peripheral spaces in conversations about models, theories and practices of our disciplines. Remember the times when that pain became so much that we refused to be lied to any more about our history. Remember our meticulous uncovering of story, the piecing together from the many fragments of memory. Remember the time when the pain of exclusion became so much that we stood up and claimed a central placing. Remember that!

The pain carried by women and peoples of subjugated cultures is real. It is a result of long histories of domination. The articulation of this pain illuminates behaviours, attitudes, values, and structures of domination. At a functional level, societies, disciplines, agencies, including family therapy agencies, cannot afford the non-hearing of this pain. Structures and disciplines of domination have caused the disruption and brokenness of many families - a brokenness our societies can ill-afford. Our only home for the human family - the Earth - has even been broken by structures, values, and apparatuses of domination.

At another level, the stories of pain of the subjugated, and the meanings they give to their stories, pose an interesting question. Do we see their stories and meanings equivalent to the stories and meaning of domination? We have referred to "preferred meanings" (Waldegrave 1989) as those that are articulated by the people who have been unjustly treated.

For example, if we want to understand what has really happened in South

Africa over the last century, we must listen to the meanings black people and their movements give to events, more so than to the stories in the white community. Because they experienced the pain of domination directly, they know exactly what they lost. This is usually underplayed in the white community. As such, the black story offers a preferred description of events. The same can be said of the story of a woman who has been abused, when compared with the story of the perpetrator.

This is not to say one group has the whole truth. Rather, it is to recognise hidden stories and the particular association of pain with truth. The stories of pain call from us an ethical stance, for: "Every human act has an ethical meaning because it is an act of constitution of the Human World" (Maturana & Varela 1988).

Accountability as Vulnerability in Trust

After hearing the cry of pain, one of the obstacles that block the way to creative change is the fear of role reversals. A common unspoken question is: "Will they who have been unjustly treated exercise the same control and domination over us as we have over them?" "Will they develop a blindness to our pain similar to our blindness to theirs?" These are legitimate fears, for all around us abound the culture, structures, attitudes and rituals of domination.

However, the cultural memories of the subjugated peoples hold vestiges of relationships other than the vertical arrangements of relationships that are characteristic in Western nations. These cultural memories are being recovered, for they often hold a differing value system of humility, respect, sacredness, reciprocity, and love, that underpins new structures and processes of accountability.

For example, our analysis of pre-colonised Samoa revealed a covenant relationship (*feagaiga*) between brother and sister that had the capacity to equalise the relationships between women and men (Falenaoti 1992). The Western models do not always offer the liberative new structures that people are currently searching for.

Accountability was institutionalised into The Family Centre as a result of our work with families of subjugated cultures and subsequently in our work in the area of gender. We made a commitment, in the first instance, that all our work with families of cultures, other than the dominant culture, would be accountable directly to the therapists of that culture. This was because the therapists of these cultures had the knowledge of their own people's stories, meanings, and rituals.

Our approach to accountability involves an act of humility. It requires a recognition that we don't have all the knowledge pieces to provide healing and wholeness to peoples of other cultures. Furthermore, a more critical and humble approach to the achievements of the social sciences, to date, is called for from us.

It follows from this that our models, theories, and practices in the Pacific Island and Maori sections are accountable to selected people of our communities. We hold meetings whereby we lay out our thinking and practice for our elders and co-workers to comment on.

Accountability, for us, is essentially an ethical process, a process that calls from all of us humility, respect, sacredness and love. It is required of all workers who are involved in healing, both those associated with domination and those associated with subjugation.

Cultural and gender accountability involves a dialogue between groups associated with opposite experiences. In dialogue we are mindful when we articulate, that we speak from positions of unequal power. We have created a structure that makes an open dialogue possible where hidden and exposed meanings are both addressed. It also involves a dialogue beyond the centre, whereby workers in cultural sections go to selected members of their communities.

Accountability that fosters commitment to actions makes a difference to the lives of those who suffer. If it lies in the bedrock of values like humility, reciprocity, love, and sacredness, a mutual learning process can take place, for both those who call for accountability and those who respond. It becomes a mutual learning in vulnerability.

In essence, accountability is about the building of trust with the group with whom trust has been broken. Therefore, accountability in such a process is not about a simple reversal of roles in the hierarchical sense. It is an offering of vulnerability in trust to each other, so that the pain of injustice can be transformed.

The Sequence of Events

The development of this process occurred over a decade. It may be helpful to indicate some of the historical markers. In 1979, The Family Centre was set up as a family therapy agency. When we listened intently, we learned that many families who came to the agency associated the onset of their problems with issues outside the family system. They identified issues like housing, unemployment, racism, and sexism. It was the early 1980s and New Zealand was going through an economic recession.

The agency, after reflection, was moved to respond by opening up a community development wing to work specifically on these issues. This took place in 1982 alongside the therapeutic work. Reflections from this proved to be another turning point. During this period, the community work informed the development of family therapy, and the family therapy informed the community development work. The early signs of "Just Therapy" began to emerge.

The marginalisation of peoples of cultures other than the dominant one took place even in organisations of the marginalised. Primarily, the peoples' senses of belonging were with their cultures. As a result, The Family Centre decided to move its community development work away from an issues base to a cultural base in 1986.

Three cultural sections were set up to address the issues in culturally appropriate ways, and to further develop their approaches to therapy. We removed the director position and, in its place, set up three cultural co-ordinators, one from each section, to head the agency. The Maori and Pacific Island cultural sections are self-determining. The Pakeha (European) section organises its own affairs, but is accountable to the other two sections. It was at this stage that we began to institutionalise accountability along the lines set out in this article.

We then developed gender caucuses. It became apparent in the gender area that a model of accountability needed to be put in place, given the disparity in the male/female positionings. In our caucuses the principle of collective voice is employed.

The institutionalising of gender and cultural equity is now formally reflected in our constitution of 1991. Our 10 person Trust Board is strongly represented by all three cultures, and women and men. Our constitution states: "The Family Centre is composed of a Maori Section, a Pacific Island Section, and a Pakeha Section. The sections are to be self-determining, co-operative, and are to share all resources equitably."

The following statements comprise three of the seven objectives in our constitution:

• *Advocating for justice with particular reference to the prevention of discrimination against women and cultural groups, and the prevention of all forms of poverty.*

• *Providing cultural and gender-based services in family and community development work.*

• *Articulating and safeguarding the spiritual values of the cultural groups represented in The Family Centre.*

Finally, we do not consider our story as triumphal in any sense. We have walked a path which has many more challenges and obstacles ahead. It has been very painful and, on occasions, probably prompted some workers to move on. It has also been the source of great joy. We have no illusions that we have reached some utopia of total gender and cultural equality, sensitivity, and understanding. It is precisely because we are becoming more sensitive to our own biases that we have set up these systems of accountability. There have been no models for us to go by. This approach is changing us, our relationships, and our ways of working. Hopefully, the next generation will find it easier because we and other groups have made a start.

PART TWO

Men's Development

4

Boys and Education in Australia
Christopher McLean

After years of relative obscurity it seems that gender issues, as they relate to *men's* lives, are finally hitting the "big-time". Items are regularly appearing in the mainstream media dealing with men and masculinity, and they no longer take the mocking tone previously (and somewhat understandably) directed at the drum-beating, "wild-man" manifestations of the men's movement. One of the ways in which this new-found respectability has been achieved is by linking analyses of masculinity with issues of widespread concern. Nowhere is this more evident than in the area of boys' education - a subject that was recently examined by "Four Corners", Australian television's most eminent investigative current affairs program (What About the Boys? *ABC Television*, 18 July 1994).

Concerns about schools and education are nothing new. Declining standards of literacy and numeracy, high levels of violence and vandalism, and a perceived lack of respect for adult authority, are standard fare in the media. However, what is new is the "discovery" that it is overwhelmingly boys who are "causing" these problems, and the claim that programs addressing boys' gender "socialisation" could help deal with them. Men offering such programs report an overwhelming demand from schools, desperate to do *something* about out-of-control boys. Education departments around Australia are seriously examining the need for special gender-based strategies for boys, and in New South Wales such a program is soon to be unveiled.

On the face of it, such moves could seem to be unequivocally positive and desirable. However, there are problems. Concerns felt by many people about directions taken by the men's movement are equally relevant to the area of boys' education. In fact, this is perhaps one of the first areas in which different strands of the men's movement are seeking to gain an influence over directions taken in government policy. There is indeed a lot at stake. Will these new programs be part of the backlash against women, based on notions of men's "oppression" and pitting the needs of boys against those of girls? Or will they be informed by a pro-feminist analysis, and seek to develop ways for boys to act in partnership with girls in the larger struggle for gender equity and social justice?

This paper in no way claims to provide definitive answers to the issues confronting people interested in this topic. It is my contribution to what I believe is a debate of vital importance. It is informed by my own experience as a secondary teacher, 14 years as a single parent, and memories of my own schooling. It is based on numerous conversations with friends, interviews with academics in Australia and the United States, with school counsellors, teachers, students (boys and girls), and therapists working with male perpetrators of violence.

In this paper I outline some of the factors which I believe are essential to an understanding of boys' experiences at school. It seems to me that many of the claims currently being aired in the media are based on analyses that fail to place schools in a larger social context, and treat gender as the only factor influencing boys' behaviour. In particular, issues concerning power, class and ethnicity are being ignored, as well as the nature of schooling itself. My goal, therefore, is to examine some of the current claims and proposals in the light of these factors, and offer some ideas as to how they might inform practical programs in schools.

There is, indeed, little doubt that there is a problem. "Youth" violence and crime is overwhelmingly perpetrated by boys, who also successfully commit suicide far more often than girls. Sexual harassment of girls by boys is widespread in Australian schools (Martin 1993 p.31), and "recorded violent offences committed on school grounds [in New South Wales] increased by 69% between 1989-92" (*NSWLCSC* on Social Issues, 1993 p.27). Boys predominate in special classes for emotional and behavioural disturbance (Fletcher 1994 p.3) and there is an increasing gap between girls' and boys' academic performance in the final years of secondary school. In New South Wales, for example, girls topped 103 subjects in the 1993 Higher School Certificate while boys topped 51 (West 1994a, p.12).

However, what is not clear is how best to understand these factors, and a number of propositions are currently being aired. Prominent among these are claims clearly informed by men's movement concepts, along with a worrying dose of "men's rights" rhetoric. However, concern is much wider than this. Many parents, and particularly feminist mothers, are worried about the schooling their sons are getting, and see an obvious difference between the energetic, forward-looking attitudes of their daughters, and the often apathetic or angry responses of their sons. There are a number of pro-feminist men who see the importance of working with boys in school, as a part of the larger context of opposing sexism and male violence. And there are women, actively working to promote educational strategies for girls, who see the importance of changing boys' attitudes. However, they quite correctly fear the possibility of boys' programs occurring at the expense of funding for girls, or even directly undermining the improvements that have been achieved with such difficulty over the last ten or so years.

The men's movement argument goes something like this: Boys and girls are equally (but differently) limited by their gender role prescriptions. They both suffer from narrow life options, and, while girls traditionally have been excluded from full participation in public life, boys have been excluded from full access to the realms of emotion, intimacy and human relationship. While strategies for girls have been put in place over the last two decades, nothing has been done for boys, and they are therefore falling behind.

The root cause of boys' problematic behaviour is seen as the messages they are being given about what it means to be a man:

> We tell boys that their lives must be risky, wild and aggressive. Many males today have a tremendous fear of not being masculine enough. This fear drives adolescent males into behaviour that 'proves' their masculinity ...
> We don't give males any strategies for dealing with conflict other than violence ...
> We need to show boys that it's OK to show their emotions ... Feminism has encouraged women to grow, but our men are still stuck in an emotional rut. (West 1994b, p.15)

The obvious answer, flowing from this analysis, is to provide boys with alternative models of masculinity. This argument stresses the need for a greater involvement of men in boys' lives, both at school and at home. Male teachers, modelling "positive varieties of masculinity" are seen as essential in schools, as is an increased bonding between boys and their fathers within the family (*The Gen*, March 1994, pp.3-4).

One of the aspects of male culture which is seen as particularly problematic is its anti-intellectual stance, resulting in boys' antipathy to school work. It is apparently just not possible to be good at school, and to be a *real* boy on the way to becoming a *real* man. In particular, humanities subjects are seemingly viewed by boys as inherently "female", thus explaining the low participation of boys in these subjects. Proponents of gender-based strategies for boys often demonstrate a remarkable belief in the transformative capacities of humanities subjects. As Cheryl Vardon (Chair of the Taskforce for the Education of Girls) says: "good language skills are a substitute for violence ... if boys learn to express themselves and to talk about emotions, they'll have a different way of relating to people ... we'll see less sexual harassment and bullying." (*The Gen*, March 1994, p.4)

While having some sympathy for aspects of the arguments outlined above, I also have strong reservations. In particular, it seems to me that these ideas are based on a rather simplistic view of what is going on in schools, and of the place of schooling in the wider society. Equating the position of boys with that of girls ignores the role of schools in perpetuating existing power relations between men and women, and significantly overstates the gains that girls have actually made. No mention at all is made of other major social factors, such as class and race, that continually intersect with gender, in forming our social experience. It seems quite likely, for example, that many boys' refusal to co-operate with adult-defined educational goals and authority structures, may have as much to do with class factors, as with gender.

The idea that language-based subjects are the answer to boys' violence and sexist behaviour is a rather curious notion, and one which is certainly not backed up by the extreme levels of misogyny demonstrated in the lives and works of many famous artists, writers and intellectuals. It denies the actual record of subjects like history, which themselves have a history of participation in gender, racial and nationalist oppression. It also denies the serious nature of verbal harassment and emotional abuse - techniques which can be (and are) effectively utilised by men with sophisticated language skills. Research into the construction of masculine culture suggests that what is most seriously absent in male social development is the capacity for empathy and emotional connectedness *with the experience of other people* - not simply an inability to express one's *own* feelings (Middleton 1992, p.190). This is certainly not *automatically* developed by language-based skills and humanities education.

It is not useful to regard men's emotional lives as "mistakes" that can be "fixed up" outside of a thorough-going questioning of masculine culture, as it is actually manifested in the institutions and practices of social power. Boys are "toughened up" (brutalised and emotionally desensitised) so that they are prepared to take their places within the machinery of oppression that makes up this society. Clearly not every man is a "winner", and most men do not feel themselves to be powerful. But they generally accept that life is about winners and losers, and participate in practices that maintain the existence of hierarchical power structures, which place *men as a group* clearly in control of the overall shape and direction of our society.

The "equal but different" argument, that equates boys' under-representation in humanities classes and cooking classes with girls' under-representation in science, maths and technical subjects, ignores the clear status difference between the subject groups. Boys are not passive beings, slavishly responding to social messages. They are actively responding to the realities of the world within which they live, and constructing a gendered identity that will serve them in negotiating the hierarchies of social power. Girls' push into traditionally "male" subjects involves a challenge to existing power structures, and implies a rise in status. Boys' entrance into traditionally "female" subjects would imply a loss of status and a decrease in potential social power. Boys recognise this clearly, and any programs seeking to change their choices will have to show them some good reasons why they should abdicate from men's traditional position of dominance. Adult men have, as yet, failed to come to terms with this question, so expecting boys to accept it unquestioningly is rather unrealistic.

Proponents of boys' education strategies consistently paint an overly rosy picture of girls' educational advances. Final year and university entrance results are a very limited indicator of girls' overall position within gendered power relations. Australia's work force continues to be one of the most gender-segregated in the world, with women occupying the least well-paid jobs (*HRSCLCA* 1992, pp.31-2). The world outside of school is still heavily stacked against full and equal participation by women, and while girls do better than boys at the initial stages of university, men still predominate at post-graduate level, and the higher levels of academic employment (*ABS* 1993, pp.101,107).

Schools themselves are overwhelmingly male-defined institutions, from their hierarchical authority structure, competitive learning styles, and combative discipline policies. As Jane Kenway says, "effective equality policies [would] mean change on a very large scale: changes in recruitment, in organisation, in curriculum content, in pedagogy" (1990, p.50). Unfortunately, "equal opportunity" or "anti-discrimination" is generally defined very narrowly, and the factors mentioned above do not even enter the discussion (Connell 1989, p.300). Equal opportunity programs for girls often receive lip-service at best, and on occasions face outright opposition. Feminism continues to be seen as a "dirty word" by many male teachers, who see it as a way for women to get an unfair professional advantage.

In this context it is no wonder that some women fear the push for "equal attention" for boys. Boy's interests are regularly set against those of girls, as clearly shown by the "Four Corners" program, which was structured around a high-school debate between senior boys and girls on the subject "that feminism has gone too far." The boys themselves grasped the idea well, as articulated by one debater: "What we all have to realise is as soon as you bring in programs for girls it must affect boys, because the more emphasis you put on girls the less emphasis there is going to be on boys, thus restricting boys even more. That's the bottom line." (Four Corners, *ABC Television*, 18 July 1994)

Advocates for girls' educational strategies correctly point out that while a small number of girls are indeed doing very well - 2,000 out of 31,000 at Year 12 level in New South Wales - things have not really changed very much for the majority. The possibility exists that the success of the few could be used to remove support from those who continue to need it. (Four Corners, *ABC Television*, 18 July 1994)

The concern that boys' education strategies could be part of the backlash against women is further strengthened when we see how well many of the ideas outlined above fit within the larger "men's rights" context. The claim that girls are doing wonderfully fits with the larger claim that women have got everything they need and that feminism is now the dominant ideology of contemporary society (said by Warren Farrell during an interview on Australian talk-back radio). The assertion that boys are worse off than girls in the area of health and safety (Fletcher 1994, p.ii) parallels similar assertions about men in general (Farrell 1994, pp.180-198).

The whole popular discussion of men's and boys' issues is oblivious to the complexities of class and race. This allows the exploitation and oppression suffered by working-class men, and men from marginalised ethnic and racial backgrounds, to be used to justify the claim that *all* men are oppressed. Warren Farrell does this to an extreme extent:

> Blacks are more likely than whites to be homeless; men are more likely than women to be homeless. Blacks are more likely than whites to be in prison; men are about twenty times more likely than women to be in prison. Blacks die earlier than whites; men die earlier than women ... Apartheid forced blacks to mine diamonds for whites; socialisation expected men to work in different mines to pay for diamonds for women. (Farrell 1994, p.39)

This is an absurd argument which is hard to take seriously (though many people do). Surely it is not too difficult to see that men are not an homogeneous group and that there are factors other than gender at work here! It is also ethically unacceptable. Using the suffering of clearly oppressed groups for one's own ends is yet another form of exploitation. This, unfortunately, is exactly what is happening in the area of boys' education, where the real problems experienced by boys from working-class, Aboriginal and ethnic minority backgrounds are being appropriated to advance the interests of men as a whole.

The nostalgia for "the good old days" of gender certainty and male bonding, demonstrated by the Robert Bly style men's movement, and the cause of much concern to many women and men, is often reiterated by "boys' education" advocates. Robert Bly claims, for example, that "the fifties male had a clear vision of what a man was, and what male responsibilities were" (Bly 1991, p.2). Dr Peter West claims that: "a generation ago, boys' lives were less complicated, because gender lines were firm ... Men looked up to their fathers with love and respect" (West 1994B, p.15).

This is certainly not the picture I have gained from my reading of histories of masculinity. "Patriarchy" has always involved a struggle for power between "the fathers" and "the sons". Freud's "Oedipus complex" represents the psychologising and universalising of conflict between the (male) generations, and popular American movies of the 1950s were often obsessed with boys' alienation from their fathers. In addition, there is a long history to men's uncertainty about their masculinity - usually focussed on the allegedly destructive effects of too much female input into boys' schooling and general upbringing.

During the late-nineteenth century there was an increasing apprehension, in Britain and the United States, that boys were being feminised due to the absence of fathers from the home. There was a harking back to the manly values of the frontier, and concern that a "long period of profound peace [would create] effeminate tendencies in young men" (Kimmel 1987a, p.147). The Boy Scout movement was created largely in response to such fears of "feminisation" and the allegedly pernicious influence of mothers and female teachers (Pleck 1987, p.23; Kimmel 1987a, pp.148-9). Fears that masculinity was "under threat" surfaced strongly after both World Wars, when it was realised how many men had been disqualified from military service on physical or mental grounds, and how many men had suffered emotional breakdown in battle. These phenomena were interpreted by many as a failure of masculinity, and blamed on the too-close relationship between mothers and sons (Pleck 1987, pp.22,28).

During the 1950s and 1960s, concern was regularly expressed about the effects on men of new occupational roles. The most popular explanation of social problems, such as juvenile delinquency, was "father absence", which was said to cause boys to experience anxiety about their masculinity. The domesticated father of television sitcoms was shown as weak and dominated by his dragon-like wife in curlers. This image is most clearly expressed in the movie *Rebel without a Cause*, where James Dean seeks advice from his father, but recoils in disgust on finding him wearing an apron and washing dishes (Pleck 1987, p.29).

These explanations for boys' behaviour are recycled by much of the men's movement and hailed as "new insights". They have unfortunately been bought by many mothers (Silverstein & Rashbaum 1994, p.88). For example, concerned mothers interviewed in the "Four Corners" program mentioned earlier, stated that boys' problems are directly due to too much input from women, and not enough from men. I find it quite disturbing that yet again women can end up being blamed, and blaming themselves, for the effects of masculine culture on boys.

None of this should be taken to mean that boys do not deserve or need attention. It is an extremely painful process learning to be a man. Boys who I interviewed talked about the constant presence of fear - fear of ridicule, fear of humiliation, and sometimes fear of physical violence from their peers. The world of men is an intimidating and often terrifying place for boys, who face the prospect of having to "measure up" if they are to find a place within it, usually without any emotional support from the boys and men around them.

In order to make any sense of the "male experience", we need to be able to keep two seemingly contradictory things together. Men as a group are firmly in control of the power structures that determine the shape and direction of this society, yet they generally experience themselves as powerless. For women and girls, who are experiencing men's culture from a marginalised position, it is easy (and understandable) to think that "it must be wonderful to be a boy" (this was said by an advocate of affirmative action for girls on a radio program dealing with girls' education). This, however, mistakes the structures of power for the personal experience of empowerment. For men and boys, who experience the subjective powerlessness that goes with being a small cog in an overpowering machine, it is very difficult to see that they are, in fact, part of a dominant group.

Much of boys' experience of gender and power within the context of school, and their resulting behaviour, is strongly influenced by their class and cultural background. From this perspective, the school curriculum can be seen as middle-class knowledge being imposed on often actively resisting students, whose resistance is interpreted as "misbehaviour" or stupidity. "Remedial" education strategies are often based on a deficit model that poses middle-class, Anglo-saxon ways of being as the norm, and labels other groups, that are unable or unwilling to compete, as defective (Kenway 1990, p.46). This is a profoundly disrespectful approach, and is unlikely to produce anything other than further resistance.

When seen through the lenses of class and ethnicity, the recent "discovery" that not all boys are doing well at school is hardly news at all, yet many advocates of boys' education strategies act as if no-one had ever realised it before. Educational inequality between males, as well as between males and females, is not an aberration, but an integral part of the system. From the beginning of compulsory mass education in the late nineteenth century, schools were designed to reproduce class-based inequality, and to protect the power and privileges of the middle and upper classes. As Bob Connell observes:

> [Schools] are set up to 'sort and sift', to give elite training to the children of the rich, to prepare others for the assembly line, and to legitimate the results. That is why we have a testing program, selective promotion to the upper levels of education, privileged private schools, and so on. To produce educational inequality is the proper business of schools performing their function of reproducing an unequal social order. (Connell *et al.* 1982, pp.189-90)

The official ideology of "equal opportunity" in modern education systems hides deep-seated and persistent structural inequalities, and the organisation of education in terms of individual competition operates to hide these inequalities. Our society has been convinced that success at school is primarily to do with individual intelligence and diligence, rather than class, gender or race-based access to power, privilege and resources. Boys from elite private schools, and academically-oriented state schools in affluent suburbs, have always done well, and continue to do so. Feminist observers certainly seem to have a point when they suggest that while girls posed no academic threat to these most successful boys, no-one bothered themselves about those working-class boys who failed. It is only now, when girls are seen as a real threat to the job prospects of privileged boys, that working-class boys are martialled on behalf of men as a whole.

Historically, there has been a clear and direct link between the part played by schools in the reproduction of class privilege on the one hand, and the reproduction of masculinity on the other. The elite English "public" schools of the nineteenth century were concerned with forming upright Victorian gentlemen, ready to take their rightful place as the ruling-class of the British Empire. The "manly virtues" were vigorously instilled, often with the assistance of considerable amounts of violence and brutality. The prevailing ethos of schools today continues to be essentially male, despite the predominance of female teachers. Men continue to fill most of the top positions, and they are generally the disciplinarians. Secondary schools reflect the hierarchical structure of all patriarchal institutions, with a (usually) male principal and deputy, who have wide powers over both teachers and students.

This hierarchical structure is central to the school's construction of masculinity, which, rather than being monolithic, is characterised by a range of competing masculine "styles". "Cool dudes", "swats", "wimps", "jocks", "nerds", "toughs", "bullies", and "uncontrollable louts", are all terms describing masculine styles among students, each with their own position within the school hierarchy. This hierarchy, however, is much more complex than is generally accepted, and the argument that academic success is incompatible with masculinity is far too simplistic.

Sports prowess and physical strength certainly provide a definite prestige and potential access to power. However, academic success, in itself, need not preclude a boy from high masculine status. There are a whole range of behaviours that enter into establishing a masculine identity, and boys are highly skilled at manipulating them. An academically-successful boy who smokes cigarettes, misbehaves in class and has an attractive girl-friend will not be treated by his peers in the same way as a boy whose only interests are chess and computers. Within elite private boys' schools, a great emphasis is placed on academic success, including on the humanities, languages, drama and music. This is certainly *not* seen as incompatible with masculinity. A combination of sporting achievement and academic success is usually essential in the "head boy", who is expected to personify the school's image of desirable masculinity.

This combination of masculinity and academic achievement is possible within ruling-class schools because they are: "the locus of what is usually a mutually-supporting set of family, school and peer practices. The production of a specific kind of masculinity, and the process of class formation, are virtually one and the same." (Connell *et al.* 1982, p.98)

Academic success and the competitive abilities associated with sporting prowess (particularly in team sports) provide middle- and upper-class boys with a direct path into the adult male world of the professions and business.

The reality is quite different, however, for working-class boys. The inevitable result of individual competition, within a curriculum based on middle-class knowledge, is failure and the feeling of being stupid; and it is no wonder that working-class people often experience their time at school as humiliating and disempowering. However, the class-based nature of this failure, and the resulting alienation and conflict, is effectively hidden by individualising and psychologising practices. "Badly" behaved students are defined as "problem children", their families are blamed, and psychologists and school counsellors certify that the problem is, in fact, internal to the child.

During my visit to the United States researching this article, a worker in a juvenile psychiatric institution described this process to me. In her area, when children's misbehaviour reaches a certain serious point, they are initially ordered to participate in her institution's programs. If this is not successful, they are then handed over to the juvenile justice system. Apparently, almost all of the children coming within the ambit of her institution are diagnosed as having "Oppositional Defiant Disorder". Here in Australia, families are often blamed for the problematic behaviour of students, avoiding any suggestion that schools, the educational system, or the society at large might bear some responsibility. This attitude was clearly expressed by Dr Ken Boston, Director-General of education in New South Wales, who was reported as telling a seminar on conflict resolution:

> We have children in our schools who, for one reason or another are not receiving effective parenting. They may come from very unstable families, they may be underfed or undernourished, they may be poorly clothed, they may be inadequately supervised, and these kids all come to school, to a degree, unteachable. (*Advertiser*, 5 August 1994, p.7)

This approach, however, hides the realities of what is going on. For working-class boys, the school is the representative of a hostile, class-based authority, and "getting into trouble" is often a "process of constructing masculinity through conflict with the institutional authority of the school" (Connell 1989, p.291). The school is seen as part of a structure of authority and privilege to which they have no access; they are there only because they are legally forced to be, and they despise the "book-knowledge" that bears no resemblance to the struggles of their every-day lives.

However, behind the school stands the state - the police, the courts and the prison system, which quickly come into play if the school's authority is flouted (Connell 1989, p.294). Working-class boys' perception of being involved in a class-war is really quite accurate, and is often reflected in the hostile attitudes of teachers and school administrators.

A working-class boy who wants to do well at school is faced with some very difficult choices, which middle-class students rarely have to deal with. To perform well means embracing the ethic of individual success. This means that he "would have to break with his major patterns of relationship, and isolate himself from the interactions which build solidarity among family and friends" (Connell *et al*. 1982, p.123). Teachers often relate to the values held by working-class families and communities simply as a handicap that "motivated" students need to leave behind. Education literally requires such students to become "class traitors" if they are to be successful, and those that make this choice are often left with deeply felt, long-lasting emotional scars.

On the other hand, many students refuse what they see as a meaningless choice. They can see clearly that advancement through educational achievement is a possibility open only to very few with particular abilities, not something that is available to working-class young people as a whole. Despite the popular rhetoric that everyone can be a success if only enough effort is made, the competitive system requires losers as well as winners. Middle-class children from professional, educated families have built-in advantages that guarantee them pride of place in any educational competition.

As working-class participation in the higher levels of secondary schooling has increased in recent years, the educational requirements for a whole range of jobs have simply increased, leaving the dynamics of privilege relatively unchanged. If anything, working-class young people are probably worse off, because a great deal of the employment opportunities that existed in the past have disappeared and it has become more difficult for young people to get unemployment benefits. This has forced more students to stay at school longer in order to get government student support, while knowing that their schooling is most unlikely to end up getting them a job. It is no wonder that many such students become apathetic, hostile or actively antagonistic.

When these class and economic factors are combined with the requirements of masculine culture, all the ingredients for major difficulties exist. For a working-class boy:

> The construction of his masculinity goes on in a context of economic insecurity, or hard-won and cherished security, rather than economic confidence and expansiveness. It means that his father's masculinity and authority is diminished by being at the bottom of the heap in his workplace, and being exploited without being able to control it; and that his mother has to handle the tensions, and sometimes the violence, that result. (Connell *et al.* 1982, p.181)

This is not to say that it is only working-class boys who are problems at school. However, it is a common-place among teachers to distinguish between "good" and "bad" schools - and almost invariably there is a class basis to this division. Boys in working-class schools are much more likely to be labelled and dismissed as part of a faceless group of "bad" students, while middle-class boys are more likely to receive a whole range of individualised, "remedial" attention.

In my attempts to gain an understanding of what is going on in schools, I have found the work of American sociologist Philip Wexler extremely useful. According to him, even the best intentioned educational reform generally fails to recognise the central task that schools are actually engaged in. He sees this task as the production of meaning, and in particular "the core meaning of self-identity" (1992, p.10). In modern, Western society, the possession of a "self", which is publicly valued and affirmed, is fundamental to becoming an individual of moral worth. While educators tend to see the formal curriculum as the core activity of schools, the *students* see themselves as engaged in a project of "becoming somebody" (Wexler 1992, p.7). In this project, interactions with peers and the products of popular culture tend to be of prime importance.

Students are well aware of the need for an acceptable "image" - a need that I remember very clearly from my own schooling. It tells you what clothes to wear, what music to listen to, who to hang out with, what to do after school, and it determines your attitudes towards school, teachers, parents, drugs, and alcohol. This image is no minor matter. Creating it is a major and continuous production, and its success can be literally a matter of survival. "You have to work to become somebody; otherwise you become a 'grug', a nobody with no place, no alcove, no gym or library entranceway to hang out in and to meet your friends - your friends who confirm who you are." (Wexler 1992, p.21)

In our society, gender is central to the definition of identity. Identity is largely to do with being "different from" and "the same as", and gender is one of the major signifiers of difference. Davies and Banks, in their work on masculinity in schools, see gender as an "enterprise or even an industry" (1993, p.5). Similarly Judith Butler (1989) describes how: "[One] executes it, institutes, produces and reproduces it, wears it, flaunts it, hides it, but always stylises it on one way or another. For gender is a corporeal style, a way of acting the body, a way of wearing one's own flesh as a cultural sign." (p.256)

In dominant masculine culture, the need to "be somebody" is exaggerated and extreme. Competition and the struggle for power are central. One only has to observe young boys to see how central this is to their sense of self worth. A simple walk turns into a constant competition - the first to the next corner, jumping the biggest puddle, throwing a stone further than anyone else, walking way out in front of everyone else.

School itself becomes a testing ground for a boy's successful assumption of an appropriate gender identity. Olga Silverstein describes how: "from the first day [of kindergarten] on, he's expected to measure up to his peers, to demonstrate that he's a regular guy." (Silverstein & Rashbaum 1994, p.43)

Similarly, a boy interviewed by Bob Connell described his transition from primary to secondary school:

> When the First Form joins and all come together from all different [primary] schools, there's this thing like sorting out who was the best fighter, who is the most toughest and aggressive boy in the form, and all the little mobs and cliques develop. So it was like this pecking order stuff ... and I was really frightened of this. (Connell 1989, p.294)

The consequences of not being "somebody" can be dire, and putting others down is one of the main ways of demonstrating self-worth. Boys who don't "measure up" are at best ignored and left out of things, both inside and outside of the classroom. During group activities in the class, such boys are often left completely isolated, or forced to join in with "the (other) girls" (Frank 1993, p.55). In one study, teenage boys were quite clear about the most unacceptable behaviours: "Acting like a girl, any indication of what they considered homosexual behaviour, not participating in sports, and hanging out with the girls" (Frank 1993, p.53)

According to one boy interviewed: "I find that you have to be constantly letting everyone know that you're not going to take any shit from anyone, that you're not going to be stepped on." (Frank 1993, p.53)

This project of constructing gender identity takes place within the context of a commercial youth culture which is "viciously sexist" (Connell *et al.* 1982, p.165). One only has to watch the early morning television programs of rock music video-clips to see this sexism blatantly displayed. These video-clip shows play a very important part in setting young people's fashion trends, and their influence in schools is demonstrated in the annual "Rock-and-Roll Eisteddfod". This is a competition, which has become a highly prestigious and hotly contested event, televised nationally, in which schools produce short pieces of dramatic dance-theatre set to the latest popular music. These tend to be closely based on video-clip images, and often feature highly sexist stereotypes. Popular culture generally, on television and in films, also reinforces the idea that violence, aggression and dominance are highly valued aspects of being a man, and prestige contact-sports link violence with high status masculinity (Fitzclarence 1993, p.17). This is reinforced and reflected by the importance placed on these same sports in schools.

The school itself is "an organised production process" which distributes images of identity (Wexler 1992, p.8). and along with the obvious academic "tracks" go distinct identity "tracks". Central to this is the production of "winners" and "losers". "Winners" are created on the sports field and gymnasium, in the exam room, the school magazine and the official student councils. "Losers" are created in the detention room as well as in the competitive system itself, which condemns many to inevitable failure. These concepts do not simply describe success or failure in particular academic tasks - they take on powerful moral overtones and speak of the worth of the whole human being. Getting detention, or being suspended, are not merely punishments, they are messages from the school structure about the student's identity (Wexler 1992, p.9) - messages that can affect students for the rest of their lives.

Philip Wexler's work (1992) has focused in some detail on how this production of identity can manifest in different ways in different class contexts. It demonstrates how important it is, for anyone attempting to deal with issues of gender in a particular school, to gain a solid understanding of the larger cultural and community context within which that school exists.

Within the working-class school, Wexler identifies a pervasive sense among students that "nobody cares". Cutbacks in funding, the reassertion of "traditional values", and an emphasis on discipline in the absence of caring interaction reinforce this feeling. This in turn ensures that students turn to each other and to popular culture for the images needed in their "struggle for selfhood" (Wexler 1992, p.110-111). The school is seen as a prison - a subject which is joked about, but also felt quite deeply. It is a place where you have to come if you want to see your friends, but which is otherwise of little relevance (Wexler 1992, p.17).

In contrast to the lack of expectation in working-class schools, middle-class students have to deal with an all-encompassing demand for performance. In their schools, competition and pressure are all-pervasive and never ending. This prospect stretches out ahead of children into the future, with the knowledge that entrance to university is only the beginning - next comes competition for a higher degree, entrance to a profession, advancement within the profession and so on *ad infinitum*. Even the social education programs of "enlightened" schools, teaching about the environment, race, gender, poverty and the dangers of drugs, can be seen as yet another pressure to perform, to be perfect and to save the world. Self-worth and identity depend upon success within this competitive treadmill, and apathy, depression or outbreaks of rage are common forms of response to the pressure for achievement.

In urban "under-class" schools - attended in the US mostly by African American and Hispanic students - the struggle for identity is particularly intense. The whole of dominant culture is telling these students that they are worthless and morally inferior. This general context makes any sense of self "tenuous, and if not absent, then certainly under attack" (Wexler 1992, p.13). School is experienced as part of this attack, and "misbehaviour" is part of a life-and-death struggle to prove that they are indeed "somebody".

The depth of self-denigration and the tenuousness of identity in these schools is so extreme that there is a need for continuous "display" to establish self-worth. Rapping, verbal put-downs, loud music, dancing, language, clothes and hair-styles can all be seen in this light. According to Wexler, violence "is almost always a self defence against imputed moral inferiority" (Wexler 1992, p.133), and: "'Don't mess with me' should really have a second clause that reads, 'because I have been messed with so much and so systematically by so many people and their social apparatuses that what is left is very raw, and worn right on my sleeve'." (p.142)

None of this is intended in any way to down-play the seriousness of the violence and abuse often perpetrated by many boys on girls, other boys, and teachers. What I am arguing is that the problem is, in fact, far *more* serious, complex and deep-seated than most masculinity-based arguments acknowledge. The problem exists, not only within particular aberrant individuals, but within the very structures of our society and its institutions, including schools. If we are to effectively take action to change boys' behaviour in schools, it is extremely important that we understand this behaviour within its larger context. We need to understand the meanings that boys are themselves giving to their experiences and actions, and how these meanings relate to the realities of their lives.

Simplistic analyses that see boys' behaviour as involving relatively straightforward choices, between positive or negative "styles" of masculinity, are unlikely to be effective, and could even make matters worse. We could find ourselves reproducing existing dichotomies between "good men" and "bad men" that fail to recognise how we all, as men, participate in masculine culture, and benefit in various ways from the structural subordination of women. It also makes it easy for middle-class men and boys to self-define as "good", reproducing class-based patterns of injustice. Unless we understand that the behaviour, which *we* see as undesirable, is understood by the boys themselves to be an integral part of their identity and crucial to their survival, efforts to produce change are unlikely to be successful.

Fortunately, if the will is there to really take on this issue, there are reasons to hope that boys can be engaged in a project of change. Far from being passive receivers of gender "messages", studies have found that boys are actively involved in a continuous:

> Struggle for and against what it means to be masculine, often by the same boy, not just in their relationships with young women, but in their relationships with other men: at school, at home, in the playing fields, at the dance, simply walking down the street, going to the school washroom, and putting their hand up in class to answer a question. (Frank 1993, p.50)

The very present, contradictory and painful nature of this process means that there are potentially points of entry into the world of even the most "macho" boy. Similarly, the work done by Philip Wexler offers some hope. He found that students overwhelmingly begin school with a *strong desire for love and connection*, which is soon destroyed by their experiences of institutional indifference (1992, p.119). Some teachers might greet with derision the idea that it is "love" that children are looking for at school, but this idea has been met with enthusiastic agreement by most of the students that I have spoken to personally. It is also backed up by the shining nature of the memories that many adults carry with them throughout their lives of those very few teachers who *really cared*, when they were at school. This theme occurs in the story of one very violent boy interviewed by Bob Connell. "[This boy] felt the school did not care about him, and he 'wanted to be someone, school write-off is better than being nothing' ... 'I wasn't a nobody'." (Connell 1991, p.149)

If this is the case, then our best way forward is to turn our schools into truly caring communities. However, most of the recent trends in education are likely to make things worse, rather than better. The decrease in educational funding, increase in class sizes, heavier workloads on teachers, the push for a "return to basics" and a standardised curriculum, emphasis on "discipline", and the overwhelming sense that schooling is about preparation for jobs, with students as a national economic "resource", are all likely to make education more impersonal and less caring. As Fitzclarence says:

> Educators will have to choose whether they are to self-define as functionaries of
> the economic reformers, or as pioneers of a new, more sophisticated and humane
> form of educational practice, which aspires to produce a more stable and less
> violent society. (1993, p.18)

One of the biggest difficulties faced in engaging boys in examining gender issues is that they rarely identify "masculinity" as contributing to any difficulties they may be experiencing in their lives. They are more likely to see masculinity as a highly desirable "given", and be desperate to get more of it. Gender is only likely to be seen as a problem in terms of the "threat" posed by girls and feminist teachers who are challenging boys' privileges. If we, as adults, impose our definitions of what the problem is, without understanding and engaging with the complexities of boys' lives, we are going to lose them from the start. In particular, since boys *are* advantaged in very real ways by existing gender arrangements, they are likely to resent and resist teachers' attempts to change their "role" (Connell 1989, p.292).

It seems to me that useful pointers as to how to proceed are given by work done by some therapists working with men who abuse. An approach informed by their work would involve listening to boys' stories and affirming the knowledges and skills that they have developed in dealing with often very difficult life situations. It would involve finding ways of honouring their resistance to the many injustices that they themselves have experienced, at the same time as helping them recognise and make a stand against the injustices they have inflicted on others. The articles by David Denborough and Alan Jenkins in this book both contain some exciting and important ideas, particularly around the importance of treating boys with respect, while ensuring they are prevented from continuing to act abusively.

Group work with boys needs to start by getting to know them well, finding out about the struggles they are having in their lives, their hopes and their fears. In our society, where gender is one of the basic structural divides, it should not be too difficult for a creative teacher to eventually bring any such discussions around to issues of gender - but it would then be gender as it actually impacts on the realities of boys' lives. This will take time and perseverance and I think it is useful to take some hints from Paolo Freire's approach to liberative education. He stressed that, before beginning a program: "You have to spend six months within a community understanding the community, the language, ironing out the vocabulary, talking and making contacts ... It really means going into a community, understanding it, and then teaching as an organising activity." (Karp 1994, p.23)

The final issue that I want to address is the usually unquestioned assumption that work with boys should take place in all-male groups, led either by male teachers or by "experts" brought in from outside the school. This assumption rests on the belief that boys' difficulties stem from a lack of male "role-models", and the resulting programs focus on the need for increased masculine self-esteem. Some schools have taken the "role-model" approach to heart, and brought in rugby players to teach creative writing to boys "to break down the stereotype that men are either macho or creative" (*The Gen*, March 1994, p.5). One wonders whether a society full of creatively macho men would really be much of an improvement!

More importantly, such programs run the serious risk of being used as a weapon against women. Olga Silverstein has demonstrated how psychological theories, stressing the importance of the father's role in boys' psychological development, emerged at the same time as men were increasingly absent from the home, and needed ways of maintaining their power and influence within the family (Silverstein & Rashbaum 1994, p.87). These theories generally say nothing about the quality of the father's interactions with his children or partner - they simply stress the crucial importance of his presence. Thus, Karl Zinsmeister (1993) claims:

> What matters for social success today is less whether your father was rich or poor than whether you knew your father at all ... We know, as a clinical finding that exclusive rearing by women restricts a child's environmental exploration and delays development of some kinds of external competence ... I think it is important to recognize that the bulk of our problem with domestic and street violence today grows out of having too little masculine authority at the base of society, not too much. (pp.43-44)

This kind of approach reinforces concepts of women's inadequacies, and the need for men to be in control. As Olga Silverstein asks: "What does it tell a boy about his mother, and about women in general, if a man has to be brought in to take charge?" (Silverstein & Rashbaum 1994, p.88)

This question is equally relevant to programs which suggest that only men have anything to offer boys at school. Men already predominate in positions of authority within educational and social hierarchies, and stressing the "special" nature of masculine experience is more likely to reinforce this than to challenge it. Bob Connell (1994) has pointed out that:

> Men and boys have a material interest in patriarchy ... Persuading boys, male teachers and school administrators to follow feminist principles means asking them to act against their own interests as men. Trying to do it in all-male groups, to make the discussion of 'male experience' easier, has the unfortunate effect of highlighting their shared interest. (p.2)

This is certainly supported by my own experience of some men's groups in the past, which have started out with the intention of examining our own masculinity, and degenerated into a pooling of our anger and resentment towards women. I agree that there may be times when work with boys is most appropriately done in same-gender groups, but this should be issue-focused and as part of a larger gender-inclusive program, rather than as part of a philosophy which values "men-only" meetings for their own sake. It is important to keep in mind that the fundamental issue is *gender justice*, not men's experience, and this involves women as well as men.

When all-male groups are deemed necessary, it is vital that we find ways of making the work done in them open and accountable to women and girls. It is important for men working in this area to recognise that we do not stand outside of men's culture ourselves, and it is always possible for us to *think* that we are doing good work, while unwittingly reproducing dominant and unhelpful ways of being. Unfortunately, in a culture that sees gender relationships as a "battle of the sexes", any suggestion of "accountability to women" is likely to produce negative and defensive responses from men and boys. However, it is a crucial issue that we cannot afford to ignore simply because of the difficulties involved. The best way to ensure that boys' education strategies do not become part of the backlash against women is to actively involve women and girls in those programs. This means working to build a genuine partnership between the genders in a context that recognises the realities of structural power differences. (For a discussion of accountability processes see other chapters in this book).

I believe that such "partnership-accountability" practices have an immense amount to offer men and boys. I agree whole-heartedly with Olga Silverstein when she says that "the real pain in men's lives stems from their estrangement from women" (Silverstein & Rashbaum 1994, p.25) - but I would add "and from their oppression of other less powerful groups in society". Men will only be able to heal their own relationships when they cease acting oppressively towards others. Boys' interests will best be served by helping them to see this, not by encouraging them to see themselves as oppressed, and setting their interests against those of girls. However, before we can expect boys to believe us, we need to be demonstrating it as adult men in our personal lives and in the world at large.

I certainly believe that there is an important place for gender-based programs for boys in schools, but such programs have little chance of success unless they are part of a broadly based attempt to deal with the realities of students' lives and the society in which they find themselves. Schools will have to come to terms with the fact that they are part of the very system that is creating their problems. However, as well as being institutions involved in the reproduction of inequality, schools have often been sites of struggle for fundamental social change. This political role is something that cannot be avoided - it can either be enthusiastically adopted in the interests of social justice, or left to conservative forces, which are all too keen to take it up. The current stress on the purely economic aspects of education is itself part of a powerful right-wing political push, that is successfully turning back many of the educational reforms achieved since the 1970s (Apple 1992). The backlash against feminism is a part of this conservative reaction, and we need to be very careful that programs for boys don't become part of it as well.

Abbreviations:

ABS: Australian Bureau of Statistics
HRSCLCA: House of Representatives Standing Committee on Legal and Constitutional Affairs.
NSWLCSC: New South Wales Legislative Council Standing Committee

5

Healing the Mother Wound
Maggie Carey

Why is it that young boys aren't allowed to remain connected to their mothers in the same way that girls are? I heard a story recently of a small boy and his mother. The boy needed to cross a large busy road in order to get to where he was going, and as they came up to the road, the little boy still holding his mother's hand, the mother withdrew her hand and said to the boy that it was time for him to cross the street on his own, that he was a big boy now, and had to be brave and not be a "mummy's boy". The feeling of complete desertion and isolation as his mother withdrew from him, stayed with this man into his middle age where he was now presenting in therapy over relationship issues.

One of the dominant themes of the present-day manifestation of the men's movement is breaking down the constraints of alienation and isolation that is the common experience of so many men. When I heard the story of the little boy having to cross the street on his own to show that he wasn't a "mummy's boy", I caught a glimpse of some of the setting in place of that isolation, and here I would like to challenge the beliefs behind the practices that have allowed and even encouraged that isolation to happen.

By doing so, I would hope that some of these long-held practices might be scrutinised through the lens of new understandings that are currently available regarding the ways in which gender is constructed. Whereas in previous generations there were commonly accepted beliefs about the "nature" of masculinity or femininity, now these beliefs can no longer be attributed the status of unquestioned and unquestionable truth. The raising of our boy children must be looked at in the light of our cultural discourse around gender and, in doing so, we can hope to find new ways of bringing up our children that are closer to the ideal of a non-sexist society, where neither gender is subject to demeaning or dehumanising practices on the basis of their gender.

I wish to look at specific aspects of separation in the raising of boys in our culture, but I would like to do so against the broader backdrop of a process of separation that pervades our whole Western nucleated society. This is the notion of individuation that is based on the necessity of separation. It is the idea that to be an "individual" is a highly prized state of being, and that independence and autonomy are necessary requirements in the process of individuating up the ladder of self-actualisation. It is a story about a way of being that we have been enlisted into believing is a true and necessary way.

Part of the story seems to equate difference with separateness, that somehow because we are different and know ourselves to be different, we believe we must also be separate. In our culture there doesn't seem to be a lot of credence given to the idea that we can be different and connected at the same time. Our experience of individuality based on separation contrasts sharply with instances of individuation happening within a collectivity where the good of the whole group is put before the good of any one individual. Those cultures that operate within such an understanding are noted particularly for their tolerance of difference, and we get some inkling of how prescriptive and normative the ideas of individuality are in our "aggressively individual" culture.

Notions of individuality have obviously served the capitalist system well. Separation is a necessary prerequisite for competition, as isolation and alienation are for war. Making an icon out of self-interest allows the "First World" to maintain its relationship of disconnection to the "Third World".

And so to the first and highly formative separation that men experience, separation from their mothers, traditionally as quite young boys. Any examination of the mother/son relationship in this culture has to be within the context of the Freudian framework, given that this has been the most dominant and widely accessible discourse on the raising of boys to be available this century. How many mothers, if not having actually heard the term Oedipal complex, are aware of cultural inhibitions around demonstrating an overt closeness to their sons beyond a very young age? How many women stop themselves from doing what they feel to be right in terms of remaining close, in order to do what they are told is right in not letting a boy grow up to be a "sissy".

Freud's account of how a boy's Oedipus complex is put in place is relatively simple and straightforward. The boy's pre-oedipal attachment to his mother becomes sexually charged and the boy then comes to see his father as a rival for his mother's love and wishes to replace him. The boy dreams about killing his father, or at least castrating him; he then develops a fear of retaliation from his father for having these desires, specifically that he himself will be castrated. The fear of castration is such that he gives up his sexual attachment to his mother, and represses and sublimates his feelings toward her. The reward that he receives for his sacrifice, apart from not losing his penis, is "identification with his father, and the superiority of masculine identification and prerogatives over the feminine" (Chodorow 1978, p.94). To lose one's penis is to become a female, and in Freud's topology that is to become the object of contempt.

The overwhelming desire for a penis is the driving force of the female Oedipal complex. At about three years of age little girls realise that they do not have a penis, which automatically leads them to think that they have been castrated and are therefore inferior, in Freud's words, they "fall a victim to envy for the penis." They develop contempt for their mothers whom they realise also don't have a penis, and whom they blame for their own "atrophied" state. The blame and anger and contempt causes them to turn away from their mother to their father, who does have a penis. Eventually they change from wanting a penis from their father to wanting a baby from him, through somehow unconsciously equating the penis and child.

The Oedipus complex serves to provide men with very strongly developed superegos, the internalised voices of paternal authority, because: "In boys ... the complex is not simply repressed, it is literally smashed to pieces by the shock of threatened castration, whereas Girls remain in it for an indeterminate length of time; they demolish it late and, even so, incompletely." (Freud 1925) Freud uses these observations as a basis for conclusions about women's lesser moral character and lesser ability to be objective: "I cannot evade the notion (though I hesitate to give it expression) that for women the level of what is ethically normal is different from what it is in men. Their super-ego is never so inexorable, so impersonal, so independent of its emotional origins as we require it to be in men." (Freud 1925, p.257)

He further claims that women have a less developed sense of justice than men, that they allow themselves to succumb to the emotions of shame and jealousy, are conceited, are in effect "unable to submit to life's requirements, and have made no contribution to civilization. (With the exception of weaving and plaiting - which women developed on the model of their pubic hair to further cover their genital deficiency from the world." (Freud, 1925, p.143)

These are not, Freud assures us, new knowledges about female nature, but rather "characteristics which critics of every epoch have brought up against women", and which he can see follow logically from his theory of the "psychic effects of genital differences" (ibid, p.143).

In his later writings, fully aware of the political setting of the time, he argues that "the feminists' demands for equal rights between the sexes does not take us far"; that "we must not allow ourselves to be deflected from such conclusions [about women's sense of justice etc.] by the denials of feminists, who are anxious to force us to regard the two sexes as completely equal in position and worth" (Freud 1925, p.258).

It would seem then, that Freud's psychological framework for the establishment of masculinity is heavily predicated on not being a woman. A boy must separate from his mother in order to join the superior ranks of manhood, and the separation is steeped in fear and contempt - fear of castration and thus ending up a woman, and an inculcated contempt for women would make that the worst fate possible. So the mark of "normal", healthy development of masculinity becomes the ability to separate from and reject that which is feminine. In this way men are coerced into not having any sense of empathic identity with any women.

If we look once more at the "individualistic" backdrop against which this "separation from" has been increasingly played out in the latter half of this century, we get a clearer understanding of the forces that are at work to establish a condition of isolation and alienation that most particularly pertains to men. In the Piaget-type developmental studies, we encounter very directly the idea of separation as the end point of childhood development. Independence and autonomy are the perceived goals. The infant at birth is seen as being in a state of undifferentiated ego mass with the mother, and the task is to evolve a separate ego self.

In Maslow's hierarchy of needs (1968), self-actualisation is at the top of the ladder. In all of the "human growth" psychologies there is reference to finding the truly unique individual self that is free from the accumulation of interdependencies, co-dependency being its most recent and most alarming manifestation. It has become psychologically unhealthy now to want to be involved in the lives of your loved ones, and it's interesting that this "malaise" primarily affects women. Feminist family therapist Marianne Walters points out how this latest addition to the plethora of self-help possibilities "suggests that women have overdone their roles, that they have gone too far in taking care of others, that they do too much loving, helping, reaching out, protecting, nurturing" (Walters 1993, p.64). Women are being told to extricate themselves from the lives of their children and partners, and the message is one of containment, of "don'ts". Don't love too much, don't be too involved, or responsible, or emotional. Don't do any of the things that have been traditionally ascribed to woman's roles as mothers and daughters; "these behaviors have entered into the language that is used to describe dysfunction, that has taken on meanings associated with problematic interaction" (Walters 1992).

And while women are being encouraged to let go, men, under the dictates of the mythopoetic men's movement, are being persuaded to take up the cause of regaining men's lost power, by discovering the ancient and primitive wild man that lives in the depths of the male psyche, and which has been lost to men through the industrialisation of our society, that saw fathers become unavailable to sons as true models of masculinity. The raising of sons mostly by women, because of the absent father, has contributed to men becoming "soft" and to their losing their sense of primary identity as men.

Bly opens his best-selling formulaic for reinstating patriarchal culture with the declaration that "something is wrong" with the men who have gotten in touch with their feminine side through their contact with women. They have become "soft males", anomalies in a system that only rewards those who are hard and ruthlessly competitive, and, by page four, he is inciting men to drop all that and to get in touch with something within themselves that is really "fierce". Once again, male identity is being defined in terms of not being feminine and there is an overt contempt for being "too soft" or "feminine." And the process prescribed for unlocking the Wild Man: "Stealing the key from under your mother's pillow ... the key is under your mother's pillow - just where Freud said it would be." (1990, p.11)

According to Bly, it is essential that boys make a complete break from the locus of their first love, the mother, for "when women, even women with the best intentions, bring up a boy alone, he may in some way have no male face, or he may have no face at all" (ibid, p.17).

This is the same old script of masculinity being named only in opposition to anything female, and carries on the sense that boys are somehow deeply contaminated by their mother's child-rearing. What is not included in the analysis is a grasp of how it is traditional gender role structures that force women to do all the child-rearing, while at the same time co-opting most men to avoid it.

The incidence of softness and femininity in boys is of such concern to fearful parents in North America that clinics have been established to deal with this problem:

> Run by "male mothers" such as Richard Green, author of "The Sissy Boy Syndrome", these clinics force the boy into conforming to "masculine " norms, inciting him to kill anything remotely "feminine" or motherlike in himself, often through bizarre behavior modification techniques. "Feminine" behavior, such as playing with dolls is punished, while "masculine" behavior, such as pulling all the hair off of a female doll, is rewarded. One "sissy" boy was deemed cured after he beat his mother and sisters with a stick. (Caputi & MacKenzie 1992)

It is instructive, in terms of contextualising Bly's attitude toward women, to look at what he was engaged in prior to his work within the men's movement. In the latter half of the seventies he was actually writing and performing poetry on the theme of the Goddess, and touring the United States giving readings of these poems. Although these readings were purportedly in accordance with the growing interest in Goddess religion, it seems that Bly had a fixation on the more extreme "Teeth-Mother Naked" versions, that saw women as "essentially devouring and rapacious". As Charlene Spretnak (1992) points out: "the symbol called "vagina dentata", so important to Freud and other patriarchal theorists, has never been found in excavations of nonpatriarchal cultures. Woman the Devourer, in short, is a projection of the patriarchal world view."

The solution for Bly to the problems facing men and their understanding of masculinity follows in direct line from Freud and other patriarchs, and continues an ideology that damages us all. Alternative solutions might involve critiquing this idea of a masculinity that is defined as 'not-woman': to let boys stay connected to their mothers until they are ready to cross the big streets on their own; and to encourage a sense of masculinity that is in partnership with women, rather than in opposition to them.

But where does all this leave those men who as boys were denied a full relationship with their mothers on the basis of society's demand that they prove themselves 'not-woman'? I cannot help but be struck by the way the cutting-off from mothers equates in some degree with an experience of that relationship dying, and how the grief associated with that death might impact on an individual. What would it be like for men to reflect on how they would have been different if they had not had to separate, if that relationship had been allowed to remain alive?

I wonder about the loss of self that may have happened when the door was shut on that relationship, and what it would be like for men to now be invited to reclaim what was important to that sense of self that came from their early relationship with their mother. Michael White, in his article "Saying Hullo Again: The incorporation of the lost relationship in the resolution of grief" (1988), describes an interview with a 39 year old man whose mother died when he was seven, in which Michael invites this man to reconnect with those things about himself that his mother had seen in him. He asks:

What did your mother see when she looked at you through her loving eyes?

How did she know these things about you?

What is it about you that told her about this?

What can you now see in yourself that had been lost to you for many years?

What difference would it make to your relationship with others if you carried this knowledge with you in your daily life?

Would this type of questioning be helpful, I wonder, in enabling men to reclaim a relationship to themselves that was denied them? Would it be useful to bring this lost sense of themselves forward, and would this then make it less likely that their sons, and their son's sons, would be denied it?

6

Step by Step:
Developing Respectful and Effective Ways of Working with Young Men to Reduce Violence

David Denborough

Issues of gender equity, and girls' and boys' education strategies, have generated much debate throughout education circles over the last 12 months, and have involved a diverse range of groups and positions.[1] This paper seeks to explore some of the issues involved in working with young men to reduce violence, and describe an approach that Sydney Men Against Sexual Assault (MASA) has begun to develop in conjunction with various women and women's groups.[2] It is hoped that such an approach may open up space for women and men to work co-operatively with young people on issues of violence and gender.

The paper consists of two parts. The first explores my own experiences of schooling, and through such an exploration attempts to draw out various theoretical threads upon which our current work in schools is based. The second details the framework of the sessions that Sydney MASA currently run in schools, outlines possible future directions for such work, and invites schools to take on the broader responsibilities involved in order to adequately address issues of gender and violence.

Back in the Old Schoolyard

Multiple Masculinities

I spent most of the years of my childhood in an Anglican, private all boys school in Canberra. There, despite a relatively narrow cross-section of the male population (particularly regarding ethnicity and socio-economic status), I came across many different ways of being and becoming men. In my day-to-day wanderings through classrooms, sporting fields, and family homes, I ebbed and flowed within and between differing masculinities. Within my school there existed three key masculinities: the "cools", the "squares", and the "poofs"[3], and a great diversity of others, some of which were defined primarily by racial or class backgrounds, with still others defined by particular sporting preferences and skills.

A Hegemonic Masculinity: "Cool" and "Tough"

Despite such diversity, there was also clearly a dominant, hegemonic masculinity - that of the "cools".[4] This was the group of boys that I wanted to belong to more than the others. The benefits, privileges and prestige of such membership outweighed all the rest. After about Year 9, when I began to see my peers' approval as in some way competing with that of my parents, much of me desired to be "cool".[5] The key attributes that one had to demonstrate in order to achieve such membership consisted primarily of excellence at football, drinking, "sleazing", and remaining always in control. In order to "be cool" one had to, in many ways, become cold.

Such messages are also played out on broader arenas. The same strands of the dominant versions of masculinity in our culture at this time seem all too often to work themselves around the following themes:

1. The importance of dominating and controlling others. The more power and influence you wield over others, be it expressed on the football field, in the bedroom, the office, or in the international arena, the more of a man you are seen to be.

2. The justification to use coercion, force, and, in many cases, even violence to achieve such control and power.

3. The abdication of responsibility for acts of coercion, force and violence.

4. The importance of rejecting and denigrating the feminine.

5. The importance of rejecting and denigrating homosexual expression.

It is such dominant messages of masculinity that this paper and Sydney MASA's work in schools attempts to address and move beyond. It seems reasonable to suggest that such messages contribute to the incidence of interpersonal, structural, and even international violence prevalent in our society and, in the vast majority of instances, perpetrated by men.

Many Levels, Many Messages

In order to deconstruct such messages and create new meanings and ways of being men, it will be important to understand how such a dominant masculinity is formed and supported on a number of different levels within a school setting.

In my school, such a dominant masculinity was supported in many ways, including through peer power relations, which played themselves out in constant insults, threats, and occasional violence against those boys who dared create alternative ways of being men. It was also sustained by the privileges that the adoption of such a masculinity brought, such as admiration, time and space to occupy, the right to speak, status within the school, and also, of crucial importance, the status it brought within our sister school. The dominant masculinity was also supported by the school structure in its hierarchical staff and student leadership and decision-making patterns, its rewards for sporting excellence, its discipline regime (which still included at that time the cane), and, perhaps more subtly, by the fact that the curriculum itself was generally taught from the perspectives of white, middle-class, heterosexual, dominant men.[6]

On an even broader level, our playground banter and the dominant messages of masculinity were informed by the representations of global media, the inequitable distribution of wealth, and inequitable representation of women in positions of power, the construction of language, imperialist ideology, and even our capitalist economy which, in itself, supports an individualistic, competitive masculinity and justifies power over others.[7] The very ways in which we were learning to use our bodies within such contexts inscribed such dominant meanings within our sinews, blood and bone.

Clearly the dominant masculinity playing itself out in our private school was receiving plenty of support and was, in turn, recreating the very systems just described.

Alternative Messages

It would be misleading to think that such support was universal or essentially enshrined - far from it. At the very same time as receiving the broader and social messages outlined above, we were also exposed to the androgynous and camp popstars of the eighties, the social movements of feminism and the anti-nuclear movement, Nelson Mandela, the lesbian and gay Mardi Gras, and the mixed messages of our families. All such factors found their way into our conversations and into our minds. On the school level, blatant abuses of power between students were harshly punished (albeit by methods that reinforced the power of adults/teachers over young people/students), and various individual teachers promoted very different, non-violent and non-dominating ways of being men. We were receiving a multitude of often contradictory messages about being men.

Thus our gendered identities are not formed simply through our families, nor simply through our peers, but through relations with individuals, communities, and institutions. In order to bring about change, our approaches will therefore need to operate on all these levels. There are a number of dynamics upon which we can work. There are alternative messages about being men available in the broader community, and even within the schoolyard there are multiple masculinities constantly challenging one another. Such realisations open up space for change.

The contradictory nature of the gender messages that we receive has further implications for the way we understand identity formation, and therefore the strategies that we develop.

Active Negotiation

One way of understanding gender construction is to recognise that, as we receive such contradictory messages, we constantly actively participate in negotiating our identities.[8] Such a perspective allows us to notice and take seriously how we adopt very different positions and ways of being in differing contexts. Our masculine identities, never fixed, always in formation, are far from universal or consistent. Instead, they are riddled with cracks and contradictions. It is such a realisation that brings further hope and directions for change.[9] Such an acknowledgement means that even boys and men who are identifying strongly with an aggressive masculinity can be seen to have cracks and contradictions within their ways of being, which open up space for bringing about change.

An example was demonstrated by a Year 7 boy I knew when I was in year 12. His name was Paul.[10] By Year 12 I had achieved a high status masculinity (a complicated negotiation between "cool" and "square"), with an accompanying profound isolation - from my family, from all but one of my peers, and indeed from large landscapes of myself. I spent most of my days at school, when not in class, with younger boys. They seemed to have such a vibrancy and a sense of life that I was missing in myself and my contemporaries. In particular I recall Paul, a twelve year old kid, who was always in trouble, fighting, appearing from nowhere with a black eye, broken nose, or arm in a sling. He was notorious for smoking cigars and drinking port on school grounds. Around his peers he was always trying desperately to assert himself, often in extremely violent ways, and yet with me in different contexts it was often quite a different story.

I remember an incident one particular afternoon very clearly. It has almost a sacred feeling for me. During lunch times whole groups of Year 7 boys would occasionally attempt to jump on top of me (I considered this quite a sign of friendship, while various teachers saw it as degrading the role of prefects). This particular afternoon Paul had spent the lunch time as my bodyguard from the other Year 7s. A little later on, as we were walking through the cloisters of the quadrangle, he reached up and held my hand. It was an unheard-of situation in a relatively competitive and cut-throat school. I'm sure the institution would have found it far easier to deal with his violence than with such tenderness between boys.

Such an act was a clear contradiction, a clear exception. It showed me another way of being a man and it came from the most violent kid in the school. It could have been seen as a moment of resistance to the dominant ways of being men. It could have been recognised as such and built upon. Unfortunately, such acts of resistance were not built upon at my school. Instead, he was punished more and more for those times when he identified with a dominant aggressive masculinity. The last thing I heard of the boy who held my hand in the cloisters was that he was facing court in New Zealand on charges of violence.

Such exceptions are used in our approach as openings to new ways of being. Recognising how we act differently in different situations allows us to acknowledge that we make choices regarding our gendered identities and actions. This seems to me a more empowering way of understanding gender and identity formation than some of the theories that posit individuals as passively socialised into a certain sex-role.[11] The realisation that we actively negotiate our identities opens up the possibility for inviting and taking responsibility for the gendered ways in which we act.[12]

Power

It must be remembered that the choices we make, and the gendered identities that we construct, are located within intricate power relations.

As we played on the monkey bars, the old tractor, and in the fort, we were organising our identities around and within the power dynamics of our society. Our insult vocabulary, whom we invited to and excluded from parties, and how we felt about ourselves, were all influenced by sexism, racism, heterosexual dominance, and economic inequalities. They were also influenced by the positioning of young people in our culture, as will be discussed later. Our identities are suffused with issues of power and control. Identity, far from a universal or essentialist entity, is therefore a political construction. This also means that the choices we make are not totally free - rather, they are inter-relating with far broader power relations, restrictions, and options.

There are a number of intersecting power relations that play themselves out, and indeed are created, in the schoolyard. These include the power relations between boys/men and girls/women, the dynamics between the differing masculinities (the "cools", the "squares", and the "poofs"), and between adults/teachers and young people/students.

Race and class power dynamics are of crucial significance and yet are not discussed in any detail in this paper. This is a significant deficiency in our approach up until this point. What follows is therefore limited to a brief discussion of how gender, sexuality and age power relations played themselves out in my schooling, and their implications for our approach.

Relations with Women

Although we had little contact with women of our age during school hours, girls and constructions of femininity flowed constantly through our conversations, and influenced the ways in which we positioned each other and ourselves. From interactions at the bus stop, to the division of labour in our homes, to our relationships with sisters and neighbours, to our symbolic interaction with women in our fantasies, books and television shows, girls and femininities were always present. A number of formative dynamics stand out in my mind.

On the football field in the early years of schooling, no girls were visible, but their presence was summoned up whenever someone was insulted for playing badly. The fear of being identified as a girl meant that we carried pictures of girls, and the need to be unlike them, in our minds, from the earliest of days. This is an obvious example of men defining themselves as superior to women, while at the same time organising power relations between the various masculinities. Later, as the constant cliched banter of scoring and the magnificent fables of sexual conquest filled the prefects' commonroom every Monday, it was clear again that our identities as men were being formed in relation to women. The scorn shown towards various older female teachers, and the positioning of younger female teachers as sexually available for our conquest, all illustrated that, despite a single-sex environment, we boys were constantly defining our identities as separate from, and superior to, girls and women. The dominant theme was clear - girls were to be seduced for our pleasure, and the power that came through such seduction was seen to be the ultimate turn-on.

There were also contradictory messages available. Close relations with mothers, in particular, sisters, and/or girlfriends, were eliciting and indeed creating profoundly different ways of being men and relating to women in other circumstances. Even so, the dominance of particular ways of relating still ensured that our identities and even our sexualities as young men were enmeshed within power relations.

Recognising that the overall relationship between men and women is one of oppression and domination, and that this dynamic is a crucial definer of masculinities, will be imperative for any approach attempting to address violence. So, too, will a recognition that the relationship between men and women is multi-dimensional and not limited to this dynamic of power and oppression. Men's relations with women include emotional and sexual relationships, divisions of labour, and co-operation in work, just to name a few complicating and, at times, contradictory dynamics.[13] Once again such contradictions appear to be the most productive openings for change.

Homosexuality

The power relations *between* masculinities were perhaps most apparent in the ways the "cools" positioned homosexuals and homosexuality. The one (courageous) openly gay boy in my form was subjected to constant abuse, ostracism, and occasional physical violence. As always, there is an alternative theme, however, as I have heard more recently that he also enjoyed some of the best sex of his life while at that school - a constant stream of willing participants, almost all of whom were publicly homophobic!

In an all boys school in which many of the students were too unsure of the unknown entity called "girls" to consider intimacy with them, and whose parents and family life often offered little in the way of emotional or physical intimacy, homophobia played a key role in isolating young men from their own desires and each other. It was certainly a key dynamic in enforcing and privileging the dominant masculinity, and is often the first response of young men when one in any way challenges masculinity. Indeed, once in a workshop, even before I had said a single word, a boy came up to me and warned me about another guy in the class being gay! If we wish to reduce men's violence, it will be imperative that we find effective ways of challenging heterosexual dominance. A first step, for me, is to acknowledge both the privileges I receive as a heterosexual and the sexual attraction I feel to men in my life.

Young People's Powerlessness

It seems important also to recognise that the identities of young men and women are formed in a context of relative powerlessness. Most young people in our culture are without financial independence, have little control over their own learning (what goes into their minds!), and often spend much of their waking hours in rigid hierarchical institutions (schools). At the present time, such factors are exacerbated by extremely high levels of youth unemployment and government policies which decree that young people are entitled to substantially less welfare support than adults. Into this picture one must also, of course, factor the outrageous incidence of both physical and sexual child abuse in our community.

Young men receive the dominant gender messages that they ought to dominate and control others in this context. In such an atmosphere, the messages are understandably powerful and seductive. If young boys are able to position themselves with the dominant masculinity to a large degree, they gain attention, air space, and a greater say (power) over their lives and those of others. At the very least, they are less likely to be targets of abuse, and will have themselves easy targets to pick on: girls and those boys who do not fit the mould.

Again this matter is not simple, as the common occurrence of adolescent boys harassing female teachers demonstrates how dominant gender messages can be accessed by boys over women.

Acknowledging the power differentials between adults and young people does not mean excusing boys' violence; it still allows room for adults to invite young people to take responsibility for their actions. What it does mean, however, is that, as adults working with young people, we have a responsibility to develop respectful ways of working.

Respectful Practice

Acknowledging that issues of gender and violence, and indeed even our identities, are infused with power relations has implications for the very ways in which we work. Some members of the welfare field are recognising that working respectfully across race, cultural, class, gender, and even sexuality divides involves a great deal of work.[14] We must acknowledge our position within such power relations, and consciously structure our work in ways that ensure that it is respectful. For me this means acknowledging my place in the world as a white, middle-class adult who receives all the privileges of heterosexuality.

I have been very slow in recognising my place within the power dynamics of race, class and heterosexual dominance. As such, what follows is limited to a discussion of some of the implications for respectful practice that flow from acknowledging that I am an adult working with young men, and a man working on gender issues.

Adults' Responsibilities when Working with Young People

Working respectfully with young people might include the following:
-   Trying out the program with a number of young people and honouring their feedback, indeed ensuring that the program did not go ahead until all of their concerns were addressed.
-   Ensuring programs are voluntary.
-   Learning about and respecting young people's culture.
-   Teaching about how young people are treated, and honouring their resistance.
-   Moving towards supportive, self-determined, peer education programs.
-   Allowing space to name and expose the silences associated with young people's powerlessness, including child abuse, and acknowledging young people's rights.
-   Ensuring programs and workers are transparent, open and honest about all that they are trying to achieve and the processes involved.
-   Breaking down any idea that we as adults are "experts" with the answers,

and instead working from young people's agendas, acknowledging their knowledge and expertise of their lives.

 - Ensuring that one's theory and practice is informed by analyses of power. That is to say, recognising that young men's violence is located within class, race, gender and sexuality dynamics, and recognising young people's powerlessness in relation to adults.

It also seems important to question our motives for working with young people. To place oneself in a position in which one has much power over a number of people is a decision worth questioning. Similarly, it is an important question to answer for activists. Education of the young is always seen as the first response to any global problem. I suspect this is not because it is the most effective means of social change, but because it is the easiest. Often such a perspective abdicates adults' responsibilities for change, and is used to justify the lecturing of young people about the new "correct" ways of living. In many cases, such an approach simply makes young people feel more and more powerless, and is a perpetuation of injustice.

Men's Responsibilities when Working on Gender Issues

As a man working on issues of gender, I feel I have a responsibility to acknowledge that I am prone to reproduce the very systems such work is trying to dismantle. With such a recognition comes the responsibility to ensure that our work as men is open to the voices and experiences of women. Similarly, we have a responsibility to acknowledge the work of women, both past and present, upon which our work is based.

Through a number of recent conversations[15], it has become clear how easy it is for us as men to be unaware of how our work is being positioned, both by ourselves and others, in ways that are disempowering to women. This can include taking up scarce airspace and resources, not acknowledging women's work, being positioned in ways that are condescending or patronising, or speaking on issues about which we have no right to speak.

There is no doubt that such issues will be ongoing for us as men who wish to work with other men and boys on issues of gender and violence. We must ensure that we do all we can to address such issues, and to build partnerships rather than enclaves.[16] This area offers exciting work but, if it is not done respectfully, we will be replicating all we are trying to alter.

Working in Schools

What follows is a description of Sydney MASA's approach for working with young men to reduce violence, that builds upon the understandings outlined above. It draws upon the work of Michael White and Bob Connell, and our experiences of a number of one-off workshops that we have run in schools throughout New South Wales, Australia. The approach ought to be seen as just that, however, an approach that could be adapted for use within differing educational settings over differing periods of time. As shall be discussed later, one-off workshops are a profoundly inadequate response to the issue of violence. They can, however, be a starting point.

The approach that follows recognises that when one walks into a school to conduct a workshop with boys on sexual harassment or violence, one is walking into a contested field of power, contradiction, and constantly contested identities. Our approach seeks to acknowledge multiple masculinities and the power relations between them. It also seeks to acknowledge and work with the power relations between men/boys and women/girls, and between adults/teachers and young people/students. It seeks to build upon understandings of contradictory and contexted identities, and also the contradictions *between* various masculinities and *within* various masculinities. In doing so, it seeks to open up space for young men to take responsibility for issues of violence, and to negotiate with each other, with girls, with the school and broader systems, new preferred, non-violent ways of being boys and men. It is an approach dedicated to respecting power differentials, working respectfully, and being accountable to both young people's and women's experiences. As such, it recognises that change must occur on many levels, and that we must refrain at all times from positioning young men as "the problem".

When we are invited into a school, it is often to deal with a "problem" year group (invariably Year 9). In order for our work not to participate in the pathologising and individualising of what is a broad societal issue, we must ensure that our work does not remain at this level. Year 9 boys are *not* the problem - the problem is the ways in which gender, race, class, and sexuality dynamics are organised in our society. If our work is not at this level then we will be participating in the blaming of relatively powerless boys for far broader social systems.

As is outlined below, we attempt to enter the problem at the level which the school so desires (Year 9 boys), but through our process we broaden the layers of responsibility until they reach the entire local community. We insist that we talk not only with the boys but also with the parents, the staff, and members of the local community. First, though, we must make connection with the young men.

1.   *Introductions.* The first step of our workshop is to introduce ourselves. I generally run such workshops with Mark D'Astoli (a youth development officer), and we take the opportunity to give a short spiel about our personal backgrounds and that of the organisation. Incidentally, I always mention my work in a maximum security prison, which generally fascinates and opens some

space for questions and answers.

In our introductions, we are keen to acknowledge that young people are often lectured by adults, and that we don't believe in that way of working. We are keen to acknowledge that they are the experts on their lives and that we'd like to learn from them about their situations, while at the same time offering all we have picked up along the way.

When working across class, race and/or cultural differences, further acknowledgements are necessary, and adjustments must be made to ensure that our ways of working are as respectful as possible to the culture we have been invited into.

(a) *A game of sex and lies.* At times we play an introductory game in which we ask each member of the group to tell us one lie that they've ever told about their sexuality. We do so knowing full well that few stories will be volunteered. Primarily this game gives Mark and me the chance to express some of the lies we told while at school. Somehow this intrigues, and we instantly become objects of curiosity.

Sometimes we ask all those who have told such a lie to raise their hand. Only Mark and I generally have our hands raised. Then we ask those who have *heard* such a lie to raise their hand and the room is filled with waving arms!

Through this exercise, we show that we are willing to discuss issues not usually discussed. We immediately somehow step outside the normal process of being checked out - somehow we move the boundaries. It is also the source of great laughter. It seems that self-disclosure of this nature is a way of respecting where the young people are coming from. It illustrates how we have thought about the pressures on young people, and recognise their need for support.

Talking about sexuality is also a process of addressing one of the key areas in which young people's experience is denied. The unavailability of condoms in schools (a particularly pertinent issue in country areas where the local chemist knows everyone) highlights the denial of young people's sexuality.

(b) *Addressing the climate.* The next thing we establish is why the young men think we have been asked to talk to them, and what they've been told. At times principals have introduced us to the boys in a most authoritarian manner, while at others we have entered a climate in which the boys have just been told how badly they are performing, the recent suicide figures for young rural boys, and how being a boy now is so impossibly difficult.

2. *Mapping violence.* We ask the group to list the different sorts of violence in their lives. Generally, violence between boys, police violence, and violence of fathers takes a very short time to be articulated. It often takes further questions to elicit answers pertaining to violence against girls, against women, and homophobic and racist violence. We try to learn about the history of the area in which we are working, so as to link present violence with past acts of violence - especially in relation to violence against Aboriginal peoples.

Once we've got a list covering a wide range of violence, we ask if the group likes this violence, if it is good for their lives, and whether they'd like it to stop. Generally it is quickly agreed that they'd like at least some of the forms of violence to stop. Often it is stated that the level of violence is getting out of hand.

At one high school, when we began this part of the workshop, we were told that there was no violence in that area. We thought we might have to pack up and go home - and we said as much. After a few further questions, however, we had soon filled a whiteboard with different types of violence, including a recent car-bombing!

3.   *An articulated invitation.* Having heard this, we ask if they'd like us to stay and talk about these issues - if they think it might be useful for them. We state that it would be very useful for us, as we're sure that they would have a great deal to teach us about their situation and about violence in this area. After such a question, we have always been invited to stay. From here at least we have a foot in the door and some space to explore issues together - on the same side.

4.   *Gendered nature of violence.* The next step is to ask the group who it is that commits the violence just listed. It often takes an extraordinarily long time for the young men to articulate that it is *men* who overwhelmingly commit such violence (if exceptions exist, we consider and explore them).

We then ask more questions to make the gendered nature of violence more and more visible and problematic. We ask what might be some of the reasons why it is men who commit nearly all of the violence that we have just listed on the board. Incidentally, we have found it very important to write such discussions up on either a board or on butcher's paper. In some way it assists the group to discuss the issues in ways that are less threatening, while at the same time helping focus the group and providing an instant reference to what has just been said.

Through asking questions as to why it is similar in lots of schools and areas across Australia, we gradually build up some sketch of the dominant masculinity and various messages that it entails. If genetic arguments are brought up, we ask questions as to how then can we explain that some cultures are less violent than others, or how levels of violence differ throughout history. If victim-blaming answers are offered, we often switch to asking questions about different forms of violence - particularly male-on-male violence. We try to elicit answers that articulate the messages that boys receive that may be relevant to why boys and men are violent. (Examples of these types of messages are those listed earlier in this paper.)

5.   *Naming the dominant plot.* The group is then asked what they call this particular way of being a man - the way that ends up with such violence. Often

the phrase they use to describe it is "being tough". This is referred to by Michael White (1993) as "the dominant plot".[17] By this stage, we have externalized the hegemonic/dominant form of masculinity so that the group is given some space to separate it from their very identities. This enables discussion of these values and ways of being without such a conversation being experienced as a personal attack. The task now is to find more space for the group to be able to argue against those forms of masculinity to which they have expressed opposition, and to create new preferred ways of being men.

6. *Mapping the effects.* From here we proceed to map the effects of this dominant plot for children, for men, for women, for gays and lesbians. We take care to include any positive effects of violence for young men and any contradictions articulated are put up next to each other. We believe it is important to illustrate how gender systems result in gross inequalities of wealth and decision-making power, as well as interpersonal and international violence. It soon becomes apparent that the dominant messages of masculinity and their links to violence bring major negative implications for all groups, although they also bring men various significant entitlements and benefits.

7. *Inviting an articulation of the need for change.* We then seek an articulation that this system, this way of being men, needs to change for the sakes of women and children and, crucially, also ourselves. This articulation is vital as it means that we can work together. Without it, respectful practice would be impossible. Fortunately it is generally not too difficult to illustrate the advantages for changes in masculinity for *young* men, which often offers considerable leverage.

Particular advantages that changes to the dominant masculinity would bring for young men include:, reducing the violence directed towards young men by older men (fathers) and by their peers; not having to witness violence in the home directed towards their mother or sister(s); improved relationships with one's peers in which one can talk about issues and reduce loneliness and fear of not fitting in; increased access to certain sports or activities that are presently seen as "wussy", such as drama; a more pleasant home and school atmosphere; improved relations with sisters and/or girls in the school; and a world free of war and violence. If the groundwork has been done sufficiently, then such articulations are generally relatively quick in coming.

8. *Finding exceptions.* As outlined earlier, our identities and ways of being can be seen as containing contradictions.[18] Our task is to find the places and times in the boys' lives where they are not acting in accordance with the dominant "being tough" plot, and to co-operatively build new ways of being around these exceptions.

Such exceptions are everywhere - we are just not used to looking for them.

Even the most aggressive young man demonstrates exceptions to the "being tough" mode of being. As a group, a common exception revolves around the earlier part of the session. They have often co-operated with one another, even supported one another, and have shown considerable insight into gender relations in their lives. These are all exceptions, and we point these out to the group.

If these particular sorts of exceptions are not so apparent, we ask individual young men about exceptions in their lives. Often times with their mothers, sisters, girlfriends, or times alone, are brought up as times where they don't "act tough". At these times they often state they are quiet, sensitive, and operating in totally different ways. There are always exceptions. It is our responsibility to be skilled at finding them and creating space for them to built upon.

9. **Name the counterplot.**[19]   Having articulated such exceptions, we explore what they mean. We explore both what the existence of such exceptions means, in terms of hope and scope for change, and also what their existence says about the individuals and the group (see point 12 for more discussion).

Having gained some expression of the positive traits that such movement entails, we then seek to name these exceptions into a counterplot - a plot of resistance against "being tough". Michael White (1993) describes this as a process of co-authoring new stories and ways of understanding.[20] We ask the group what they call this other way of being men. Often this other way of being a man is seen by young people as "being yourself". It is a common counterplot. There are, of course, many counterplots, but we are concerned with articulating and strengthening just one for the time being.

At one school, the young men called the old way of being a man "cool and tough" and the new way "a *new* cool and tough". It was imperative for them to still use these particular words, so they skillfully changed their meanings!

10. **Articulation of preference.** We then need to establish if the group believes it would be a good thing to move in the direction of "being yourself" and to move away from "being tough". Invariably, by this stage, it is agreed that it would be a good thing. Establishing this articulation is imperative. If it is not apparent, more work is needed to be done in mapping the effects of violence and the "being tough" ways of living for the young men themselves. Strategies used by Michael White (1993) include forecasting where "being tough" will lead - "What is the career path of toughness?"[21]

Working in a maximum security prison is again useful leverage! At times I have shown a video made by a number of maximum security inmates who describe the dominant masculinity and its links to crime as a "scholarship to nowhere". Such a video has proved a remarkable resource in isolating the dominant masculinity and outlining its effects on those (working-class) men who have adhered to it perhaps better than anyone else. It is clear to the young men that the guys are as tough as one can get, and that such toughness has resulted in violent crimes and prison. Even the toughest guys are seen to be repudiating toughness!

Once both a dominant plot and a counterplot have been articulated, attitudes and behaviours can be seen in the light of either moving towards "being yourself", or getting stuck in "being tough". They are set off against each other. Down the track questions can be asked, and indeed ought to be asked, about issues of sexual harassment, homophobia, responsibility for violent acts, and a whole range of other discriminatory beliefs. These can then be located within the struggle between the plots, and one can work *with* the young men against the dominant plot.

Room to move is being created. However, as the broader culture largely supports "being tough", in order for the counterplot to even survive, a great deal of support needs to be found for it.

11. *Building on exceptions.*

(a) *Building on strengths.* The first place to build such support is within the exceptions articulated earlier. These are the openings to new ways of being. We ask questions deciphering the small steps that it took to step outside of "being tough". We endeavour to explore, in some detail, how the exception was possible and what strategies they used to defeat "being tough". We ask what or who helped them to overcome the "toughness" in that circumstance. We ask how they did it, who supported them, and how they could find further support. We are particularly interested in exploring ways in which members of the group could support one another against "toughness".

(b) *Building on histories.* Importantly, these new ways of understanding themselves also need a history - just as does the dominant plot and dominant masculinity. We search for times in the past where the young people have acted in accordance with the counterplot - either as a group or as individuals. This history will already exist; we are simply articulating it in a new way, opening it up to be used as a resource for change.

(c) *Communities of support.* Identities are not formed in isolation. They are dependent upon relationships with other individuals, with institutions and social movements. We need to locate support for these alternative preferred stories ("being yourself") through significant others, including family, staff, friends, and communities.

We ask what these people would think of their attempts. We search for significant people who would approve of their attempts - be they in their history, in their present life, or even public figures or cultural icons. We endeavour to find ways that people could offer practical support and encouragement, while all along the way checking out with the group if such support would be useful.

It is important to remember that these new directions have been identified as preferred by the group itself, so we are not pushing them but are instead building support underneath their work in accordance with their own desires. This process of thickening and building support for preferred counterplots is never-ending.

12. ***Reflecting on strengths.*** We continually ask the young men to reflect on what characteristics it takes for young men to step outside of "being tough". We ask what it says of them that they can, even for short periods of time, challenge the dominant gender messages. Often the young men, after some questioning, reply that it takes courage, caring intelligence, or guts, to "be yourself".

Throughout the process we ask what it says about these young men that they are attempting to step outside the dominant destructive ways of being men. We ask questions such as:

What does it say about you that you could act differently than "being tough" in those circumstances?

What does it say about you as a group that you have supported one another despite these messages that pit you in competition with one another?

It is questions such as these that seem to open the most space for boys to move. They allow young men to articulate their resistance to dominant gender messages as examples of strength, often for the first time, rather than as examples of weakness. This is particularly empowering when young men articulate that it takes courage, guts, and strength to move away from "being tough", as these are the words and attributes deemed so necessary to traditional manhood. It is taking the old language and using it against itself.

Michael White (1993) refers to these questions as operating on the "landscape of consciousness"[22], and it is an apt description. There is often a striking silence after one has asked questions such as the ones above. One can almost feel the space opening up when they reply, "I guess it takes a lot of guts". We are building a new language of resistance. It is their language.

At this stage (or perhaps a little later), we often invite the group to consider the following question:

If it takes strength and courage to move away from the dominant tough ways of being a man, then what does it say about those boys who have <u>always</u> stood outside of such ways of being? What does it take for those boys who are hassled and taunted day-in and day-out for being different, to stay in school and not to give up?

After such a question, the "cools" and the "toughs" - if we have done our work thoroughly, will have enough space to acknowledge that those boys who they hassle every day are courageous and brave for standing outside the dominant masculinity. For these boys - the butt of constant jokes and often violence - to hear this has, at times, been profoundly moving. Indeed, after some sessions, boys have thanked us specifically for asking this question.

It is crucial for us to ensure that we do not put pressure on the young men to achieve what is not possible. For us to suggest that boys have the power to change their identities and ways of behaving, without support from family, school, and the broader culture, is to do more harm than good. It is to encourage boys to feel powerless and at fault when their attempts at change are blocked or unsupported. We must ensure that our work is conducted in such a way that it eliminates, as Michael White (1993) describes, "the possibility of failure".[23] In order to ensure this, instead of making grand predictions about how fantastic they will be when they overcome future hurdles, we simply point out the strengths that it has taken for them to be where they are now. We aim to stand behind them rather than in front of them "blocking their view".[24]

13. *Broadening the responsibility.* Once resistance has been identified, and preferred ways of being boys and men have been articulated, there is still an enormous amount of work to do. Indeed, it has just begun. Identities and behaviours are not formed in a void. Young people are in an extremely powerless position. Even with this articulated desire to move in new directions, without support for these new stories about themselves their attempts will be in vain.

Such support needs to come from a whole range of areas. The rest of this article will focus largely on the role of schools, but families, and indeed whole communities, need to take responsibility for these issues and for supporting young men in their endeavours to find new ways of being men.

Having heard the young men articulate their desires for change, we ask the group to state what the staff and families, and indeed the local community, could do to support these alternative ways of being men. We make it quite clear that we believe this issue is the responsibility of the entire community - particularly the male community - and that they cannot simply change gender relations on their own. We collect the ideas of the young men and take these to the parents and staff of the school.

Taking these suggestions to the broader systems is enormously empowering for the young men who were, up until now, being labelled as the "problem". Suddenly they are the ones offering solutions! It profoundly challenges both the school and the community to re-evaluate their collective responsibilities. Later in this article, I will focus particularly on the responsibilities of school systems to support these young men in their struggles.

14. *Summary and evaluation.* Before we take the young men's suggestions to the broader systems, we generally summarise all that we have been through, and ask them for a fairly detailed evaluation of the day's events. The evaluation includes both the process and content of the workshop, and also any videos, slides, or other props that we used. This is an important part of the process, and has led to many improvements to our approach.

Summary of the Workshop Process

1.   Introductions:
(a)   considering notions of respectful practice.
(b)   a game of sex and lies.
(c)   addressing the climate.
2.   Mapping the extent of violence in their lives.
3.   Eliciting an articulated invitation for us to stay and discuss these issues.
4.   Gendered nature of violence. Identifying messages and beliefs of the dominant masculinity and exploring why it is that men are the ones who are violent in the vast majority of instances. We look at some key gendered messages and how boys are encouraged and coerced into positioning oneself within them.
5.   Naming this dominant plot - e.g. "being tough"
6.   Mapping the effects of this dominant plot on children, men, women, and homosexuals.
7.   Inviting an articulation of the need for change.
8.   Finding exceptions - exploring what it means that they exist, in terms of hope and in terms of what it says about them.
9.   Naming the counterplot.
10.   Asking for an articulation that moving towards this counterplot - a plot of resistance - would be a good thing (for men, women, young people, homosexuals).
11.   Building on exceptions:
(a)   building on strengths - exploring how they did it.
(b)   building on histories - instances in the past that would support thinking of themselves in this new way.
(c)   building communities of support - who supported them, how they could find other support.
12.   Reflecting on strengths:
(a)   what it says about them.
(b)   what significant others would think.
13.   Broadening the responsibility - taking their suggestions as to how they could be supported in their attempts to move towards "being themselves", by staff, the school, families, and the local community.
14.   Summary and evaluation

If one was to watch us work, one would observe a process that looks far less clear-cut than the one above - especially with Year 9 boys! Nevertheless, all those steps are crucial in our work. Our demeanour is one of curiosity - we are full of questions. We are constantly checking out what is preferred to them, what a certain development in one way or the other might mean for them. We are endeavouring to find culturally-appropriate ways forward. Each situation is different, so all we can do is go searching with each particular group for contradictions and strengths on which to build.

This process is still in embryonic stages. However, each time we conduct a workshop, the results are improving. At our last attempt, a number of young men who had previously been seen as the "problem ones", once given room to move and argue against certain gender prescriptions, ended up selling white ribbons around the school and the town as part of Sydney MASA's White Ribbon Campaign! It was an inspiring day according to all concerned. A day of laughter and movement - step by step.

The Broader Responsibilities of Schools

There is no time-frame for this process. It must be made clear that building new ways of seeing oneself takes time and thoroughness. Schools at times seem to hope that a one-off workshop will hold solutions to centuries of entrenched oppressive gender relations. Much much more is required. As yet, we have not spent enough time working intensively, and over long periods of time, with school systems and communities to support young men's resistance to dominant gender messages.[25] Such work is essential.

The suggestions of the young men to the school body, the staff, parents, and local community will obviously vary greatly, depending on the local context. Connell (1994)[26] has clearly shown how there are gendered meanings throughout all facets of school life. There are gender implications in particular uniforms, in the decision-making processes, in the gendered make-up of the teacher population, in the content and process of the curriculum, in the distribution of school resources, in sexual harassment (between staff, from staff to student, and from student to staff), in disciplinary regimes, indeed, in every facet of the running of a school.

All of these elements must be studied and then reworked so that they support home-grown, alternative, co-operative gender meanings. Curriculum materials could be developed that tap into the language of resistance and support young men on their quest for non-violent ways of being. Teachers and schools could develop whole projects celebrating positive examples of masculinities. Young people could be given power over their own lives in ways that would encourage them not to need to have control over others for their sense of self-worth and power.

Once the boys are articulating and arguing for gender change and "being themselves", then the schools could, and indeed must, fall behind them and support these new ways of being, if they are to succeed on a broad scale. In terms of teaching young men on issues of gender, the work of Margaret Clark (1989)[27] and Bob Connell (1994)[28] gives us some directions.

Teaching About Gender

The first obvious direction to take is to teach young people about the process of gender construction. This would empower young people to understand, to some degree, the ways in which gender relations are making an impact on their lives. It would aid them in developing strategies to address issues that they feel need addressing. Such teaching would undoubtedly involve research at the individual school level as to how gender relations are played out in each particular school.[29]

Teaching from the Viewpoint of the Disadvantaged

The second direction that Connell advocates is to adopt a "counter hegemonic" approach.[30] What this means is to teach from the perspectives of those groups that are currently disadvantaged. History, for example, has been traditionally taught from the perspective of white, middle-class, heterosexual men. A counter-hegemonic approach to history would involve teaching from the perspectives of the indigenous peoples of this country, women, the working class, and gays, lesbians and queers.

In terms of gender, this means addressing all subjects and facets of school life in relation to the experiences of women, and the ways of being a man that are currently subjugated, such as men who achieve prominence in traditionally non-male areas, homosexual, bisexual, queer men, indigenous men, peace activists, etc. It also means teaching from the perspectives of young people, teaching about how young people are treated, and giving control to young people over their own learning.

Local Solutions

There are no limits to such an approach. What is imperative to remember is that there are no generalised solutions. The construction of gender depends on history, geography, race, and class. It is somewhat different in every school. There are different solutions in every school. In order to find them, adults, teachers and parents will need to have genuine commitment to challenging power relations between adults and young people.

We will need to develop trusting working relations in which the young men can articulate preferred ways of being male, ways that benefit themselves, women and children. There will already be examples of such ways in front of our eyes - if only we are looking for them. They are our hope, our magic. They are where our young men are resisting and overcoming, if only for a short time, and if only in some places, with some people, the gendered messages that have caused such harm over countless centuries. We must find them and support them. Our young people have the answers to bring about a world free from violence. We must be willing to listen to them and to work with them.

Working Together with Boys and *Girls*

It is misleading for this paper to be subtitled *working with young men*. It is named that way because our role as an organisation is to work with boys and men to take responsibility for ending men's violence.

We will never bring about an end to violence simply by working with boys. Gender is negotiated. Boys are defining their gender identities in relation to the girls and women whom they know. The only reason we are even thinking about working with boys is due to the energy, commitment, and intelligence of the feminist movement. Because women have changed one side of the relation, men are now having to renegotiate their identities. The energy, drive and commitment for gender justice and new ways of being has come primarily throughout history from women.

The greatest catalyst for changing men's and boys' ways of being is a chorus of women's voices standing up against the tide of sexism and oppression. Because the women's movement has done, and continues to do, just that, there is enormous hope for change that will benefit girls and boys, women and men.

It would be an enormous error for energy and resources to be poured simply into working with boys, while ignoring the value and extreme importance of working with girls on gender issues. It is the girls who need support to deal with the gendered behaviours and attitudes that we are endeavouring to change. It is the girls who will know all about such behaviours and will have developed strategies of their own to counter them. Just as with the boys, we will need to bring institutional and community support behind such strategies. We need to work with our boys *and* our girls - together. They have much to learn from each other, we have much to learn from all of them.

The potential for programs in which boys and girls listen to one another's experiences, and develop strategies to work together against out-dated notions of gender, are perhaps the most exciting of all.

As previously mentioned, at times we have run our workshops in conjunction with various women's groups working with the girls.[31] This has much to commend it, although we have much work to do to truly co-ordinate our approaches.[32] It would be wonderful to create space for the boys to support the preferred ways of being articulated by the girls, and for the girls to support the boys "being themselves" in some way. It also seems imperative to create space for boys to value their friendships with girls and to acknowledge this, as well as to challenge the boys' dominant beliefs about women and femininity. In order to constructively challenge the fundamental element of boys defining themselves against girls, such interactions and co-operative work will be crucial.

Our Responsibility as Men

Most importantly, however, in the broader scheme of things, adult men must begin to take responsibility for ending men's violence and creating new positive masculinities. Girls' education strategies have all had the support of the broader women's movement and, as such, have proved remarkably successful in some areas. In order for boys to be able to take up new ways of being men, there needs to be strong vocal community articulation that such new directions are welcomed, encouraged, and rewarded. It is the responsibility of all men to ensure that our young men can hear such a chorus of support.

In Context

Around Australia, at present, there are calls for new boys' education strategies and, at the same time, threats to the funding of programs and resources for girls. This is within a context in which there is still widespread sexual harassment in schools, and discrimination in the general community. Any work being conducted with boys must be placed within a theoretical and political framework. In no way should working with boys be prioritised above, or indeed be placed in competition with, work with girls. They are part of the same process - to move towards gender justice, a world free from men's violence, and a world in which gender ceases to limit the experiences of girls and boys.

Summary

This paper has endeavoured to explore some of the issues involved in working respectfully with young men to reduce violence, to describe the process Sydney MASA has developed, and to outline future directions for such work.

It is clear that, if we are to significantly reduce men's violence, men will need to begin to forge new, non-oppressive masculinities in a multitude of sites and cultures. The work described in this paper aims to use the site of the school as an entry point for respectful work with young men, which will then filter out into the community through staff members, families, and local groups.

Recent understandings in gender theory, and recent debates in education circles, seem to indicate that there will be many openings for women and men to begin to work in partnership on issues of gender and violence. It would appear an exciting time. We must acknowledge young people's resistance. We must go out looking. If, in our searching, we find a time when a girl and a boy, or a group of boys and girls, are working together - especially if they are ever working together against violence, then that is our starting point. We ought to consider it a miracle, for in many ways it is, and ask: "How did you do that?" "How can we help it to happen again, and again, and again?"

Acknowledgments

This paper would never have been written without the influence of a whole host of people, particularly my friend, Mark D'Astoli, with whom I co-facilitated the sessions described.

Much of the theory and approach described by this paper has been influenced by the work of Michael White and Bob Connell. Their insights have not only greatly assisted my work, but also totally changed the ways in which I understand my own life and relationships.

I'd like to thank Bob Connell, Andrea Allard, Cheryl White, Pia Van de Zandt, David Newman, Lori Beckett, Van Davy, and Steve Fisher for their feedback on my initial draft. Chris McLean's detailed suggestions (although they led to a major rewrite!) were particularly helpful.

The ongoing encouragement and feedback of Cheryl White, Michelle Swift, Claudia Vidal, Samantha Wood, Lee Bell, Van Davy, Michael Flood, Natalie Green, Miamh Nic Stiofan, Lyn Manor, and Cath Muscat, have proved invaluable in many areas including, but in no way limited to, the work described in this paper.

I'd also like to acknowledge the role played by my parents and siblings in creating the space for me to imagine other ways of living, and setting the example of taking risks in order to get there.

Of course, my work - indeed all work in the area of gender - has only been able to occur due to the work of generations of women activists, academics, teachers, mothers, sisters, and friends. The ongoing feminist movement offers continual inspiration and hope for new ways of relating. It offers so much to us as men. I only hope we are beginning to realise this.

I'd also like to acknowledge the suggestions, insight, and openness of the young men with whom we have come in contact throughout this work. Their enthusiastic responses, feedback, and questioning has, in many ways, built our approach.

Finally, I'd like to thank the young man who held my hand in the cloisters of a private school quadrangle, for showing me another way of being a man.

Notes

1. See Kenway (1994) for a summary of such positions.
2. Throughout the year, Sydney MASA conducted a number of workshops in conjunction with Younger WEL. Their advice and co-operation, along with the input

from Claudia Vidal, Michelle Swift, Miamh Nic Stiofan, Natalie Green, and Samantha Wood, has proved invaluable.

3. Australian colloquialism for gay men, i.e. faggot. Such descriptive terms are those that were common in the schoolyard I attended. The term "poof" was used both to define groups and power relations between groups (i.e. there was more or less discrete "poofta" group), as well as to define members and power relations *within* all groups.

4. See Connell (1989) for a detailed description of multiple and hegemonic masculinities in a school setting.

5. The hegemony of "the cools" differed over time. It was particularly strong from years 8-10. In Years 11 and 12, however, the looming HSC, and the importance placed upon academic success, challenged the authority of the "cools", and opened more space and acceptance for those previously regarded as "squares". Due to the importance of those earlier adolescent years, however, in negotiating my identity, it was the particular masculinity enshrined by the "cools" that remained pivotal in terms of my experience and, I suspect, that of many boys.

6. See Connell (1994) for further exploration of the gender regimes of schools.

7. See Connell (1993) for exploration of global implications of masculinity formation.

8. For a more detailed exploration of young people's constant negotiation of gendered identities, see Davies (1993).

9. It was the work of a one-week intensive with Michael White in 1993 that introduced me to the ideas of contradictory identities, and that opens up the possibilities for the approach our work takes.

10. Not his real name.

11. See Jenkins (1990).

12. See Carrigan, Connell & Lee (1987) for a more detailed description of multiple and dominant masculinities, and the differences between such a way of viewing masculinity and masculine identity formation, and those described by sex-role theory.

13. Personal communication with Bob Connell.

14. See Hall (1994).

15. Many of these considerations have flowed from conversations with a number of women, including Cheryl White, Samantha Wood, Pia Van de Zandt, Lyn Manor, Niamh Nic Stiofan, Claudia Vidal, Michelle Swift, and Cath Muscat.

16. See Hall (1994).

17. Michael White's 1993 one week intensive.

18. See White (1992), pp.42-44, for an elaboration of this point.

19. Finding exceptions and naming the counterplot is possible due to the contradictions and diversity in masculinities. Bob Connell pointed out to me that there are two somewhat distinct sources for the counterplots which we attempt to build. The first are those that are generated from the existence of alternative masculinities. We build, for example, upon cultural constructions of masculinities, or on the existence of the "squares", and the complex dynamic between them and the "cools". This allows the opportunity for alternative masculinities to claim air-space and credibility, and thus

challenge the construction of the dominant masculinity. A second type of counterplot is created from the contradictions *within* a particular masculinity - most commonly within the dominant masculinity.

20. Michael White's 1993 one-week intensive.

21. Michael White's 1993 one-week intensive.

22. White (1991), p.10.

23. Michael White's 1993 one-week intensive.

24. Michael White's 1993 one-week intensive.

25. Such work will be the focus of a research project in 1995 funded by the Anita Morawetz Scholarship from the Melbourne University.

26. See Connell (1994) for a more detailed exploration of the gender regimes of schools.

27. See Clark (1989).

28. See Connell (1994).

29. See Clark (1989) for research ideas into gender relations in schools.

30. Connell (1994), p.12.

31. Including Younger Women's Electoral Lobby.

32. Such co-ordination will also be the subject of next year's research project mentioned above.

7

Moving Towards Respect:
A Quest for Balance
Alan Jenkins

Jeff is a 29 year old man, court-mandated to see me, after assaulting his marriage partner and breaching a Protection Order served following a previous assault. Jeff's partner, Sue, and their two children, David aged 5, and Kirsty aged 3, have lived under a reign of terror imposed by Jeff through a variety of controlling, threatening, intimidating, and humiliating actions. Jeff's physical assaults upon Sue began after three weeks of marriage. Jeff slapped Sue twice on the face when she laughed at a critical comment he made about her friends. He later apologised and wanted to have sex with her. Sue refused and he subsequently raped her. Over time, Sue has been increasingly isolated from her family and friends whom Jeff sees as "trouble makers". Sue has become increasingly fearful for her own and her children's safety. The children are extremely worried and insecure, having witnessed Jeff's violence and abuse towards their mother. When Sue decided to leave Jeff, he stalked and assaulted her. This behaviour eventually led to the serving of the Protection Order, which was immediately breached by Jeff when he assaulted Sue once again, and threatened: "You can't stop me".

Jeff is enraged by the court mandate and reluctant to see me. He protests: "She's a bitch." "She can't do this." "She's the one who should be here." "It's her bloody friends that are the problem." "I'm not violent ... she's making a big fuss out of nothing."

Later in the interview he discloses, "I've had a rough life you know", and alludes to having been physically assaulted as a child: "she ought to try to put herself in my shoes and see what it's like".

Steve sexually assaulted his partner's 12 year old daughter, Karen, over a period of three years. Karen recently disclosed the abuse and is extremely distressed. She feels used and violated, and has made two recent suicide attempts. Steve acknowledges the abuse but appears preoccupied only with avoiding justice consequences and reuniting with his partner. "I don't know what all the fuss is about"; "I think she's just doing it to get out of going to school"; "Anyway, I've had a cunt of a day".

Peter is a 15 year old boy who physically and sexually assaulted his 7 year old half-sister, Kelly. She was subjected to sexual abuse, accompanied by bullying and intimidation over a period of six months, and was terrified of his behaviour and his threats. When Kelly disclosed the abuse, Peter acknowledged his actions but appeared to show no remorse or concern for Kelly. In fact, he physically assaulted her after the disclosure, before being moved out of the family home.

Peter is reluctantly brought to see me by his mother and step-father, who are extremely distressed at his actions and seeming lack of remorse. Peter acts in a sullen manner and looks bored, frequently glancing at his watch or out the window. His response to any attempt to address him is, "I dunno".

Take a moment to reflect.

.   What is your experience as you read these brief accounts of Jeff, Steve and Peter?

.   What do you feel?

.   What do you think?

.   What do you want to do with this information?

.   What do you feel like saying and doing to each of these males?

.   How do you feel like responding to them?

In my work with males who abuse members of their families, I am constantly confronted with these stories and presentations, and with my own personal experiences and reactions to them. I am repeatedly shocked, offended and saddened, and highly challenged by such high levels of disrespect, insensitivity and disregard of the experience of others.

I would like to share my own experience; the challenges and struggles that I face in my attempts to facilitate respectful outcomes for these men and boys, and for those they have abused. In doing so, I invite you, the reader, to examine your own experience; to keep in mind your reflections of Jeff, Steve and Peter. The questions I posed above are ones I frequently reflect upon in my quest to intervene in ways which are respectful and which confront abusive behaviour.

I invite you to consider and examine, in your own experience, compelling tendencies that I, as a man, experience both in my work with men who abuse, and when witnessing injustice and abuse in the course of being a participant in a variety of communities and subcultures in a Western society; tendencies to act either as a passive bystander inadvertently perpetuating abuse and injustice by minimising its nature and consequences, or as a tyrant who advocates violence or abuse as a means of stopping such injustice.

I believe that males can cease abusive behaviours and practise respectful, sensitive and equitable ways of relating, if addressed in a context of respect, responsibility and accountability. This requires that they accept full responsibility for their abusive behaviour, and for the ways in which they relate to others. The process of acceptance of responsibility includes: full acknowledgement of abusive actions; acceptance of personal culpability for these actions; an appreciation of the potential impact of the abusive actions; accepting the consequences of these actions; and embracing the obligation to develop and practise respectful ways of relating. Men who abuse, and therapists who work with them, must be accountable, not only to those who have been hurt by the abuse, but also to justice, welfare and other statutory authorities, and to the members of the wider community.

Therapeutic intervention can be helpful and accountable if carried out in a broad social justice context in which such intervention complements a strong community response mediated via statutory authorities. Abuse is regarded accordingly as unacceptable, often criminal behaviour, which will not be tolerated, and strong sanctions should exist for those who offend. A strong community response should be complemented by strong proactive and reactive interventions which are respectful, both to men who abuse and those they have abused, and which assist these men to accept responsibility for their actions, and to develop respectful ways of relating.

The issue of respect is critical. I am convinced that interventions which are disrespectful to either party inadvertently contribute to the maintenance and even exacerbation of abusive behaviour.

There are two components to the concept of respect. Respect for others refers to a belief in the integrity of others and practices which are informed by this belief. Self-respect refers to a belief in the integrity of self and practices which are informed by this belief. Both components of respect are essential goals of helpful and effective intervention. I believe that both must be attained for a man to cease his abusive behaviour. When men abuse, they experience little self-respect, or respect for others. However, as they discover and embrace both forms of respect, abusive behaviour becomes increasingly incompatible with their experience and lifestyle.

Unfortunately, our systems of intervention, whether they be statutory or therapeutic, more often than not treat those who abuse, and those who are abused, with considerable disrespect and even further secondary abuse.

There is generally little justice or protection offered to those who suffer abuse within families. It is evident that victims and survivors of abuse are usually left to do all of the work and take all responsibility for the abuse and its consequences themselves. They struggle to tolerate, keep secret, stop or prevent the abuse, and deal with its traumatic consequences. What does it say about our systems when the only protection offered to Sue, who is being abused, stalked and harassed by her ex-partner, Jeff, is to be told by police to change her name and move to another state with her children in order to be safe?

We also treat those who abuse with considerable disrespect. We often act like confused parents attempting to discipline a naughty child. Most commonly this involves half-hearted and ineffectual attempts to punish these men in order to make them see the error of their ways. When this fails, as it inevitably does, we ignore them, perhaps writing them off as incorrigible. In effect, we expect little of these men, and we treat them as though they are completely incompetent. The less than 1% of males who are punished by the criminal justice system also have little expected of them. They may be imprisoned where, at best, they take little responsibility for their actions and, at worst, are raped and brutalised. Statutory authorities do sometimes make efforts to tell those who abuse to stop their abuse, but seldom provide any assistance or encouragement to act in more respectful ways.

Alternatively, we invent elaborate psychological explanations for men's abusive actions, and then attempt to "treat" their "pathological" conditions. The tendency to "psychologise" abusive behaviour leads to the construction of concepts such as individual personality disorders and developmental and interactional pathologies and syndromes. Such causal explanations generally serve to provide psychological excuses and justifications which mitigate against acceptance of responsibility by the men who abuse.

Whether we act like tyrants who brutalise and bully for noble causes, like inconsistent and ineffective parents or like scientists who inadvertently excuse abusive behaviour in the name of psychology, we treat those who abuse, and those who suffer abuse, with considerable disrespect. We fail to enhance integrity in either party or ourselves.

My work is based on a number of assumptions which relate to practices of respect, responsibility, and accountability. One of these assumptions relates to a distinction I draw between a man's disrespectful practices and his intentions. Most of the men I see are not wanting relationships in which they abuse those whom they love. I believe that their preferred ways of being and relating are respectful and equitable, despite their disrespectful practices. A second assumption relates to the notion that these men are not limited by pathology or deviance, but are restrained by their interpretations of popular and dominant ways of viewing the world. These viewpoints are based on socially-constructed ideas regarding notions of power, control, entitlement, and responsibility, and are reinforced by unhelpful patterns of relating and life experiences. A third assumption is that the provision of respectful invitations and opportunities to identify and challenge these unhelpful ideas can assist these men to begin to broaden their perspectives and make more respectful choices. In this way, they can develop the kinds of respectful relationships and self-respect that they desire.

This movement towards respect can only take place in a context which is respectful to both the man himself and to those he has hurt. It is the responsibility of a therapist to establish such an environment through respectful therapeutic practices which confront, by inviting the man to accept responsibility for his actions. They should never excuse the man of his responsibilities or attempt to coerce or bully him to face them.

Maintaining a position of respect is a challenging one in my work. It requires constant self-monitoring, reviewing, and debriefing with colleagues. As well as listening to my clients, I make it my business to seek information and try to understand as much as I can about the experiences of those who have been abused by them. When I hear stories like those of Jeff, Steve and Peter, with their statements of insensitivity, minimisation, blame, and avoidance of responsibility, I feel strong feelings of outrage and anger. These feelings are particularly potent when I contemplate the extent of the abuse of power and lack of responsibility, in the face of the enormous burden which is being dumped on and left to be carried by extremely vulnerable individuals who have been victimised. My outrage and anger is generally accompanied by feelings of sadness and grief associated with the betrayals, losses, and hurts experienced by those who have been abused, and by the man himself. I am sometimes reminded of events in my own life about which I have experienced loss and grief.

I sometimes feel fear and concern for the safety of others and, on occasions, for my own safety, particularly when the man appears to be taking little responsibility at all for his own actions. I also experience a sense of shame associated with being a man, and the understanding that it is men who perpetrate most abuse, but take the least responsibility for stopping abuse.

I have long understood the importance of listening to men's stories of their own hurt and pain, without regarding these experiences as excuses for their abusive behaviour. I have long appreciated the necessity to practise respectful ways of inviting men to take responsible steps in the painful journey to face their own shame, and to "wear" the consequences of their actions, in order to develop self and other respect.

However, despite my endeavours to practise respectful invitations to men to accept responsibility, I come face-to-face with my own capacity for self-righteousness and abusive behaviour - an experience which does much to break down the "us and them" mentality, a delusion which is particularly seductive for therapists working with abuse. This delusion can mask the continuum of abusive behaviour in our own experience and in the general community, and the awareness that abusive behaviour is not a consequent of individual sickness or deviance, but an over-conforming response to dominant ideas regarding power, privilege and responsibility which are regarded as normal, and which in fact constitute our societal norms and structures. It is indeed comforting to pull the wool over my eyes by surrounding myself with men who have perpetrated horrific abuses. I can easily feel smug and self-satisfied, and certify myself as "non-abusive" at the expense of my clients. It can feel heroic to prop up this self-image by perpetrating abuse in the form of self-righteous confrontation and condemnation of others, tyranny which becomes justified in the service of the noble cause of protecting the vulnerable.

When I hear denial, minimisation and justification in the face of horrific abuse with horrific consequences, I experience an "inner tyrant", a part of me which is informed by my outrage and grief. This "inner tyrant", at times, wants to "make him see sense", or even "knock some sense into him", to "make him see what it is like", to "break down his denial", or, failing that, to write him off as someone who is evil, bad, and uncaring. Such aggressive thinking and terminology has, in fact, informed much popular confrontive "therapy" for men who abuse. This thinking and behaviour is of course identical to that engaged in by the man who abuses, who experiences a desire to "knock some sense into" his "incorrigible" marriage partner.

I most commonly experience my "inner tyrant" as a sense of frustration and impatience. How can I get through to this man? How can I make him see what he is doing? This experience is strongest at times when I am finding it difficult to invite the man to challenge or take responsibility for his own behaviour. My frustration and impatience are accompanied by a desire to make the man see things the way I see them - to change at my pace and according to my framework. If I act on this frustration and begin to argue the point with the man, I invariably provoke his increasing sense of frustration and impatience. This, in turn, further inflames my "inner tyrant" which invites me to label him as "resistant" or uncaring. I then remain increasingly blind to this interactional, vicious circle, and to my own tyranny.

My "inner tyrant" operates from a position of self-righteous superiority - I am right and he is wrong. This, in turn, justifies my exaggerated sense of entitlement, blame, and even punitive vengeance. Some of the most destructive abuse is done in the service of a supposedly noble cause.

Despite practices of self-monitoring, reflection, and debriefing, my "inner tyrant" still, at times, threatens to dominate and direct my work. I remain convinced that I cannot assist a man to give up patterns of abusive behaviour by abusing him in return. I cannot assist a person to respect other's personal boundaries by violating his own. Respectful therapy involves a process of knocking on doors and waiting to be invited in, rather than breaking them down, barging in, and then expecting to be welcomed with open arms.

It would clearly be folly to wait for perpetrators of abuse to accept invitations to cease their abusive actions when vulnerable family members are being hurt. I believe it is appropriate for authorities, such as the police and welfare organisations, to take action to protect victims of abuse who are at risk of further abuse. There are times when we need to support quick and firm protective action. Consequently, I believe it is appropriate for me to report incidents of abusive behaviour to relevant authorities. I always try to involve my clients in these notifications. However, if they are unwilling to participate, I take unilateral action, even if it means threatening trust in my relationship with them. My client is informed, in the first interview, of the practice of "limited confidentiality", whereby information about any matters which may impact significantly upon the safety or welfare of others may be shared with them or the appropriate authorities. I try to find a balance in my work between respecting the wishes of my client, and those of family members he has abused. I believe it is vital for me to maintain sensitivity towards those who have been victimised, and to keep their needs and safety in the foreground. All of these dilemmas involve political choices that require consistent and ongoing monitoring of the use of power in my work.

I find that I share many of these feelings and experiences - my outrage, grief, and the "inner tyrant" - with others. I am particularly interested in the ways in which we, as therapists, deal with our experiences and our "inner tyrants". For me this has involved searching for ways to overcome many of the unhelpful ideas which are an integral part of professional training.

My early professional training was informed by behavioural psychology. I was encouraged not to feel but to experience a kind of "objective" detachment in my work. I notice that many professional workers, particularly in the welfare field, also strive to be "strong", detached, and unaffected by the stories of abuse which they encounter on a daily basis. There is a mistaken belief that tyranny can be avoided through professional detachment. The therapist is supposedly protected from the emotional consequences of the client's experience if s/he does not feel or does not get "emotionally involved" or "over-invested". Through detachment, clients are supposedly safeguarded from being harmed or unnecessarily lumbered with therapists' emotional reactions and experiences.

Such detachment requires an extraordinary amount of minimisation and denial by the therapist. Long ago I began to question: is this really healthy for the therapist or the client? Does it really prevent tyranny? Does it prevent therapist burnout?

I am convinced that the feelings and experiences that I have described, including those of the "inner tyrant" are, in fact, inevitable and appropriate for therapists who work with abuse. It is unhelpful to pretend that these experiences do not exist or, alternatively, to carry them in isolation as a secret burden. They must be identified, named, and expressed, at times in the form of serious reflection and debriefing, and at other times in the form of black humour. These practices of expression and reflection must be taken seriously in organisations and agencies, where sufficient time should be put aside for them.

I have decided that if I stop feeling in these ways then it will be time to stop working with men who abuse. If I am no longer deeply outraged and saddened by abusive behaviour, then I have become part of the problem.

The consequences of detachment are to minimise abusive behaviour, to dull our own experiences, to compromise our own self-respect, and to discount and disrespect the experiences of both those who abuse and those who suffer abuse. I try to maintain a fine balance between the need to acknowledge, normalise, and express my feelings and experiences, and the need to prevent them from dominating my practices.

I believe that therapists have a responsibility to promote social justice in their work and to contribute towards safer, more respectful and equitable communities. We do not practise in a political vacuum. We must recognise when we are acting as unwitting agents of oppression. If we assume the power and authority inherent in the role of therapist, but stop feeling and fail to regard abuse for what it really is, we are abusing that power and authority. How can we help others who abuse to take responsibility - to think and feel about what they have done - if we lose the ability to think and feel about it ourselves? How can we help men to take responsibility for abusive behaviour if we deny the existence of similar experiences and tendencies in ourselves?

I was trained in unhelpful thinking practices of psychology, in particular to minimise abuse by finding psychological explanations which reduce it to a symptom of individual or interactional psychological process or pathology. Some therapists with strong commitments to social justice also minimise abusive behaviour with causal explanations which attribute abuse to the impoverished socio-economic circumstances of the individuals concerned. The tragic consequences of abuse are not mitigated by the socio-economic status, race, religion, culture, family, or origin circumstances, or "psychological health" of the person who abuses. I have not found that any of these parameters reliably determine an individual's capacity to take responsibility for his abusive actions.

This is not to suggest that men who abuse and are members of oppressed communities should not have their histories of oppression and victimisation heard by more dominant communities. As a member of more privileged communities, I believe I have a responsibility to be active in understanding and challenging social injustice. Not surprisingly, men of less privileged communities are unlikely to take responsibility for their abusive actions, if their own experience continues to be ignored or disrespected. However, it is unhelpful to regard experience of victimisation and oppression as directly causing or as justifying abusive behaviour. Men do not take responsibility for their actions and develop more respectful ways of being under these circumstances.

However, the "inner tyrant" is pacified by causal psychological and sociological explanations. I still feel a strong tendency to justify and minimise abusive behaviour when the perpetrator of that behaviour has come from an extremely impoverished background.

I find no evidence which suggests that the advent of psychology, over the last half of the century, has led to any significant increase in accountability or responsibility with those who abuse. Instead, it appears to have fostered a significant increase in professional minimisation by therapists and statutory authorities. Those who have been subject to abuse may carry an even greater burden of responsibility, as a result of the influence of psychology.

Therapists and statutory justice authorities now tend to act in ways which are informed by psychological thinking. If we can't find a valid, psychological cause, then the person is bad and must be punished - there is no excuse or mitigating circumstance. The psychological explanation appears to be the only legitimate way to keep the "inner tyrant" at bay - to provide a *raison d'etre* for acting respectfully towards, even assisting the person who abuses - in this all-or-none, black-and-white way of thinking. We can help him only if he is "sick" and therefore not responsible for his actions.

It is indeed possible to promote responsibility without promoting blame - the two should not be confused. At the same time, therapists can protect themselves and prevent tyranny without resorting to causal psychological explanations and corresponding concepts of "pathology" and "treatment".

My work requires a continuing balance between establishing processes of accountability and practices which are respectful towards the men who are my clients. Neither Jeff, Steve, nor Peter would have made themselves available for intervention in the absence of external pressures or mandates to attend. Yet, at the same time, all three are entitled to be treated with respect, at all times throughout my intervention. I also have a responsibility to intervene in ways which are respectful, but which do not excuse my clients of responsibility or minimise their actions.

I try to be aware, at all times, of the politics inherent in the practice of therapy - the power hierarchy which is inherent in the therapist-client relationship. I find it helpful to regularly remind myself of the dangerous stance that I take if I am tempted to embrace the myth of objectivity in my work. I acknowledge that I will inevitably reproduce power hierarchies and social injustice in the very nature of my work. Wherever a power differential exists, there is potential for abuse, and the person with greater privilege has a special responsibility to monitor their sense of entitlement and responsibility with great care. This is especially relevant in a therapist-client relationship. In therapy, I try to be aware of this power differential and to use my power and privilege in a responsible manner.

As a therapist, I am in a position of authority in relation to my client who perceives me as having knowledge, influence, skills, and even magic, that he does not possess. As a therapist, I have recognised authority and status in courts, welfare, and other statutory institutions. I am clearly in a position of greater privilege and power than my client.

The client puts an enormous amount of trust in me when telling his story, and is consequently in a particularly vulnerable position whilst trusting that I will act responsibly. When individuals talk about abuse, perhaps for the first time, they take an enormous leap into the unknown, facing their fears and feelings of shame - often terrified about how they will be evaluated or judged. I am in an especially trusted, privileged, and influential position. This story-telling is also a somewhat one-sided event. As a therapist, I do not tell my story or share my experience unless I feel that it would assist some strategy for helping the client. Regardless of how I might like to idealise the therapeutic relationship, it is generally understood that I ask the questions and the client does not share this same freedom or privilege.

I recognise that I am in a privileged position in relation to the client. The client is "my client". I see him in my office, in my familiar surroundings. I strategise and consider what questions I will ask, and which client responses and behaviours I will address. I determine the time-frame: when and how often I see him, and usually when I will terminate contact.

My own values about abuse and relationships will naturally inform my therapeutic practice. I believe that abusive behaviour is never justified, and is always morally wrong, regardless of the circumstances that my client may find himself in. I believe that I have a responsibility to facilitate the cessation of abusive behaviour, and that this will generally assist my client in achieving his goals, as well as help to provide safety for others. I generally believe that my client's predominant ways of thinking, and explanatory ideas about his abusive behaviours, have not proved helpful in developing more respectful and satisfying relationships. I listen to my client's ideas and invite him to develop and consider explanatory ideas and constructs that may prove more helpful and hopeful. I hope to influence his thinking and experience so that he regards himself, his behaviour, and other people, in new ways which I believe may be helpful in achieving his goals, or, rather, my understanding of his goals. My thinking, strategies and invitations are informed by my understanding of his goals and my beliefs about individual responsibility and social justice. I make assumptions that he would prefer respectful, non-abusive relationships, and invite him to discover this preference and embrace it as a personal goal.

I try to maintain a focus on the issue of individual responsibility. This means remaining vigilant and alert to attempts by my client to attribute responsibility for his abusive behaviour to other people or external circumstances. I also look out for attempts by other family members to accept responsibility for the man's behaviour, or to attribute responsibility externally to factors over which he has no influence. All family members are invited to consider who is responsible for the abuse, and gently but firmly assisted to attribute this responsibility to the abuse perpetrator.

At the same time, I maintain vigilance for any evidence of acceptance of responsibility in the man's thinking and behaviour. I try to highlight such evidence and seek opportunities to invite the client to attribute meaning to it, and consider its relevance in relationship to his goals. He is encouraged to consider new definitions of strength and masculinity which are embodied in the painful but healing and self-enhancing process of facing responsibility.

When men who have abused begin to accept responsibility for their actions, they face powerful feelings of shame, sadness and fear, as they begin to think and feel about the harm they have caused, and the damage they have done, to the ones they love. This process can become a healing and strengthening one in which the man gets in touch with a sense of strength, courage and integrity, which comes through facing painful truths which he has not felt able to face before. He may begin to develop empathy for those he has hurt, transcend his self-centred preoccupations, and develop a greater capacity for equity and respect in his relationships.

I search for a variety of means to decline ongoing "invitations" from clients for me to consider causal aetiology for their abusive behaviour, and to participate in the pacifying quest to attribute blame to various external causal factors. When declining these invitations, I am constantly thinking of ways to invite the client to maintain a solution focus in the form of preoccupations with acceptance of responsibility for abuse, and the development of respectful and responsible behaviour when relating to others. I invite my client to link these new preoccupations with his goals, and with a growing self-respect and confidence. I invite him to consider ways in which he is beginning to embrace new concepts of justice and equity, and leave old and popular but unjust and unfair ideologies behind him. These strategies all require ongoing and careful consideration and reflection, given that they involve choices in the use of power in a therapeutic relationship.

I have become increasingly aware of the political nature of language which is used to discuss violence and abuse in therapeutic literature. Therapeutic jargon often fails to recognise power differentials, and this is especially the case in the literature relating to abuse and violence within families. Much therapeutic literature does not adequately draw distinctions between abuse perpetrators and victims, in terms of issues of power and responsibility. By and large, this language invites the diminution of personal responsibility on the part of the abuse perpetrator. Terms such as "family violence", "marital violence", and references to "violent families", "violent marriages" and "incestuous families", can suggest that all family members are responsible for one person's abusive behaviour, and that victims of abuse contribute towards their own victimisation. These terms do not promote the acceptance of responsibility by the perpetrator of abuse. Explanatory terms are powerful and influential, and help to construct beliefs about the nature of problems and their solutions.

I believe that it is vital for a therapist to label abuse and injustice as such. I endeavour to encourage my clients to use these labels themselves. Men who talk, for example, of "fondling" a child, are encouraged to relabel their behaviour as "sexual abuse", and to consider the parameters of this behaviour that make it abuse. This relabelling becomes an important part of an engagement strategy in which the man is invited to consider what it means if he is able to think about his abuse for what it really is, rather than pretend that it is less serious, or provide excuses and justifications for it. I endeavour to assist the man to focus on his abusive behaviour right from the first session, rather than becoming preoccupied with explanations, justifications, and excuses. I find it helpful to do this by first inviting the man to acknowledge some responsibility, and then responding to his achievements, rather than by directly confronting him, and provoking increasingly defensive and irresponsible behaviour.

It is vital that I continue to recognise and examine my own feelings of powerlessness, frustration, and anger during this engagement process. I may be in a privileged position; however, I do not always feel powerful, and can often feel quite powerless and frustrated. In this regard, my experience may be similar to that of my clients. Many men who abuse have greater access to resources, greater status, and are physically stronger than their victims - they are in positions of greater privilege. However, they may not *feel* more powerful. Many abuse at times when they feel frightened, threatened, and powerless. Most therapists can identify with situations in which they feel a sense of impotence with respect to their clients. This is a dangerous context in which to possess some status or privilege, as I will endeavour to illustrate.

I often get quite excited when I am working with clients, and develop novel explanatory concepts, ideas, and ways of thinking about my client's experience and behaviour. At times I discover exciting ways to ask a client a question which I believe may help him see new connections, and may be very liberating and self-enhancing for him. I find it easy to get into a world of my own when doing this, getting off on my own excitement, and becoming, at times, insensitive to my client's experience. I find it very self-satisfying to be working diligently and creatively towards the noble cause of empowering the client. I have an inevitable investment in being successful at this endeavour, and regarding myself as a catalyst for significant change. It can be hard to resist developing a sense of ownership of the client's world and experience, in this context.

Sometimes clients do not appear to embrace or even understand my clever ideas and interventions. This experience of "failure" is indeed a cruel blow when I am working "for the client". I find it easy to feel disappointed, and even angry with my client. If he does not appreciate my hard work, I may wonder if I am "casting pearls before swine". Of course, I no longer see clients as being "resistant", so it is not an easy shift in thinking to begin to blame my clients. Instead, I may resort to systems terminology, and regard my client as "unready". In other words, it is his problem - my ideas are okay.

I endeavour to monitor, with the help of my colleagues, this "I am right - he is wrong" thinking, and check the tendency to replicate the context and dynamics of abuse in therapy. I am aware of, and try to monitor, my "inner tyrant" which continues to notice the man's lack of sensitivity to the impact of his actions, and his lack of appreciation of some of my well-intended efforts. I try to monitor any desires to "make him see sense", make him accept responsibility for his behaviour, or hurt him as he has hurt others.

When my "inner tyrant" dominates my work, I become a powerful agent for reinforcing my client's initial unhelpful and irresponsible ideas. As I try to convince him of the errors in his thinking and actions - that he is wrong and I am right - he generally mounts an escalating and irresponsible argument to justify and even extend his own abusive behaviour. He may respond to my abuse with increasing irresponsible and insensitive thinking and behaviour. A profound loss of empathy and respect occurs between myself and my client, and the context for abuse is enhanced.

There is only a fine line between responsible therapy and therapeutic abuse which is "justified" in the service of a noble cause, yet much current therapeutic practice with abusive men is based on confrontation. This generally involves a kind of benevolent bullying of the man which is designed to "break down his denial". It would appear that significantly abusive and brutal practices are justified by the practitioners if they achieve the goal of forcing the client to acknowledge his abusive behaviour. Such therapy may be highly adversarial in its nature, and relies on the therapist "winning" such a battle with the client to achieve success. Even the language used to describe the process relates to violence: "breaking down denial". The actions of the therapist often appear to be little different from those of the client, who may also have believed that he was acting for a noble or justifiable cause.

However, I have also learned that nothing is totally black or white. Whilst I believe that it is appropriate to attempt to invite, rather than to force, men who abuse to accept responsibility for their actions, there are times when I decide to confront clients in an adversarial fashion. This confrontation generally takes place once a context of respect has been established in the therapeutic relationship. I may even discuss the notion of respectful confrontation with my client and seek his endorsement of this process. These are choices regarding the use of power and privilege for which I must be prepared to take responsibility for any consequences.

I have become increasingly interested in the concept of a balance between the processes of invitation, and respectful confrontation in my work. I feel that it is appropriate to avoid rigid styles of thinking and believing that there is one, and only one, correct way to conduct therapy. I have found it necessary to constantly monitor this balance in my work in order to try to ensure that my "inner tyrant" does not determine the criteria for confrontation. I find that this is most helpfully done in a context of peer review with my colleagues.

I find myself becoming increasingly interested in the paradox that is "success" in therapy. By and large, I think I am successful at times when I believe that I have influenced my client in thinking about his abuse and abuse-related behaviour in a similar way to myself. I work hard at establishing a context for the client to own his "discoveries" and see himself as the architect of his own new thinking and behaviour. Yet, all the time I am acting strategically and intervening towards this end. Is this really self-enhancement? If I am acting in a way which encourages the client's thinking to be in agreement with my own thinking, is this a context for self-enhancement, or a context for deference and dependency? Could therapy be a skilful con-job designed to trick the client into thinking that he has orchestrated and enacted his own ideas in changing his behaviour? If so, how different would this be from the process of brainwashing and constructing a reality for the victim of abuse by the abuse perpetrator, whereby the victim is taught to accept responsibility for the perpetrator's actions? I have not found clear answers to these questions. In fact, I believe they are appropriate questions to be mindful of throughout the process of therapy - questions to discuss and monitor with colleagues and clients in the process of peer review and evaluation of our work. We should at all times be mindful of the risk of insensitively pursuing our own agendas at the expense of the client's experience, and thereby passing off manipulation as therapy.

As a man I will inevitably, and often quite unwittingly, assist in the reproduction of gender imbalances and inequalities. I endeavour to notice tendencies in my behaviour in therapy which are consistent with dominant Western ideas about masculinity. One of these is the tendency to work in isolation, or cut myself off from other workers - to be an individual. This tendency goes hand-in-hand with ideas about being a "success", and doing it on my own, or toughing it out. I have to remind myself to debrief after particularly challenging or difficult interactions with clients. It doesn't come naturally to take time to talk about the impact of my work on my own life, and to consider my own vulnerability in this work. I have already commented on the compelling fantasy to single-handedly and heroically rescue vulnerable individuals from cruel and heartless villains.

The issue of ownership raises its ugly head more often than I care to imagine. I like to develop ideas and, at times, want to own them and can even get upset if someone uses them without acknowledgement. I am no stranger to the idea of competition, as to who has the best or most correct ideas and practices in working with abusive males. It is of interest that these same ideas about ownership, dominance and truth are significant in the experience and behaviour of those who abuse members of their families.

I have been particularly aware of the practices associated with hierarchy and competition in the behaviour of therapists at conferences and in other places where gossip takes place. Work with violence and abuse has been especially redolent with issues of ownership, jockeying for power, and competitive debates as to who has the cornerstone on truth and correct practice. Protagonists gather in camps which are not unlike political parties, and argue for truth. I have participated in such discussions concerning the correct way to work with perpetrators of violence. I once observed two advocates of the use of the penile plethysmograph (an instrument used by some behavioural psychologists to measure sexual arousal patterns to different stimuli in sexual offenders - the device attaches to the penis and measures degree of erection) comparing the heights of their stacks of literature in an argument about the correct technology for this application! The new economic rationalism and limited funds appear to have fuelled the perceived need for this adversarial debate.

I am quite convinced that my intervention involves political choices pertaining to the use of power. Therapy can involve a responsible use of power, or the abuse of power with clients. Decisions made and actions taken in the practice of therapy are influenced by, and have influence on, broader political structures and ideas, regardless of the beliefs of the therapists. Therapy can never take place in a political vacuum. Consequently, we have an obligation to carefully monitor the use of power and the political implications of our work if we are to avoid abusing the very people we wish to help.

Young men, such as Peter, can provide powerful invitations to the "inner tyrant", with their expressions of sullenness, disinterested boredom, and failure to take responsibility for their actions. Peter's mother and step-father had, in fact, been working extremely hard to try to make him show remorse for his abusive behaviour. Initially, when I saw them, they made frequent attempts to get him to "sit up straight" and "pay attention" in my office. The more they importuned him to behave responsibly, the less responsibly he appeared to act. It is not easy to try to interview someone who responds "I dunno" to each question, and gazes frequently at his watch or out the window.

I found it helpful to pay particular attention to my "inner tyrant" with Peter and his family, and to interrupt my desires and his parents' attempts to make him behave responsibly. I am particularly mindful of the need to avoid overloading young men such as Peter with expectations which they feel unable or unready to meet, and which simply confirm their own and their parents' sense of their limitations and inadequacies. I found it helpful to decline Peter's parents' attempts to label him as sick or deviant but, instead, to invite them to consider any evidence he may have demonstrated which would indicate that he was a person who can feel compassion, consideration, and caring for others. I encouraged a preoccupation with the dilemma. Was Peter a cruel sadist, or a person who was at times thoughtless and puts his own feelings before those of others? While there was evidence to support both contentions, I discovered more evidence which suggested that Peter could be thoughtful and considerate - a position which Peter even acknowledged himself. I became particularly interested when Peter was prepared to speak to me about himself, and invited all members of this family to comment on the meaning of this bold step.

Taking care not to overload Peter with expectations to talk further, I again invited his parents to become preoccupied, not with their concerns about what might have caused his abusive behaviour, but with an alternative idea. What might be stopping Peter from showing his caring, concern and compassion for his sister? What might be stopping him from taking responsibility for his abuse of her? Peter's mother informed me that Peter had lived 13 of his 15 years with a different step-father, who behaved in exceptionally abusive ways towards her. As a young child, Peter had tried to protect his mother, had gone to the public telephone booth in the middle of the night to call the police after he had seen his step-father fire a gun at his mother, and had worried at nights about his mother's safety. I discovered that Peter and his mother had never talked about their experiences of living with this abusive man. I invited family members to speculate about the extent to which Peter might have worried about his mother, and the extent of the hurt he might have felt about his step-father's behaviour. I invited them to speculate about what it would mean if Peter was expected to take time to think and feel about what he had put his sister through, but did not feel that others had taken the time to think and feel about what he had been put through. Would it be fair to expect Peter to do something for his sister that he had not felt others have done for him? What would it mean if Peter felt the hurt he had endured was more significant than the hurt he had perpetrated?

In time, I facilitated interviews in which Peter and his mother spoke about their experiences. Peter's mother realised the extent to which her son had been trying to protect her, when in fact it had been her responsibility to protect him. She was able to inform Peter of this realisation. This was particularly liberating for Peter who, in a subsequent interview, began to demonstrate feelings of shame, concern, and sadness about what he had put his sister through. All the time it was clearly understood that Peter's experiences, as a victim of abuse, did not excuse or justify his abuse of his sister. However, it appeared to be necessary to acknowledge his experiences to enable him to take responsibility for his own abusive behaviour.

Peter gradually began to access his own courage and inner strength as he began to consider the abusive ways in which he had treated his sister - his initial deception and subsequent entrapment of Kelly, his objectification of her, and his disregard for her feelings and needs. These painful realisations helped to constitute a new sense of integrity and self-respect, in contrast with his previous tendency to run from the truth and hide within lies, pretences, and justifications. Peter began to redefine himself and notions of masculinity as he considered new meanings of strength and courage in facing up to his actions. He compared his journey with that of his step-father in the process of deconstructing ideas about the nature of male toughness and strength, and gradually began to see himself as strong, competent and capable - as able to face up to what he put Kelly through. Peter eventually told each member of his family what he realised about his abuse of Kelly and how he thought it had affected them. He began to discover ways to translate these realisations into new respectful actions which tended to lead to reciprocally respectful actions from others, and increasing self-respect and confidence.

Peter's attendance in therapy was of course initially coerced by his parents and by a Children's Court mandate. These external pressures were necessary in order to establish some form of accountability to his sister, his family, and the general community. However, within this context, there is considerable room for respectful processes of engagement which did not attempt in any way to excuse or justify his abusive behaviour, or to coerce his active participation in therapy. Instead, he and his parents could be invited to challenge restraints which were preventing him from accepting responsibility for his actions. Peter was required to live separately from his family to ensure safety and respect for his sister. However, he could not be *forced* to accept responsibility for his actions. He could only be *invited* to embark on this journey through respectful practices and processes in both therapeutic and family relationships. Peter was eventually able to express his grief, his hurt, and his shame, both for himself and for his sister, as he travelled on a journey towards respect. To assist and witness this young man embarking on this journey - moving towards respect - was a highly moving privilege for me as a therapist: an experience which also assisted my own journey towards the discovery of respect.

Regardless of the outcome of my intervention, I continue to be challenged, moved, and inspired in my journeys towards respect with males who abuse and members of their families. Whilst it is unfashionable to dream of a safe and respectful society, and hope is certainly out of style in current practice in domestic abuse intervention, I find this work rewarding and fulfilling. I look forward to dialogue with others who embark on similar journeys.

8

Sunday Mowing
Laurence Carter

Recently, my work as an educator has led me to consider the different ways we can look at intolerance of gay men, lesbians and bisexual people. This piece of writing forms one part of a wider debate that challenges all values and prejudices emanating from a dominant culture that is intolerant of difference. Given my own context and experiences, I really only feel confident in talking about these issues as they relate to gay men. There are many important parallels for lesbians, and bisexual people, as there are important differences, but I think it's best that they write for themselves.

I value highly the notion of the celebration of difference. I have experienced and witnessed the pain of trying to conform to dominant expectations. There can be a great deal of sacrifice in doing this. The most important is the sacrifice of self worth, individuality and confidence. For this reason, I've been particularly interested in exploring the influence of these dominant expectations on the lives of gay men in Australia. I specifically mention Australia as this has been my experience. I'm always suspicious of global statements, and feel it's important to state the measure of the breadth of my cultural experiences that inform my discussion. So, enough to say that mine is relatively narrow, with perhaps just enough experience of issues in the USA and the UK to make some tentative comparisons. As a gay man and a social work trained counsellor, I have been privileged to have had, and to have had shared with me, a wide variety of experiences. This is one of the main reasons why I now feel that I have something to say.

The fact that a major part of my last ten years has been lived and worked in the time of HIV and AIDS is central to this discussion. For one thing, it has given me the most impetus to make sure something gets done to challenge the ongoing prejudice and discrimination against gay men. Witnessing the degree of suffering from the stigma of homosexuality, galvanised by the stigma of AIDS, is the stuff of powerful experience. Living in the midst of chronic illness and death is a pretty good way of adopting the resolution that 'My life is the show, it ain't the rehearsal.'

I've just turned thirty-six, and I live in the suburbs of Melbourne with my partner and our mate (and mentor) Bob the Dog. We were born in Australia, our ancestors are white, originally Irish and English, and a mix of protestant and Catholic. Sometimes all of this seems dangerously close to the profile of the White Aussie Dream-Makers - the family sedan, the house in the suburbs, the sensible career and the right number of dependants. We're close to fulfilling the dream, but not quite close enough. The fact that we're both men may have something to do with this, not to mention our dependant who has four legs instead of two.

We recently decided to move out to the suburbs and away from the gay ghettoes of inner Melbourne. If it's not already obvious to you, it should become so later that there are real advantages to the ghetto for gay men. Although cheaper housing and the need for the quintessential backyard were major reasons for the move, I also like to think of us as urban pioneers. We came out from behind the castle wall of the ghetto, and moved forward onto the new territory. I'm not sure that this colonising analogy is the right one. However, there is a sense of being strangers in a land where the 'natives', although not often openly resistant to our presence, aren't always quite certain about, or comfortable with, it either.

This uncertainty or discomfort can make me annoyed, frustrated and sometimes despairing. Which reminds me that there's a whole stereotype of the angry gay man, involving assumptions such as "he's angry because his non-gay peers will always have the advantage", "he's frustrated by not having children", and so on. On some reflection, it's obvious that such explanations, that can be used to disqualify a gay man's anger, are statements that can lead us closer to the beliefs that need challenging. One helpful way to challenge these beliefs is to move away from a focus on the individual to a focus on the contexts of people's lives.

When I move to this wide-angle, systemic position, my immediate frustration with the uncertainty and discomfort of the 'natives' diminishes. I can see their opinions, reactions and prejudices in terms of the social and cultural influences shaping their lives and opinions. Importantly, it helps me see that these influences constrain everyone, not just marginalised people, although this does not stop my intolerance of individuals who find me "depraved, pathetic and sick" (to name just a few possibilities) because of my sexual orientation.

I have long been fascinated by the systemic approach of looking at social context when assisting people to be different. It's clearly not enough to say that I was attracted to systemic concepts because they just made sense, so I've wondered about what it is about this approach that made sense to me.

The fact that I was introduced to it when I was twenty one seems significant. I was at a point where the "problem" of my sexual orientation seemed to have a life of its own. A life that was not always particularly helpful. One of my most vivid memories from this time involves standing in the vault-like photocopy room in the vault-like library of the Western Australian Institute of Technology. As I stood waiting my turn I was transfixed by a beautiful man who was already at a copier. It was in that room that I allowed myself the unprecedented indulgence of enjoying without guilt the beauty of that man, and my own feelings of sexual attraction. It was an incredibly joyful moment for me. It was also an experience that started me questioning why I had given myself such a hard time previously about something that felt great and harmed no-one. Time would clearly have rewritten every line if I were to suggest that this event was the only turning point I needed to a life of confidence and brimming self esteem. This thing called coming out is clearly a process, and not an event.

It was at this time that I met a tutor and lecturer in counselling who introduced me to the systemic approach. My fledgling attempts to conceptualise were therefore wonderfully timed with my emerging insight that I was a member of a marginalised group and my growing understanding that my sexual and relationship struggles weren't all my fault. Indeed, the notion of fault was severely challenged. Suddenly such things as society's institutions, culture, television, families and the professions were no longer just those things out there. They shaped people's being, and that included me.

My own interests in both sociology and counselling were starting to seem less and less contradictory. There was a lively debate at the time amongst social work students, that seemed to divide along the lines of those who saw counselling and related skills as the way to go, and those who were fired by socio-political insights. Although I was at times concerned about the possibility of being a fence sitter, I was most excited by the ways in which these two approaches intersected. Rather than treating different approaches to the human condition like differences of party political persuasion, I saw that my learning was giving me two approaches, each of which could inform the other.

This brings me to the present and my interest in social context. In exploring this wider picture, I am often confused by some of the debates that go on. For example, the terms *homophobia* and *heterosexual dominance* are currently used, somewhat interchangeably, to describe the widespread prejudice and discrimination targeted at gay men, and those assumed to be gay. There is a debate as to which is the better description, presumably in the hope of enhancing our understanding of this prejudice and discrimination, so that we can more effectively challenge and minimise it. I have battled, for some time, with this debate. Then, once again, it struck me I was misguided in assuming these approaches were mutually exclusive. The understandings and experiences that lead people to use one or other term are reinforcing of each other, and reflect varying views on the same concern and challenge for change.

Homophobia certainly has currency with most people and with the media (the part that bothers to think about it). Its connotations of rejection, active discrimination, and violence are useful in maintaining a focus on the realities of living for many gay men. It is important in any debate in this area to have constant reminders that, when all is said and done, this is a problem that has devastating consequences for gay men. The accounts of the violent bashing, raping and murdering are all too clear reminders of the consequences.

The term *homophobia*, and its adjective *homophobic*, directs the attention to the individual perpetrator of discrimination. Literally it describes these people as possessing a fear of the same, although the common understanding is defining an individual by their *hatred* of gay men, lesbians, or bisexual people. Many people who are justifiably angry and dismayed by homophobic acts of aggression and rejection argue that this focus on the perpetrator is an important way to bring individuals to justice, and as a way to reinforce individual responsibility. A lesbian friend who had experienced an attempt to burn her home down, because of her sexuality, was understandably less than interested in a sociological analysis of the factors that led to the crime. A gay man, sick with AIDS, was more concerned to know something was being done about the neighbours who were scrawling "GET OUT YOU FILTHY FUCKIN' POOFTER[1] WITH AIDS" in 2-metre-high lettering on his fence.

The *heterosexual dominance* understanding is marked by a curiosity to comprehend the cultural and social context of the injustice. It is a way of challenging the supported values and imperatives that maintain the injustice. This appeals to me. Lots of examples come to mind when I think about this one. The values officially defining the main Christian churches seem to take pride of place on this list. The nature, or lack, of discussion of sexual orientation in primary and secondary schools. The vast majority of television programs, and Hollywood movies that either ignore gay men or parody them. The complete play lists of top-rating radio stations that never broadcast a melody of two men in love. The fact that two men holding hands on the street of any Australian town says more about their courage and political will than about their love for each other. The yearly tax form that my relationship won't fit into. The stranded partner who isn't allowed to migrate to Australia to be with his lover. That moment of suspense, waiting for the reaction, when two men register for a double room at a hotel. The vision of men, knowing they will now die from their HIV infection, lying in their hospital beds crying and scared that their sexuality and disease will send them to hell. The football star who has an obliging female friend who "fills in" at the yearly award nights. The employer who rejects the leave application when a man is caring for his dying male partner.

I'm tempted to go on and on and on and on with this list. It seems such a powerful juxtaposition. Heterosexuality is, every day, in every way, referred to, marketed, assumed, and celebrated. Homosexuality is yet to be noticed, let alone celebrated, on such a scale. The power of the everyday reference to heterosexuality in terms of an individual's self-esteem is enormous. Enormously useful to heterosexual people; although the constant nature of it can make this difficult to see clearly. Constantly constraining for gay men who often have to censure their own lives, loves, and selves, in the spotlight of the *status quo*.

I need to explain what I mean by the constant nature of everyday reference making its significance difficult to see. One of the best science lessons I had in high school was when the question was raised as to whether humans can feel gravity and the weight of the air above them. This initially puzzled me, and many others in the class, because it didn't feel like there was any great sense of weight on top of us. The answer that, because it's always there, we don't notice it, was amazing to me. My counselling role is often focussed on assisting gay men to see the constant censoring they have to do to avoid appearing different to these assumptions and images.

One of the common responses on hearing the argument of *heterosexual dominance* is for the audience to personalise the analysis, and retort defensively with examples of their own liberal attitudes, acceptance, and sensitivity. This happened to me recently when I was outlining some of the points discussed here to a group of child psychiatry trainees. At the time, I pondered on what it was in this session that nearly cornered me into a defensive position on these understandings. I think it is the notion that, not only do these understandings help us see the way gay men are marginalised, they also highlight the position of privilege and power inherent in heterosexuality. People seem to find this notion difficult to accept. However, like other dynamics of injustice, it is not until the powerful see their role in the injustice, and acknowledge it, that the injustice can really be challenged.

Along the lines of the earlier discussion on assumptions about the "angry gay man", it seems extraordinary to me that the desire not to be complacent about injustices, borne of suffering, is so often disqualified, and pathologised, as the irrational impulses of an overly-emotional person. Once again, what, when seen in context, is an important message for change is in fact turned against a person, or a group of people, on the basis of weakness. Anger can be such a strong litmus test for injustices and lack of control. To respond meaningfully to demand for change, whether it is support or opposition, seems to me a whole lot better than the inhumane disqualification of a person's experience. It is the ultimate double-bind.

I placed the Christian churches at the beginning of that long list. In thinking about their general position on homosexuality, their constraining influence on gay men seems so obvious. A speaker at a national AIDS conference, years ago, said something that seemed to sum it all up for me. He was a gay man, with AIDS, and he spoke of being sure that the churches would, if needed, care for him as a sick man, as they would for others. What he also knew was that what they would do to help stop the spread of the virus would be constrained or contradicted by the official values and approach of the church on homosexuality. He was someone who knew the public health wisdom of not marginalising, or punishing, those people who were deemed to be most at risk.

That, without acknowledgment, understanding, and education, they would remain at risk of HIV infection. His point - that the effective proscription of homosexuality by the church was placing many at risk - hung in the stale air of that auditorium. Perhaps it is my own wishful thinking for rapid and desperately needed change, but I have a sense that many churches are now facing a crisis of relevance and reputation as a result of many points of justice and equity, such as this one.

It has always intrigued me that, unlike myself, many gay men are active members of churches that have, at best, ambiguous positions on their sexuality. It is a sad reminder of the time that a friend, with a fine mind and sense of social justice, who was also active in the Anglican church, died recently before we were able to have our planned discussion about this intriguing fact. The other day, a woman who was a participant in a session I was running on stigma came up to me after the session. She was keen for me to suggest some responses to the argument against gay men's rights that refers to its proscription in the Bible, and the associated teaching that it's unnatural. I have to say that my own frustration and impatience with the dominant churches, and my consequent disinterest, makes me less than an expert on these matters. I suggested someone else who may have been able to advise on appropriate theological gymnastics, that may have helped her respond appropriately.

This instance raises an interesting point. Many people I've worked with who would describe themselves in their adulthood as lapsed Christians, or even atheists, find themselves struggling with constraining Christian values and beliefs at times of life crisis and reflection. The earlier example of the man fearful of hell after death, because of his sexuality, was one of these people. This highlights for me the influence and power of Christian doctrine for many Australians. The fact that this doctrine remains internalized, where it can lead to anguish and self-doubt years down the track, is proof of its significance.

I have already mentioned examples of the way mass media and entertainment contribute to ignorance and pejorative representation of gay men. It is this area that seems to most clearly, although not solely, illustrate the power of prejudice through omission. Such things as movies and popular music are central to cultural life in Australia. The passive appreciation of them is increasingly the most common way people experience cultural representations of life's themes, joys, and struggles. I worked with a couple who would often comment on the way a movie or a song they came across would strike a chord for them in an inspirational way, either for themselves or for their relationship. It seems no coincidence that they are a heterosexual couple. One of life's struggles for gay men is to find such sources of inspiration in the vast supply of popular creativity. These sources are conspicuous in their paucity. It is no surprise that the larger cities in Australia have gay and lesbian film festivals. Although I am not arguing against them, their very existence seems in one way to further marginalise the cultural experience. It is the day-to-day nature of mass media and entertainment that so potently informs people, and symbolises what is acceptable. The general omission of homosexuality in this entertainment wonderland results in continued ignorance for many heterosexual people.

The example of the football star who hides his homosexuality, by taking a woman friend to the awards night, is an important one to talk about. It takes only a little imagination and understanding to see that self-worth can be constantly challenged for people who frequently have to censor the sharing and demonstration of their love, sexuality, emotions, and uniqueness, for fear of repercussion. I have borrowed from a colleague and used a powerful exercise in awareness for people who do not identify as gay men, lesbians, or bisexual people. In workshop sessions, I often ask participants to ponder on their lives, imagining that one or more of their emotionally-important relationships was proscribed, and that they had to censor their references to it, and curtail their experiences in relation to it. One of the insights gained by many who do this is to appreciate the constant and daily nature of censorship and disqualification for gay men, lesbians, and bisexual people.

It is important to look at the changes, and the differences, too. I've just watched a television current affairs program and, unusually, I was heartened by it. It reported on a poll of the general population concerning views on homosexuality and homosexual relationships. There was a very significant increase between 1992 and 1994 in an accepting attitude towards homosexual men and women. This increasing was similarly, although to a lesser extent, mirrored in their acceptance of the equality of gay relationships compared to heterosexual "de facto" or common-law relationships.

I was heartened by hearing something that supports an optimistic outlook for the chances of gay men and women achieving greater equality in their lives. I must admit of late to an outlook on this matter that has been less than promising. Perhaps this was as a result of spending much of my time recently focussing on this very issue. All this focussing had given me too studied and narrow a focus on the way our Australian culture responds to homosexuality. I've been concentrating on all the things (and there are many) that impede our progress towards equality for gay men, lesbians, and bisexual people.

I fell into the trap that is a trademark of our culture: to look only at the problems, and the sociological aetiologies that contribute to an injustice. Watching that current affairs program tonight made me remember that significant differences have occurred over the last few decades, that have all contributed to improvements in the lives of gay men, lesbians, and bisexual people. It is important to remember these changes, and for their significance to bolster the efforts of all the people who continue to contribute to this change.

I have a sense that our culture is starting to more openly and frequently reflect and engender changing understandings and "acceptance" of gay men. I have deliberately placed the word acceptance in quotation marks. It is the ambiguous nature of much of the current acceptance of gay men that marks this time of change. A somewhat bleak description would be that gay men have moved, on the whole, from being objects of scorn, prosecution and persecution, to ones that are "accepted" as long as they don't get too obvious about it all. One of the common ways people get support and encouragement in our society is to do just that - to be obvious about "it". A common example is the modern wedding day which is surely a ritual of profile and obviousness. I shudder at the idea of ensuring gay men's equality through wedding days, but this example highlights the invisibility that can be so damaging to a gay man's confidence.

Changes rarely occur without reactions that strive to maintain *the status quo*. This is the Year of the Family. Homosexuality has long been condemned as a threat to the traditional family. (Well, only so in my experience if traditional families persist in mowing their lawns at 8am on a Sunday morning.) Those who oppose equality for gay men are therefore milking this year for all it's worth. In the face of this, the Sydney Gay Mardi Gras deliberately chose to push the theme of "We are family" this year. Recent experiences in the USA show a highly organised movement against gay rights that comes from a middle-America position of traditional values. You have to hand it to the propaganda and political machines of 1950s USA. It's a dream of a *status quo* that many hold to dearly. Even in the face of huge inequalities, community disintegration and conflict, and environmental damage on a huge scale, they hold it too dearly. The values were pretty much the same in Australia, and many people of influence today were nurturing and nurtured in the glowing hopes and dreams of this time. Its ideals and beliefs should not just be dismissed as no longer relevant.

Although I have no hard evidence (and couldn't imagine how you'd get any), levels of acceptance seem to vary with where you live, and with whom you associate. Factors such as education and social class seem to play a part here. In Melbourne, the Western suburbs are commonly seen as the home of the working-class. Counsellors, and AIDS educators I have spoken with, talk about a different scenario for gay men living in this region. It seems to be characterised by a greater invisibility, more traditional values (often arising from traditional theologies, as discussed earlier), life circumstances that constrain people in so many ways and are a marked pattern of "emigration" of openly gay men out of the area when possible. I'm aware of not wanting to perpetuate a stereotype here. However, my experiences would concur. They would also remind me of working-class people from the Western suburbs who I know who don't fit this description at all.

A counselling colleague, with many years' experience in working with gay men, shared an observation years ago that I found particularly interesting. We were talking about the fact that many gay men migrate interstate within Australia in their late adolescence, or early adulthood. There was a sense of needing to create their own social context. A social circle that was not hampered by the legacy of school, family, and other long-term associations which were proving to be constraints to their own development and self-worth. Perhaps even a case of the grass being really just that much greener on the other side of the fence. He was also noticing that many of the men with whom he was working were attempting to make a "socio-economic migration". They were often getting into hazardous circumstances of debt and over-commitment in their aspirations to join the upper middle-class.

Now, this is not a scenario unique to young gay men, given the passions of our consumer world and the power of advertising. Any financial counsellor can tell us that. However, for many gay men, regardless of their socio-economic background, it appears to me to be a sign with particular meanings. Just like other marginalised groups, its members have to try that much harder to be accepted. The irony, as with other groups, is that sometimes "even that don't help in the long run". There's a joke amongst the team of counsellors with whom I work that I'm always the one to raise the significance of money in people's lives and relationships. So, just to keep true to form, I'll talk about it some more! Its significance as a factor in social status may seem obvious. Yet it's amazing the number of people who don't think about it when contemplating low self-esteem.

Given many gay men's struggles with self-worth, it seems understandable that some would be zealous in their desires to attract social status through material and financial means. Hollywood recently had stars portraying gay men, in nearly every instance, as upper middle-class, successful professionals. Hollywood doesn't challenge the idea that, as someone must have said in a bar somewhere, someplace: "there ain't nothing more pathetic than a poor queen". It's surely an idea that needs challenging. In this context, the recent commercial advertising and marketing that overtly targets gay men may not just reflect the increasing acceptance of male homosexuality. It makes me think of the manner with which capitalism engulfs alternative movements. The way the early feminist movement in the USA engendered cigarette advertisements targeted at women who had "come a long way", and the environmental movement spawns countless dubious claims to "green" products.

There's a growing momentum amongst gay men that challenges some of these imperatives, and is developing alternative ways of constructing meaning, and aspirations. It seems a natural progression for some members of the gay community to actively develop alternatives. The general cultural and economic imperatives and institutions have either ignored them, discriminated against them, or are now starting to woo them. Of equal significance to this momentum are the sharply-honed skills many gay men have had to develop for addressing injustice, and for not taking the *status quo* at face value.

My sense of this momentum is that it highlights and celebrates difference amongst people. The "queer movement", whatever that actually means, seems to reflect this sort of response. Many people I've talked with, who identify with this movement, do not see gay men's integration and acceptance into the *status quo* as the goal to strive for. They value the freedom of non-conformity, and enjoy the experiences of difference.

I have often heard, and wholeheartedly agree with, the argument that a developing celebration of different is beneficial to everyone. The fact that discrimination against gay men constrains heterosexual men, too, is important to realise. A man's creativity, emotional expression, and flamboyance are often critically interpreted as signs of homosexuality. The number of men who consciously and subconsciously constrain themselves, for fear of such interpretation, must be significant. Many Australian observers and writers who have lived elsewhere in the world comment on the ferocious limits constantly placed on men's intimacy, warmth, and expression, in Australian life. I see it mostly when assisting men in counselling to further discover and nurture these aspects of their lives.

So, in thinking about my way of being, the benefits of casting my eyes and ears over the whole picture of my life are immense. I believe there are benefits for everyone in doing this. Indeed, the sources of discrimination and prejudice that are discovered when viewing this picture are important learnings for all people. The motivation to challenge them must essentially come from those not personally marginalised. Those in positions of greater privilege, because of their heterosexuality, need to acknowledge their responsibility to challenge the wide variety of ways gay men are disqualified and discriminated against. The continued presence of prejudice and discrimination against non-heterosexual people is surely a presence that effectively constrains all people.

Note

1. Australian colloquialism for a gay male, i.e. faggot.

9

Growing Up as a Man
Peter Lee

My conscious experience of male culture goes back to my schooling at a single sex boys' school, with a heavy emphasis on very stereotypical masculine roles, encapsulated in attitudes to women and men's dominance over them, and in aggressive interactions between students. This stereotype was reinforced at every turn, in the classroom, on the ovals, and in the social relationships between the boys, where homophobia, not surprisingly, was rife.

I never felt entirely at home in this environment, not being particularly good at sport, which was the passport to acceptance and therefore, at least for me, to self-respect and confidence. My recollection of my school life is that I spent a great deal of energy trying to win this acceptance, but never quite succeeding. Ironically, given my later conversion to the anti-war movement, the one arena at which I did succeed was in the school cadet corps, where I reached the pinnacle of becoming an officer. This success was somewhat leavened, however, at the final ceremonial parade, where I committed the unpardonable sin of leaving my platoon of thirty boys "at ease" while the other seven platoons stood rigidly at attention in the middle of the school oval in front of assembled parents, friends, and the odd military officer!

My very traditional socialisation continued at university and in my first jobs in the workforce. Still trying to establish my credentials as a red-blooded Australian male, I played football after I left school, no doubt because it seemed the traditional way for young men to display their masculinity. I was very much concerned at that time with outward appearances, and this was usually in some way connected with my understanding of what was appropriate behaviour for a male of my age and social class.

I had very little self-awareness, and even if I had doubts about the cultural messages I was receiving, I didn't have either the ability or the confidence to articulate those doubts. As I moved into a career and marriage, I took these expectations with me, and my relationship with Trish was initially a model of a traditional middle-class marriage. However, I soon became aware that my expectation that she would see me as her only source of emotional support would not be met. She had a range of female friends and she put considerable energy into ensuring that these relationships prospered. On the other hand, while I had male friends, with none of them did I feel confident that I could trust them with my innermost fears - about lack of self-confidence and doubts about my own self-worth. Not surprisingly, these friends didn't confide in me either, confirming my view that other men didn't have these concerns and therefore were more self-confident than I was. This tended to reinforce my belief that Trish was the only person with whom I could really be honest about myself.

As she began to explore feminism, and to develop her own self-awareness, I began to realise that I was really missing out on something. She would come home from the women's group she had joined, as high as a kite, and I found it very difficult accommodating to the fact that she was able to have such a good time without me! Of course, at this time other things also began to change, beginning with her expectations of our relationship. There was increasing pressure for me to contribute more equally on the domestic front, in terms of basic domestic tasks, and particularly in relation to child care. This I found very difficult to deal with, given that I was working full time supporting the household, while all she had responsibility for was the domestic tasks and our two year old, Anna. While I later recognised error in my view, at the time it did not seem too taxing, as she had time to spend with her friends, and even sometimes to play tennis during the day! What I wouldn't have given for such freedom. Of course, the fact that I didn't have any really close male friends with whom I wanted to spend such time escaped me.

As the conflict over roles developed, I realised that I was at a decided disadvantage, since Trish had a range of supportive friends to whom she could turn, while I had a sense of total isolation! I had begun to see that, in terms of social justice, she had a point, but I found it extremely difficult to accept that I should give up what little power I seemed to have. I was still tied into the model of masculinity which was premised on man's superiority over woman, and hence any concession to those over whom I was supposed to exert power was an open admission of weakness, and a challenge to my masculinity. Of course, my appreciation of this situation has only developed with hindsight - at the time I was really struggling to understand why I was finding life so difficult.

It was at about this time that I joined a men's group. I'm not really sure of my motivation for this move, but at least in part it was to feel as though I also had someone to whom I could turn for support. Little did I realise where this would lead! Of course, the process of developing closer relationships with the men in this group did not occur overnight, but the experience of being a member of a group of men who were all committed to examining their masculinity and to sharing that exploration with other men was a revelation. I had never shared my innermost feelings with any man in this way. Up to that point I was prepared to change, essentially to accommodate Trish's now openly-stated feminist ideals, to ensure that our relationship continued on a more or less even keel. In the men's group I slowly began to realise that I actually wanted to change for me and that such changes would have lasting benefits which would go far beyond enriching our relationship. The men in that group provided quite a different model of masculinity from those provided by my school and work experiences. Here were men who valued personal relationships for their own sake - no longer were such relationships a means to an end, but they were an end in themselves.

How well I remember the night I summoned the courage to tell the group that I often had feelings of lack of self-confidence and therefore found relationships with other men difficult to sustain, given how confident they seemed to be. I was absolutely astounded at the response - every one of them at times had had similar experiences. So perhaps I was not so unusual after all. In any event, the experience convinced me that I had found a group of people to whom I could relate with absolute honesty, sharing my innermost fears, without being ridiculed or put down. It also provided me with what has proved to be an invaluable tool in dealing with men who adopt the familiar aggressive male posture where they feel threatened - I visualise them as scared and as unsure of themselves as I feel in such situations. I find that this often gives me the confidence to treat them as equals, no matter how unequal I might have felt at the outset.

At about this time another significant change occurred in my life when, with Trish and our three year old, Anna, I moved into a community with four other adults and four children. Immediately the pace of change in my life escalated enormously! There had been much discussion prior to the move, about the philosophical basis for the community, so we all entered the experience with our eyes open, or so we thought. We believed that we should share equally the domestic tasks, in terms of child care, cooking and the other household jobs, while our incomes would be pooled in a joint account, to which all the adults had individual access. There was one other man, Jo, who was also a member of the men's group, and four women, and we were absolutely clear that we were strong supporters of feminism.

As I was the only full time worker, I was much more heavily committed, in terms of time, to activities outside the community. Nonetheless, the clear expectation, which I shared, at least in theory, was that household tasks were to be equally divided. Well I remember riding home from work on the nights that I, along with another adult, was rostered to cook, hoping that by the time I reached home he or she would have made a decision as to what to cook that night. It was an enormous leap, moving overnight from a situation where I was beginning to share cooking with Trish, to one where I was jointly responsible for a meal for six adults and five children two or three times a week!

I very quickly learned that there was a difference between my taking responsibility for a task, either alone or jointly, as opposed to helping someone else with the task, but not seeing myself as responsible for it.

One of the major advantages for me of the two years in the community, was the opportunity to look at myself and my life in an environment very supportive both of self-analysis and of the change which such analysis often engenders. Within six months of moving into this situation, I had given up my full time job and found a half time teaching position, allowing me to focus my energies on things other than work.

Until then my socialisation had strongly reinforced the stereotype of the male breadwinner, developing a career which would provide me with a sound base on which to build my self-image, while at the same time providing a reasonable income for "the family". I began to realise that a career was not necessarily the most important thing for which to be striving, particularly when our second child was born and I had the opportunity to be involved in his upbringing from the outset.

I quickly realised that having responsibility for children was not the breeze I had imagined it to be, even if it did mean I had more time at home. However Jo, the other man in the community, was also sharing the upbringing of his daughter, Bronwyn, and the support we provided for each other was essential in developing our confidence in caring for children. This confidence was not always shared by others with whom we came in contact. The Mothers & Babies nurse had considerable difficulty in accepting that Jo or I knew as much about our children's feeding habits as did their mothers. My developing skills in areas which were traditionally considered "women's work" led to an increasing self-confidence, as I recognised how much I enjoyed learning new skills and how relatively helpless I had been in the past. I had been a classic example of what has been termed "learned helplessness", and I relished becoming more independent and less reliant on Trish, at least as far as the practical aspects of my life were concerned.

Having moved out of the community, we were back in a suburban house, with Anna and Diarmid, who by then were seven and two respectively. We had chosen the house because it was very near to another couple with whom we had developed a warm association and, to a large extent, Peter and Fiona took over from the community in terms of both practical and emotional ties. The amount of time and attention required by the children was beginning to drop, with the advent of school and child care, and Trish and I began broadening our horizons again. We had now been together for ten years, this being the first intimate relationship for either of us. We were confident of our capacity to deal with conflict, after life in the community for two years. This had been a very positive experience, but one which required a great deal of energy from us all in reaching consensus on issues ranging from child care to use of the car. Imbued with this confidence, we decided we wanted to experience a wider range of relationships and plunged into two years of turmoil!

Perhaps not surprisingly it was Trish who first developed another relationship. I was soon to discover that there are many levels of independence and I had not even reached first base in terms of emotional independence. I realised that for all the work I had done and the changes I had made, I had not begun to develop any real emotional independence from her. While there were times when I think I dealt with this new situation appropriately, often my actions were based on a mixture of possessiveness, jealousy and, underlying each of those, insecurity. We were both convinced that multiple relationships should be possible and that we wanted to try to make it work for us, but, while this was all very well at an intellectual level, we found the reality somewhat different. No longer was Trish either able or prepared to deal with the demands I was making, largely because I was equally unable to cope with her demands for some physical and emotional independence. My conditioning about women being subject to the masculine will was extremely powerful and, my reaction to that position being challenged, even though I was intellectually opposed to monogamy, was the classic reaction of a male under threat.

There was anger, frustration, and lots of self-pity, and I suspect the only thing which brought us through was that I had agreed to this experiment before it began - I could not ever claim that I had been deceived or misled.

I also became involved in other relationships which, for a time, meant relative calm on the home front, as we each pursued our own version of true independence, within the parameters of our marriage. However, these liaisons did not last for long and I was forced to face the fact that I needed to look for affirmation from within, rather than seeking it through intimate relationships. In retrospect, I have no doubt that it was the love and support of my male friends which nurtured me through this process. They were endlessly patient as I poured out my woes, and I shudder to think how self-centred I became. They listened, responded, challenged, and supported me when I needed it most and, while I quickly realised how much my self-confidence was tied to my relationship with Trish, changing that position was a much more long-term process.

As I look back, I realise that our vision of being able to maintain a number of intimate relationships was, and is, too difficult for both of us. However, I found the experience enormously valuable in demonstrating the benefits of not putting all of one's emotional eggs in one basket. What my men friends provided was an alternative model to the masculine stereotype of cool emotional detachment and iron will, with neither of which was I particularly well endowed! I choose now to have close friendships with a range of people, particularly men, in order to share more deeply than my socialisation might have taught me was appropriate. This model provides me with a structure within which to enjoy a deeply fulfilling relationship with Trish, without losing my individuality and sense of self, and which enables me to go on growing and learning with the support and encouragement of other men.

PART THREE

Partnership and Practice

10

Perspectives on the Men's Movement
Maggie Carey

The men's movement. New constructions of masculinity. A change in consciousness. A response. A backlash. A movement. There is no one men's movement. There is, rather, a plethora of loosely connected groups and individuals who hold at times very different and often contradictory stances on the basic objectives of what a men's movement should be about. But there is a common understanding that unites these men, and it is the belief that traditional definitions of masculinity no longer work, that the models of masculinity that today's men have inherited are no longer desirable or appropriate, and that they need to be challenged and reworked.

To understand something of the phenomenon we are discussing, it is necessary to consider the very wide range of beliefs and attitudes that the different groups involved in the movement encompass. There are men who name themselves as anti-sexist and pro-feminist who see the role of the movement as one of working against sexism in all its forms. There are other men who see a need to reclaim some of the "power" men have lost to women as a result of feminism. Some men march in the streets and lobby parliamentarians to give voice to issues of domestic violence, rape and abuse, while others rally for "men's rights", claiming women are responsible for the breakdown of the family, and that women's rightful place is in the home. There are men who believe that the primary aim of this type of work is to "liberate" themselves from the constraints of masculinity. There is the gay men's movement which has been in operation since Stonewall, and which surely must be the first large-scale mobilisation of any group of men to challenge the dominant mores of masculinity.

There are men's groups which are searching for an essential masculinity, believing this has been lost or at least diluted in modern society. These men place great emphasis on primitive masculine ritual and on close readings of early mythologies in the anticipation of getting back to a clearer understanding of what it is to be a man.

There are men who choose to stay at home. One of the outcomes of new definitions around gender has been a revisioning of the part men are able to play in rearing children and in being involved in the domestic sphere. Because of the private nature of family life in our culture, these men are not readily visible, and yet they would have to represent one of the most profound changes in attitudes toward masculinity to have yet occurred.

In considering the array of attitudes, aims and objectives of this broad sweep of men's activities, it is important to be aware of the fact that few groups or individuals fall into any one category. Though there are extremes at either end of the spectrum of particular ideas, most groups take bits and pieces from various perspectives and deal with them in different ways.

The great majority of men involved in the movement are middle-aged, white and middle-class. The mainstream movement is also decidedly heterosexual in its orientation toward issues of masculinity. This is the cause of a great deal of frustration on the part of gay men who have worked over the last twenty years or so on some of the very issues that so concern "straight" men, on expressing sensitivity and caring toward men, on allowing themselves to reflect on and express their feelings, and most importantly in confronting the old definitions of masculinity and coming up with new models that worked for them.

In terms of ideological alignment, it seems that liberalism is the dominant ethos of the men's movement. The lack of any revolutionary agenda is decried by radical activists who see no avenue for social change in investing in liberal notions and thinking them to be progressive when in fact they are the ideology of the ruling class:

> Using liberalism to change doesn't work. Liberalism is enshrined in the ruling-class laws. If you start to look at an agenda that's actually revolutionary then the men's movement could be in men's interest, but I don't see that happening. There have never been any active revolutionaries in the movement, only liberals. (McCann 1992)

Having looked then at which men comprise this movement, I would like to briefly deal with the particular perspective that I bring to this discussion, not only as a woman talking about men, but also in terms of the framework in which I situate my reflections.

The body of ideas known as postmodernist or constructivist thought presents a perspective on the construction of our reality that allows us to see how we have been recruited into particular ways of being that may or may not be useful or helpful. The possibility of developing new ways of being, that are more in line with what we would prefer, is opened up. We give meaning to our lives by interpreting the experiences we have in the light of the beliefs that we have about ourselves, and we largely dismiss those experiences which do not fit these beliefs. But these beliefs can be changed, they are not fixed or based on any essential truth about human nature. Our beliefs about gender are particularly seen as a social constructs rather than as inherent and essential truths about our nature.

The process of deconstruction within this arena of gender involves looking at where our particular values and beliefs about ourselves as male or female come from, and making some conscious choices about what is no longer appropriate, and what we wish to incorporate into a new identity. John Stoltenberg, in *Refusing to be a Man* (1989), challenges us to see our sexual identity as our primary construct and that this construct is, by nature, political. The ascription of human nature into the separate categories of male and female, Stoltenberg believes, involves the almost full-time effort on everyone's part to maintain it, though some people, he points out, "work at this project with more fervour than others". We behave in ways that identify ourselves as male or female, and we carefully avoid behaviours that don't. Stoltenberg likens this aspect of our behaviour to a faith:

> A particular system of attaching values to conduct without the slightest comprehension of how or why people believe that the system is true. It is a creed whose articles never really require articulation, because its believers rarely encounter anyone who does not already believe it, silently and by heart. The valuation of human actions according to the gender of the one who acts, is a notion so unremarkable, so unremittingly commonplace, and so self-evident to so many, that its having come under any scrutiny whatsoever is a major miracle in the history of human consciousness. (1989, p.20)

It is within this spirit of a common humanity that I would like to proceed. The understanding of how our sex-roles are the products of our socialisation, and not our inherent nature, helps liberate us from the constraints of those separate roles, and in that freedom is the room to construct new identities that better serve our commonality.

Although, as was earlier noted, there is no one unified men's movement that can be easily discussed, there do seem to be two main categories of men's activities into which a lot of groups fall. These are the groups who see men's "liberation" as the primary focus of concern on the one hand, and on the other, the anti-sexist and pro-feminist groups. I hasten to reiterate that few groups are exclusively one or the other (though there are extremes in either case), and my aim is not to polarise, but to set up a framework that makes discussion possible by talking about these groups separately, as the values and belief systems that underlie the two groups are different and at times contradictory.

It is useful to locate historically the current thinking in the men's movement, and Barbara Ehrenreich, in her book, *The Hearts of Men* (1983), gives an excellent contextual account of the background to what I have here identified as the men's liberation perspective. Much of the literature surrounding the issue of a new masculinity seems to lack any awareness of historical antecedents to particular ways of thinking, and treats the issue as something that has come out of the nineties. Ehrenreich's analysis of the "men's liberationist" perspective takes us back to the fifties in white, middle-class North America, where conformity to an idealised image - the house in the suburbs, the wife, the kids, the husband-as-bread-winner - were all components of an excessively prescribed way of being to which most people conformed, and through which people expressed their psychological "maturity". Indeed the prescriptions for healthy psychological maturity were clearly spelt out, and to not complete the "developmental tasks" of early adulthood - getting married, settling down, starting a family (for women), embarking on a career (for men) - was tantamount to being un-American and therefore in that time, either a Communist or, more adversely to one's mental health, a homosexual. The role of man as bread-winner, able to support wife and family, had become linked to definitions of masculinity that saw not competing in the "rat race" as not being a "real" man.

Those who lived by the rules, however, found that life was not the smooth graduation into calm and successful waters that the well-adjusted maturity of the psychology texts suggested it might be. By the early fifties a malaise associated with living by such rigid prescriptions came to be the topic of lead articles in both popular magazines such as *Look*, *Life*, and *Reader's Digest*, as well as of academic, sociological treatises. The problem was conformity, and, most pertinently to this discussion, the emasculation that came with white-collar work. New skills were being brought into play as work in corporation life became more and more working with and on people, rather than things, and this sort of work necessitated characteristics that had been traditionally and very strictly associated with being feminine. These middle-class men were clearly becoming effeminate, and it was a worry to them.

One of the first open rebellions against societies' demands for men to conform to expectations of responsibility, work, and the attendant emasculation, came from that small band of writers and poets known as the Beat group. Kerouac, Cassady, Ginsberg and others, in their writing and in the lives that they outrageously led, presented an alternative to those ready to rebel against the constraints of "grey-flannel conformity". The beatniks who followed in their path (but to whom they bore slight resemblance, being "cool" and laid back, whereas the Beats were "mad to live") represented a large-scale turning away from the traditional ties of marriage and the soul-destroying, mind-numbing monotony of white-collar work.

The Beats found their "mad to live" people in the underclass of mid-century America, though this underclass was largely unacknowledged until the sixties and seventies. Supposedly at this time, there was "only the great middle class, and somewhere off to the side, the rich, still known benignly as 'high society" (Ehrenreich 1983, p.58). The Beats were not men walking away from white-collar anxiety, being themselves from mostly lower-middle-class backgrounds and working as labourers if they worked at all, but they found that their particular sympathies toward non-conformity most naturally lay with the underclass and the outsiders. And it was clear to the Beats, and to those that followed them, that the overt masculinity that had been lost to the middle-class grey men, was alive and well and living in the underclass. Here men had not had to grapple with the existential ennui of endless back-yard barbecues, of daily commuting to work, of having to read the "right" authors, see the latest films, own the latest commodity.

The lives of men in the working classes were hard and shaped hard men who never doubted their own masculinity. Hollywood in the fifties honed in on the overt sexuality of tough working class male rebels like James Dean and Marlon Brando, and the image took off. The music industry was irrevocably shaken by the introduction of rock and roll, whose "king" was a truck driver from Mississippi, singing black people's music. Psychological maturity, as a defined aim in life, quickly lost its appeal to a whole generation of Americans and to those of us living in America's cultural colonies.

The era of personal growth psychologies, of Fritz Perls' Gestalt Therapy, and Abraham Maslow's processes of self actualisation in the sixties and seventies, further distanced this generation from thoughts of "doing the right thing" and laid before them the much more appealing dictum of "do your own thing". In fact, to not do your own thing, to not "grow" and develop to your fullest potential, was declared psychologically unhealthy, and to be labouring under obsolete notions of guilt. Titles such as David Viscott's *Feel Free (How to Do Everything You Want Without Feeling Guilty)* became popular, as did the ubiquitous "I do my thing, and you do your thing ..."

Then came the countercultural revolution, the "age of Aquarius", flower power and hippies. The most striking aspect of this revolution was the embracing of an apparent androgyny that saw the virtual jettisoning of the traditional overt semblances of masculinity. Long hair, beads, flowers, loose, flowing clothes - it was as though these men no longer wished to be aligned with an aggressive masculinity that was, at this time, seen to be running amuck in places like My Lai.

The first murmurings of an actual movement directed toward men's liberation came early in the seventies and the idea quickly spread. It was to some degree a response to feminism, but following on as it did from the human potential movement it presented men's "growth" and freedom from constraints as its primary focus. Denouncing any suggestion of there being privilege attached to the male role by focussing on the threat to men's lives from heart-attack due to stress and the emotional destitution of men, leading spokesperson Herb Goldberg urged men to realise the extent of their own oppression and that guilt toward women was "one trap from which the liberated man must free himself."

Meanwhile, a new area of research had opened up within the realm of academia which added "scientific insight" to men's call for liberation. In the schools of psychology, researchers responded to what the feminists had brought to light by focusing on theories of sex-role behavior. They "discovered" the existence of sex-roles in men and women, popularly known as stereo-types, and that they were essentially expectations that each gender has of themselves and each other. These theories, however, did not contextualise the roles of men and women in our culture. In behaviour laboratories, no allowance was made for the constraints of inequitable access to power or privilege in forming sexual stereotypes, and indeed the impression was given of men and women being in equivalent positions in terms of the restraints put upon them by sex-role stereotyping. By not taking this into account, it was possible to concentrate on how men were being hurt by their roles, and to develop a "masculinity therapy" to deal with the hurt.

Widely popular books, such as Warren Farrell's *The Liberated Man* (1975) and Jack Nichols's *Men's Liberation* (1975), counselled that it was a necessary and seemingly straightforward task to change men's roles. Men's liberation differed from women's in that it was not deemed to be political or social but was intensely personal and therapeutic. All that it required was the stepping outside of the old roles, responsibilities, and habits, and a new age would dawn for both men and women. What these early groups, and those that followed into the eighties and now into the nineties, failed to take into account was and is the systems nature of society.

Social structures are comprised of more than just the actions of individuals, and there are institutionalised imbalances of power associated with being male or female that are not addressed by simply "undressing" one's self of the unwanted aspects of masculinity. Within the context of the imbalance of power, and within the context of actually looking contextually at what's going on, men's cry for liberation becomes a cry for what? More freedom? More equality? More power? The notion of "liberation" that our culture holds so dear is intrinsically tied to beliefs in the efficacy of individualism - we should all work toward our own liberation, it is our right and our due to be fully-realised beings. There could be another reading of liberation that goes something like: "none of us will be free until we are all free".

I would like to look now at what I consider to be the other main stream of men's activities in this movement of men, the groups and individuals that would call themselves pro-feminist, or Men Against Violence. In the early seventies, groups of men who had listened to (and heard) what women had to say, formed into consciousness raising groups, somewhat in parallel to women's groups, and looked at eliminating sexism in their lives as well as addressing issues of gay rights. The first attempts were made by men to look at and redefine their roles in respect to the impact of those roles on women. Men became involved in child-rearing, started attending the births of their children; domestic tasks were taken on as well as support given for partners to re-enter the work force or academic institutions. Fathers raising children on their own were no longer unheard of. The idea of exploring the "feminine within" and giving credence to that other, previously untapped part of one's self, were taken on.

These groups recognise that the roles that men are socialised into are limiting of men's potential, but an equal and sometimes greater emphasis is put on how these roles have led men to be oppressive to others. The solution is still one of men learning new roles, but this is located in the wider context of the institutionalised power and privilege over others that exists and that needs to be dismantled in order to liberate not only women, but also those who are on the receiving end of other oppressions such as class, race and sexuality.

Current strategies for change include education and consciousness raising that challenges the individual's sexism, as well as working for wider societal change in the areas of health, schooling, welfare, the law etc. Open support is given by these groups to the activities of the women's movement, and there is a growing sense of working together in order to bring the issues of domestic violence, sexual harassment, pornography and child abuse to the fore in the general consciousness. The idea of men being responsible for doing something about men's violence is indicative of this group's approach to the problem aspects of masculinity.

"Men's Studies" as a recently developed stream within Women's Studies in universities, has evolved out of feminism and Marxism, and takes an extreme feminist line. Men's Studies "delights in describing and tracking down the institutionaliza-tion of masculinist values and attitudes. It is concerned not with masculinity in the broader psychological sense, but with a domineering or hegemonic masculinity [or patriarchy], and with how 'ingrown' hegemonic masculinity is in Western culture. Patriarchy is so subtle that we don't always see it; it sinks into the unconscious and conditions our sense of what is normal and normative." (Tacey 1991)

This group approaches the issue of masculinity from a purely sociological perspective and gives little or no attention to the experience of individual men.

Robert Bly and the mythopoetic men's movement represent the continuation into the present of the ideals of men's liberation. The notion that men need to "become more free", and that they won't do this by pleasing the women in their life, is posited early on in Bly's immensely popular book *Iron John*. The "masculinity therapies" of the seventies opened the way for Bly to be able to pose the question "What do men really want?", as if men getting what they "really want" was the answer to the dilemmas of sexual politics. Bly takes men back to the old issue of emasculation that had been so prominent in the fifties, only this time he lays the blame for men becoming "soft" at the feet of the "strong or life-giving women who graduated from the sixties, [who] played an important part in producing this life-preserving, but not life-giving, man" (Bly 1990, p.3). In his opening examination of what he sees as the problems facing men today, Bly makes no mention of post-Industrial society as a factor in changing our understanding of what is appropriate behaviour for men, or women, but chooses rather to concentrate on how women have somehow drained men of their energy.

Bly's outline for reform centres on separation from women in order to re-establish a sense of the true masculine, and a "fierceness" in men. His work is predicated on the belief that there is a true and essential masculinity that can be recovered by going back to the formative mythologies and folk tales of our culture, or by appropriating selected visions of masculinity from primitive peoples, or by going "deep within" one's self and "getting in touch with" a core sense of what it is to be a man. By not recognising that what they will find at the "core" is what they have introjected from the dominant available discourse around them, and that our mythologies and folk tales have been the primary means of forming and carrying those particular, and mostly patriarchal, discourses, they close off the possibilities of creating new stories that are more appropriate to this time.

Shepherd Bliss, one of the self-espoused leaders of the mythopoetic movement, continues to hold out that women are the privileged ones in our society. When asked if he saw the movement eventually taking a more political line against structural inequalities in our culture, to do with racism or poverty, he responded that the main inequity that bothered him at this time was that "men die eight years younger in this country. The bottom line is actually when you add it all up, the abuse and the violence and so on in this country..."

Taking men's concerns in isolation from the social context in which they exist, looking only at what men "really want", without looking at the impact of those wants on others, is a continuing thread of the men's liberationist ethic that with the advent of the mythopoetic men's movement seems to have become enshrined as a golden, glowing ideal. Even within the less extreme groups there is a degree of blurring of the personal and the political. The act of making the personal political (which men frequently state that they are doing), is not the same as personalising the political. There is a political that exists "out there" that is not necessarily affected by what happens within the personal realm, and something else other than the personal has to be done to change that political. What can happen when the two positions are equated is that men can take as a personal indictment that which is the challenging of a political or social injustice, and when that happens there is no move to change, only defensiveness and denial.

New York activist, editor and writer, Michael Denneny, makes the point that, given that masculinity in Western cultures had reached a point in the forties and fifties of being defined as what it wasn't - that it wasn't gay, that it wasn't being a woman - and given the subsequent women's and gay liberation movements in the sixties whereby both of these groups took on a new definition of themselves, Denneny points out that there could not help but be a re-alignment of definitions of masculinity. Two major reference points by which men understood themselves (not to be) had shifted.

In talking of the possibilities and nature of gay culture, Denneny emphasises that it is a culture which has very few historical antecedents and that it has to be created in this time, and appropriate to this setting. He rejoices in the lack of "cultural baggage" that this leaves gays with, especially in the light of the collapse in a Nietzschean or Kierkegaardean sense of Western European culture. "In the new situation we're in (as the remnants of a collapsed society), we are going to have to create out of ourselves and out of whatever bits of the past we can find useful or helpful, a voluntary culture." This "voluntary culture" is obviously not one tied to old models of masculinity, and it is in the creation of new possibilities for ways of being as men, that Denneny would like to see gay and "straight" men working together. He presumes (and admits that it is only a presumption) that dealing with homosexuality would have to be on the agenda of the men's movement, that homosexuality has to be dealt with and incorporated into the re-visioning of masculinity, or it will go on being a source of panic, fears and phobias for "straight" men.

Gay men within the movement have, for more than a decade now, strongly voiced their sense of not being taken into account in terms of their different experience as men. Their voice is loud but seems largely unheard. The crisis of AIDS in gay communities is significant for the absence of "straight" men involved. In the words of Tim McCann, "it's a bloody emergency, a disaster. Heaps of people are dying every day and there's lots and lots of work to do" (1992), and yet it seems that women are more willing to get involved with the gay men in this work.

Class is another concern that is drawing more attention amongst some groups of the men's movement, as it becomes increasingly apparent that if the movement is to attract other than middle-class men, some work has to be done in looking at what issues are important or even relevant to men from the working classes. Adam Hughes, in his 1992 article, takes note of developments over the last decade in the women's movement, where "middle-class white feminism" has been strongly challenged as being capable of interpreting the experiences of all women. It is not necessary, he suggests, for men to "go through the same learning process, or for that process to be as long or as painful".

Women are definitely looking with hope and expectancy for new developments in the understanding of masculinity. If ever there were need for such a change, it is right now, as women's shelters, rape crisis centres, domestic violence groups and others dealing with the rising incidence of male violence toward women, children and other men continue to have to turn hundreds away because there are not the resources to deal with the flood.

There is a lot of work to be done to address the gender inequities within our society, and as Bob Connell puts it: "It is not an agenda for the nervous. These issues are tough enough to engage the energy, fierceness, and creativity of a vast number of men. Maybe some of the warriors would care to come down from the hills and lend a hand in the cause of social justice." (Connell 1992)

The work that needs to be done is not going to be easy. It is actually going to be quite stressful for men because it involves their going against their own immediate best interests in order to achieve a society that is just and equitable for all. Connell sees that the networking and emotional support that has been developed in the men's movement could be of great help in "sustaining a campaign of genuine social change", but feels that making "the exploration of emotions among the privileged in society the overriding issue in sexual politics is to move a long way toward narcissism, with damaging consequences for social justice" (Connell 1992 - in response to Shepherd Bliss and others' responses to *Drumming up the Wrong Tree*).

The fact that men have begun an exploration of masculinity has opened a space for the possibility of new ways of being for both men and women. It would be hoped that the redefinition of gender could be a task that was embarked on jointly, and that the new constructs could be ones of equity and justice. It is a challenging prospect to say the least, but one that has to happen.

11

Men's Culture, the Men's Movement, and the Constitution of Men's Lives
Michael White

In part, this paper is the outcome of some reflections on my experience of what is generally referred to as the "men's movement". It is also the outcome of some reflections on the situation that men are finding themselves in as they increasingly observe the very negative effects of the dominant men's culture, and as women's protest of this culture becomes more generally effective and pertinent to men. Also, it is about the predicament in which men are finding themselves as they attempt to respond to these observations and to women's protest.

I propose that this predicament is the result of the terms of reference that inform the attempts of many men to bring about some transformation of the dominant men's culture. These are terms of reference that put men at risk of reproducing problematic aspects of the dominant men's culture, and that make it very difficult for men to bring together the personal and the political. I suggest alternative terms of reference for men's work in the transformation of the dominant men's culture, and include some exercises that are intended to assist men to explore the real effects of these.

Concerned, alienated, dismayed, aware and dissatisfied men

I meet many men in different places who are very concerned about what men have done, and are still doing, to women, children and other men. Most of these "concerned" men experience a great deal of distress, shame and outrage on behalf of men in relation to those acts of men who wreak havoc in the lives of others; distress, shame and outrage in relation to the actions of those men who abuse, rape and at times kill women, children, and other men.

I meet many men in different places who are increasingly finding themselves at odds with, or alienated from, many aspects of their own culture - that is, the dominant men's culture. These "alienated men" are at odds with male privilege, with the institutionalised violence of this culture, and with the subjugation of women and men that is the outcome of distinctions that are drawn around gender, class, race and religion.

I meet many men in different places who are dismayed about the social injustice of poverty, about the extreme inequality in the distribution of wealth in our societies, and about the quality and availability of health services for those who are disenfranchised. These "dismayed men" are aware of the extent to which women, many of whom are sole parents, and members of other marginalised groups and races, are entirely over-represented in this group.

I meet many men in different places who are becoming increasingly aware of, and alarmed about, the extent to which the dominant culture of men has been so wholly toxic to this planet. These "aware" men are those who are refusing to allow material incentives and the rewards of social status to distract their attention from the wholesale destruction of our environment, from the systematic poisoning of our life-support systems, and from the extent to which the planet is now threatened with oblivion.

I meet many men in different places who are experiencing a great deal of dissatisfaction in their personal lives. These "dissatisfied men" are those who are beginning to identify the real effects of the lifestyle into which they have been recruited and in which they participate as members of men's culture. These real effects include the pervasive sense of isolation that is so often an everyday feature of men's experience of men's culture, and the burden that they carry (albeit, one that tyrannises others) in being unable to acknowledge error and to express humility.

I also meet many other men who experience all of the above, and, of course, I meet many men who appear concerned about none of the above. And it almost goes without saying that I meet many, many women, who are also concerned about all of the above, and much, much more - but this essay is about my reflections on the men's movement and on the predicament that men are now facing.

The men's movement

A great number of these concerned, alienated, dismayed, aware and dissatisfied men are associated in some way with like-minded men in groups that make up the "men's movement". However, at this present time, the term "men's movement" is hardly of any descriptive value - homogeneity is not the hallmark of this movement. Diverse orientations and a wide range of activities are encompassed by this description.

Some men are organised into politically oriented groups that are explicitly pro-feminist and anti-sexist. These groups favour various forms of activism that focus specifically on challenging the oppression of women and children by men. Other men are organised into groups that are "personal growth" or "self-help" oriented. These groups put primary emphasis on the idea of "men's liberation" and on the "reclaiming of masculinity". Yet other men, many of whom have experienced marginalisation because of sexual orientation or race, are involved in groups that are organised around issues that are quite specific to their experience of the dominant men's culture.

That there is some conflict of ideas and purposes between these different groups is only to be expected. However, for some groups of men this conflict of ideas and purposes takes on gulf-like proportions that make collaboration impossible. This gulf makes it very difficult for men to develop the sense of affiliation and collaboration that is so necessary to the task of bringing about any of the required transformations of men's culture. The gulf to which I am referring exists primarily between those action-oriented political groups that are pro-feminist and anti-sexist, and those groups that have a personal growth and self-help orientation.

Those groups of men that are more oriented to the political frequently argue that those groups that are personal growth oriented usually privilege the well-being of men at the expense of social justice. This is an argument which has also been very strongly articulated by groups of women (for example, see *Women Respond to the Men's Movement* [Hagan 1992]). Those groups of men that are more oriented to personal growth and self-help frequently argue that other groups ignore the extent of men's suffering as well as men's need to develop and engage in processes that are healing of the male psyche; that the politically oriented action groups neglect or do not sufficiently address men's experience of men's culture. In the men's movement it is apparent that the bringing together of and the reconciling of the personal and the political is fraught with difficulty.[1]

This gulf, and the difficulty that men have had in joining the personal and political, is unfortunate for many reasons, not the least of which is the extent to which it divides men from men and men from women. I believe that a significant part of this difficulty has to do with the taken-for-granted terms of reference for men's personal work; the terms of reference that frame virtually all of the personal growth and self-help oriented activities engaged in by groups of men, and the terms of reference through which the more politically oriented groups so often construe "personal work".

In this paper I will discuss some of these terms of reference - which I believe to be informed by the foundationalist tradition of thought - and will review the real effects of these terms of reference in the shaping of men's lives and in the shaping of their relationships with others. I will then argue for an alternative perspective on the personal, a perspective that brings the personal and the political together.

Foundationalist Thought

The taken-for-granted terms of reference to which I am referring are those that are informed by foundationalist thought. Despite its taken-for-granted status in our world, it is in fact a tradition of thought that is culture and period specific - the foundationalist tradition of thought became dominant in recent history in Western culture. It is a tradition of thought that assumes objectivity, essentialism, and representationalism:

(a)   The assumption of objectivity proposes that a direct knowledge of the world is possible, and that through this we can determine the brute facts of nature; that it is possible for us to obtain an objective account of the world, one that is not mediated by our language, by our interpretations, by our location in the field of social structures and so on.

(b)   The assumption of essentialism proposes that we can know the truth about the very nature of material and psychological existence; that we can successfully reduce the complexity of the world down to particular elements upon which all else is built; that we can get to the "bottom of things" and discover the essence of human nature; that these discoveries about nature constitute global and trans-cultural truths - uncontestable truths that hold for all times and in all places.

(c)   The assumption of representationalism proposes that the descriptions or stories that we have of the world and of life are reflections of the actual world and of life itself; that, to the extent that these descriptions are a mirror of the world and of life, they can provide us with an accurate account of the world and of life.

In the history of foundationalist thought, the physical, biological, social and psychological sciences have all been spectacularly successful in the manufacture of global, unitary and timeless "truths" about nature and about culture. This tradition of thought has enabled the various disciplines of the social and psychological sciences to establish truth statements about life, and it is these truth statements that constitute the professional and expert knowledges.

Despite this success, the truths and knowledges that have been manufactured in the foundationalist tradition have never been received unproblematically and gone uncontested. In recent times, there has been more interest in the history of resistance to foundationalist thought and its methods. And there has been a greater awareness of the real effects of this tradition of thought, particularly in terms of the extent to which the global and unitary truths disqualify alternative knowledges and subjugate many persons and groups of persons (Foucault 1973, 1979, 1980).

The assumptions of foundationalist thought have now been rigorously critiqued and refuted in many areas and upon various grounds. Alternative systems of thought and methods are usurping its authority. For example, witness those contributions of feminist scholars who are engaging in the archaeology of alternative knowledges of women's ways of being (e.g. Gilligan 1982); those developments in anthropology that relate to the new ethnography (e.g. Geertz 1983, 1988); the emergence of social constructionist and narrative theory in psychology (e.g. Parker & Shotter 1990; Sarbin 1986); and, in family therapy, the call for qualitative research (Atkinson & Heath 1987).

However, despite these developments, foundationalist thought still has currency in many of the academic disciplines and with many groups whose activities are informed by popular culture. And not the least of these are many of those groups in the men's movement that are committed to notions of personal growth and male liberation. These groups tend to be preoccupied with the question of men's nature, and with attempts to determine global and unitary truths about the essence of "masculinity" - so that men might uncover this, reclaim it, perform it, and live a life that is true to it (e.g. Bly 1992; Keen 1992). For it is argued that masculinity is an essence that exists deep in the psyche and which has been repressed, and which if not reclaimed will surface in wild ways, accompanied by violent and other destructive acts.

In the following discussion, by referring to what I call "the essentialist project", I will review some of the real effects of foundationalist assumptions on the men's movement.

The essentialist project and men's culture

The essentialist project has played a central role in the long and inglorious history of patriarchy in Western culture. Throughout this history, essentialism has been resorted to consistently by men in order to justify the oppression and disenfranchisement of women, of children, and of other races. Essentialist notions have also played a key role in the marginalisation of gay and other minority groups.

In the field of gender, men have persistently and tirelessly worked to establish a case for the superiority of men's essential nature over women's essential nature in all of those domains which are said to determine the "real" worth of a person - from superiority in the moral sense through to superiority in regard to the possession of those highly regarded capacities of logic and rational argument. This case has been central to the maintenance and extension of the inequitable arrangements between the genders - to the justification of the oppression of women, and for the support of male power, privilege and violence.

Over time, this essentialist project has gone through a series of revivals or renewals. Often these renewals have been in response to those women's rights movements that have challenged or threatened the established social order. For example, take the primary responses of the dominant men's culture to the suffragette[2] movement at the turn of the century - an extraordinary flurry of essentialist activity; activity devoted to distinguishing the truly masculine from the truly feminine, and to the meticulous elaboration of pre-existing notions about the true and natural role in life for each gender. In this way, the established social order that disadvantaged women was preserved and significantly strengthened.

More recently there has been a further renewal of the essentialist project. Albeit, this renewal is one that has been justified on different grounds - one that is judged to be in the service of overthrowing the dominant men's culture - but it is a renewal of the old project nonetheless. This renewal is most clearly evident in the activities of many, but not all, of those groups in the men's movement who privilege self-help and personal growth. Following Bly, Keen, and others, many of these groups, through various means, have the explicit agenda of pursuing, discovering, disseminating and performing the truth of men's nature - of the essential masculinity. Not surprisingly, this essential masculinity so often turns out to be fierce and warrior-like.

In view of this most recent renewal, and in view of the history of the essentialist project, is it all that surprising that many women and many men are alarmed by those developments in the men's movement that are informed in this way by essentialist notions? Is it all that surprising that there is a very significant concern that these developments may be reproducing, however inadvertently, some of the really problematic aspects of the men's culture?

I believe that an appreciation of the history of the dominant men's culture provides us all with good enough reason to deeply mistrust the essentialist project as a vehicle for the transformation of men's culture. Further, I believe that there is all the more reason for this mistrust upon reviewing *some* [3] of the real effects of this project as it is expressed through developments in some areas of the present day men's movement. In the following discussion, I will attempt such a review. The points that I make here are not speculative, and they are not "academic" - they are derived from events that I have directly witnessed and personally experienced. Needless to say, this review forms a critique that emerges from a non-essentialist perspective.

Real effects of the essentialist project

- To the extent that the essentialist project identifies certain "truths" about men's nature, it privileges a particular knowledge of so-called "authentic", "real" or "masculine" ways of being that we must learn from other men. Those men who possess this knowledge both assume and are recruited into an expert and leadership position in relation to other men, and the phenomenon of guruism and its associated hierarchical organisation is inevitably the outcome.

- To the extent that the essentialist project privileges certain knowledges and excludes or disqualifies those rival observations and knowledges about men's ways of being from the "outside", as well as critical feedback, it establishes a closed field - an inner sanctum. This is isolating of us, and the risk that we might be reproducing the dominant men's culture becomes extremely high. Isolation from alternative knowledges and from the direct feedback of those who have most keenly experienced subjugation and oppression at the hands of the dominant men's culture (that is women, children, and men of marginalised groups and those of subjugated races and cultures), makes it possible for us to continue to avoid the issue of accountability.

- To the extent that the essentialist project establishes unitary and global truths about men's nature, it specifies and totalises men's ways of being. We are incited to enter into certain operations on our lives, relationships, bodies, souls and so on, operations that establish us as persons of moral worth in the men's community - to enter into a form of dressage in order to achieve a particular presentation of the self that is one that meets the specifications of "authentic masculinity".[4] Other knowledges and practices of men's ways of being are marginalised and discriminated against, and thus rendered unavailable for our consideration.

- To the extent that the essentialist project suggests that the achievement of some natural condition requires a recapturing of what has been lost, a return to basics, it is inherently conservative and provocative of a paralysing form of nostalgia for what never was. This is a form of nostalgia that romanticises the history of men's relationships with other men, and particularly the mentoring of younger men by their seniors.[5] One outcome of this is the determination that there is some "universal need" for sons to have a particular sort of relationship with their fathers.[6] Since the absence of this relationship is considered to bring about dire consequences, sole parents who are women are perpetually at risk of failing their sons because they provide an "incomplete" context for their lives. This provokes a certain anxiety, insecurity and conformity in these women, who are ever more likely to submit themselves and other family members to highly subjugating experiences in attempts to provide a "good enough" context for their sons' lives - in their attempts to engage a man who will meet this "universal" need.

- To the extent that the essentialist project promotes a dream that men can wind back the clock through time to rediscover the basics, it recruits us into a mytho-myopic account of men's nature. This renders it virtually impossible for us to recognise the critical role that these very myths have played in the constitution and the justification of men's culture in the first place - to recognise that these very myths are essential to the survival of patriarchal culture.[7]

- To the extent that the essentialist project preoccupies men with a search for settled certainties about the truth of their identity, it deprives us of a basis for action in the social domain. "Need" as a criterion for action so often replaces the recognition of injustice and cruelty as a basis for action, and this allows us to avoid confrontation with issues that relate to our commitments in life - to evade recognition of the real effects, upon others, of our way of living. In short, the essentialist project enables us to avoid the moral and ethical implications of, and responsibility for, what we think and what we do. It blinds us to our complicity in the maintenance of the domination and abuse of others, and to our support of economic, political and social structures that preserve and further men's privilege.

- To the extent that the essentialist project references behaviour to a self that is considered to be an underlying, fundamental, precious and somewhat fragile entity, it encourages men to interpret many of their cruel and destructive actions as responses to threats to this self. Such actions are construed as the outcome of fears that this self may be "engulfed", "swallowed", "wounded", "crushed", "pierced", "punctured" and so on. According to this scheme, many of men's cruel and destructive actions towards women and minority groups are considered to be the outcome of certain threats that invoke such fears. In order to circumvent facts that might otherwise shipwreck this analysis [8], a special form of mental gymnastics has been necessary. These gymnastics have lead to spurious theories about the "power of powerlessness", and have made it possible for us to hold women and minority groups responsible for their own subjugation and oppression. In the culture of psychotherapy, this analysis has also supported and justified the disciplining of women, and particularly of mothers.

- To the extent that the essentialist project provokes a preoccupation with biological, genetic, and psychological explanations for the predicament in which men are finding themselves, it can deny us historical and political analyses of this predicament. For example, the theory of repression that so often accompanies the more psychological explanations of men's actions makes it very difficult for us to face what we have done, as a gender, to others in terms of subjugation and oppression, and to take responsibility for this. Furthermore, such theories distract us from any articulation of the political or class dimension of our own experience of men's culture - including those that relate to inequality of opportunity and to exploitation.

- To the extent that the essentialist project emphasises a theory of repression in its analysis of the disembodied and circumscribed ways that men speak [9], it diverts our attention from the degree to which this disembodied speech form is one that we have learned to enter and one that shapes our lives - that constitutes who we are, that creates what we experience as "self". In emphasising a notion of the repressed masculinity, and in sponsoring the cathartic discharge of emotions as a remedy, one considered to be paramount in the healing of men, the essentialist project renders invisible to us the processes of power associated with the more disembodied ways of speaking. The disembodied speech form privileges men's knowledges, while simultaneously masking the very processes of power at work in this privileging. Further, this theory of repression conceals the degree to which this way of speaking is considerably determined by men's situation in the social structures that they inhabit.

• To the extent that the essentialist project blinds men to the degree to which identity is something that is negotiated and distributed in communities of persons and within the institutions of our culture, it perpetuates and reinforces the very isolated forms of individuality that have been so impoverishing of our lives. These "isolated individualities" are the outcome of a denial of community, and this severely limits the opportunities for us to join collaboratively with others in the working out and in the determination of what might be our preferred desires, qualities, purposes, hopes, values, beliefs, commitments in life, and so on - in the working out of more affiliative or connected individualities.

• To the extent that the essentialist project makes it possible for men to deny the degree to which the domains of gender are distinct social worlds, it renders it impossible for us to engage in dialogue with women in relation to our experience of men's culture and women's experience of men's culture. So often the blurring of this distinction appears to reduce men to what is experienced by women as a highly competitive and enraging position of "we were also oppressed", and "it hurt us too". In that this blurring facilitates the co-optation of women's descriptions of their experiences of men's culture, and of the terms that they have relied upon for a political and social analysis of their position, it disqualifies these terms and descriptions, and is bound to enrage. This blurring of the distinction that pertains to the social domains of gender is in the service of oppression.[10]

• To the extent that the essentialist project provides for a radical distinction between men and women in terms of their essence - one that juxtaposes men's and women's natures - it incites men to separate from and to distance from women. The real effects of this incitement are devastating of our lives. We are split apart from the contribution that our mothers, daughters, partners and other women have made to our lives, and in this process we disqualify these contributions as well as the women concerned. This is impoverishing of the lives of men - we are left to proceed in life bereft of our experience of these women's experience of us. Furthermore, this distinction supports and reinforces misogynist accounts which encourage male separatism.

- To the extent that the essentialist project proposes the crucial recognition of sharp distinctions in identity based on gender, it inevitably locates identity in anatomy. In so doing, it prescribes for us a preoccupation with genitalia, and contributes very significantly to the phallocentrism of men's culture. The dominant "phallocentric" form of masculinity is one in which penile insertion is tantamount to the achievement of personal acknowledgment and intimate contact with others - other forms of sensual, sexual, and intimate contact are discriminated against as inconsequential, insufficient or insignificant.

- To the extent that the essentialist project obscures the structures of privilege and power that have ensured men's dominance, it makes it possible for us to construe and reduce the history of women's discontent, protest and resistance, and men's reaction to this, as a "battle of" or "war between" the sexes in which we are struggling to hold our own against "competitive women"; in which men's aggression against women is justified by citing women as co-antagonists. The construction of a "battle of" or "war between" the sexes is a ruse that blurs the power differential, conserves the status quo, and burdens women with equal responsibility in the creation of a state of affairs that they have not been free to partake equally in.

This review of the real effects of the essentialist project is by no means exhaustive. However I do believe that this is sufficient to encourage a thorough mistrust of the renewal of the essentialist project - regardless of whether or not men justify this renewal on the grounds that it will contribute to the overthrow of the dominant men's culture.

In the following discussion I will present an alternative to essentialist notions of self, one that brings together the personal and the political, and one which brings with it very different real effects in the lives of men and in their relationships with others. For the want of a better word, I will refer to this alternative as a "constitutionalist" perspective.

The Constitutionalist Perspective

Historically, philosophy has been oriented towards what Foucault calls "the formal ontology of truth" through questions like "What is the world? What is man [sic]? What is truth? What is knowledge? How can we know something?" and so on. However, at the end of the eighteenth century a new question emerged in this arena:

> This question is very different from what we call the traditional philosophical questions: What is the world? What is man? What is truth? What is knowledge? How can we know something? And so on. The question, I think, which arises at the end of the eighteenth century is: What are we in our actuality? You will find the formulation of this question in a text written by Kant. I don't pretend the previous questions about truth, knowledge, and so on have to be put aside. On the contrary, they constitute a very strong and consistent field of analysis, what I would like to call the formal ontology of truth. But I think that a new pole has been constituted for the activity of philosophising, and this pole is characterised by the question "What are we today?" And that is the field of historical reflection on ourselves. (Foucault 1988, p.145)

It is this new pole, posing questions like "What are we in our actuality?" and "What are we today?", that introduces us to what I refer to as the constitutionalist perspective.

Constitutionalism brings with it the proposition that, upon entering into life in the social world, persons become engaged in particular modes of life and thought - or, according to Foucault, particular practices of power and technologies of the self, and knowledges about life that have achieved or been granted a truth status (Foucault 1979, 1980, 1984). According to this perspective, these practices, technologies and knowledges are not radically invented - the individual person does not simply "dream them up". These practices, technologies and knowledges have been negotiated over time within contexts of communities of persons and institutions that comprise culture.

This social formation of communities and institutions composes relations of forces which establish rules that determine which ideas, of all those possible, are acceptable - they determine what is to count as legitimate knowledge. The specification of who is authorised to express these ideas, how they are to be expressed, in which contexts they might be expressed, and to whom they will be expressed, is also a function of these rules. In this way, power relations govern the production of truth.

It is not my intention to articulate these processes here more fully, nor the intimate relationship of knowledge and power, which I have discussed elsewhere (White & Epston 1990; White 1991). However, I will emphasise a central proposition of this constitutionalist perspective: these modes of life and thought are actually shaping or constituting of persons' lives and of their relationships; persons' lives are made up according to these knowledges and practices which are in fact specifying of a life. For all persons living in specific cultures, these dominant modes of life and thought come to reflect the truth about human nature, about authenticity, and about identity.

In proposing that persons' lives are constituted through specific modes of life and of thought, this perspective encourages the refutation of foundationalist assumptions of objectivity, essentialism, and representationalism. It suggests that:

(a)   an objective knowledge of the world is not possible; that knowledges are actually generated in particular discursive fields in specific cultures at specific times, and that it is impossible for persons to avoid complicity in the production of their accounts of the world.

(b)   all essentialist notions about human nature are actually ruses that disguise what is really taking place; that essentialist notions are paradoxical in that they provide descriptions that are actually specifying of life; that these notions obscure the operations of power at work in the constitution of persons' lives.

(c)   the descriptions that we have of life are not representations or reflections of life as lived, but are directly constitutive of life; that these descriptions do not correspond with or mirror the world, and that different accounts of life are not equal or neutral, but have real effects in the shaping of lives and of relationships.

The constitutionalist perspective presents us with an account of identity which is not premised on the idea of a "true", "unitary" and "fixed" nature that is unchanging, bounded, coherent, and trans-cultural. Instead, this perspective suggests that the knowledges and practices of our culture, of our social structures and communities of persons, are significantly determining of the very stuff of identity: of desires, preferences, interests, intentions, motives, values, beliefs, hopes, goals, commitments and so on.

For some, this account of identity has raised significant questions: Doesn't this claim about the determination of identity reduce persons to the level of "dupes" who blindly replicate the lives of those who have gone before, and who, simply, automatically, and mindlessly reproduce culture? Doesn't this propose a rather bleak account of identity, an account of identity as fate; one that is "fixed-up" ahead of our birth into this culture, and one that consigns persons to a passenger status in life? And doesn't this claim propose a denial of agency, and a denial of the subject?

I think not. The achievement of identity requires that persons be active in the negotiation of the different experiences of the ways of life and of thought that are to be had at the different sites of culture; at the different positions in social structures, and at different places in communities of persons. And this achievement also requires the interpretation of experience and the structuring of self-narrative. Rather than deny agency and the subject, I believe that this perspective emphasises agency and the subject.

Identity and the negotiation of subjectivity

If, as I have argued, identity is constituted through a myriad of contexts, then it is multi-sited: work, recreation, marriage, family and so on. At each of these sites, certain modes of life and of thought will be privileged, and each of these will bring forth specific experiences of self - specific "subjectivities". Many of these subjectivities will be overlapping and informed by the same dominant discourses of our culture, but some will not be.

Furthermore, at each of these sites, more than one experience of self will be available. And some of these experiences of self will be contradictory, giving rise to "alternative subjectivities". Although some of these subjectivities will be more pervasive than others, and some just fleeting, none will be total. Thus we can expect that each of these sites of identity will give rise, at different times, to competing subjectivities. For example; as teachers, persons will experience an authoritarian and an egalitarian self; as students, persons will experience a knowledgeable and a naive self; as nurses, persons will experience a competent and a submissive self; as therapists, persons will experience an involved and a detached self, and so on.

These considerations about the multi-sited nature of the self, and about the contradictory experiences of the self that are encountered at these sites, give rise to the notion that identity is an outcome of the negotiation of various subjectivities. In that many of these subjectivities are competing, on this account identity is necessarily "dilemmatic" (see Billig *et al.* 1988). Further, in that these considerations provide for a dynamic account of identity, they propose an account of identity that is ever available to contestation, renegotiation, and to change. Thus, as identity is both an achievement and a project for life, the role of agency and of the subject are vital.

Interpretation and narrative

The extent to which persons are self-interpretive - they are not passive in their response to lived experience, but active in ascribing meaning to this - leads us to a second consideration of the significance of agency and the subject in the constitutionalist account of identity.

It is apparent that the interpretations at which persons arrive in relation to their lived experience are very much informed by a criterion of narrative coherence (E. Bruner 1986; J. Bruner 1990). It is through self-narrative that persons give meaning to their experience and achieve a sense of their lives unfolding; it is through narrative that persons structure their lived experience into sequences of events in time - through past, present and future - and according to certain plots. These personal narratives are not reflections of lives as they are lived, but narratives that are actually constitutive of life; they are not stories about life, but stories that have real effects in the shaping of lives and of relationships.

As the interpretation of experience according to narrative is an achievement, then so is identity. There are always contingencies thrown up in life for which a person's dominant self-narrative is not tailor-made. These must be managed. As well, there are many gaps in personal narratives. Such gaps are the outcome of the degree to which ambiguity and uncertainty feature in all stories. In the living of, or in the performance of, self-narrative, these gaps must be filled. And there are always dilemmas to be resolved in the performance of self-narrative: dilemmas that arise from the extent to which inconsistencies and contradictions are a feature of all stories.

In the management of these contingencies, in the filling of these gaps, and in the resolution of these contradictions and inconsistencies, narratives not only shape life, but persons also transform narratives of self as they perform these narratives. So, although personal narratives are shaping of persons' lives, there is a certain indeterminacy to them - one which emphasises the role of agency and of the subject in the constitution of one's life.

The subject

The account of identity that is described here proposes a "subject" that is constituted through certain modes of life and of thought. However, this is not a subject that is reducible to these modes of life and thought. Rather, what is being presupposed is a subject that is capable of negotiating various subjectivities and contradictions, managing contingencies, and filling the gaps that arise in personal narrative. But this is not a subject that can be considered apart from real effects of this activity - for in the process of living one's life, the subject is transformed.

I believe that any attempt to define the existence of a subject or a self apart from certain modes of life and thought, and apart from experience and narrative, is paradoxical. For it is impossible to define such a subject without describing a mode of life and of thought, and, as well, a narrative of self. This description will be specifying of a particular subjectivity. And, in turn, this act of specifying a subjectivity will be constitutive of the subject - it will have real effects in the shaping of one's existence, of who one is.

I believe that the version of the subject that I represent here is close to the version of the subject that is presupposed by Foucault. Others have reached a similar conclusion, for example:

> I understand Foucault's project itself as presupposing the existence of a critical subject, one capable of critical historical reflection, refusal and invention. This subject does not control the overall direction of history, but is able to choose among the discourses and practices available to it and to use them creatively. It is also able to reflect upon the implications of its choices as they are taken up and transformed in a hierarchical network of power relations. Finally, this subject can suspend adherence to certain principles and assumptions, or to specific

interpretations of them, in their efforts to invent new ones. Foucault's subject is neither entirely autonomous nor enslaved, neither the originator of the discourses and practices that constitute its experiences nor determined by them. (Sawicki 1991, p.103)

The personal and the political

The version of identity or personhood that is proposed by this perspective challenges that version derived from the essentialist project. For the version of identity proposed here is not one that suggests an unfolding of true nature, but one that emphasises the constitution of life as it is lived. This constitution of life cannot be a process that is value-free or neutral, and because of this the formation of identity cannot be divorced from the arena of politics. Thus, this perspective on identity brings together the personal and the political - and it does so on several counts:

1.   In proposing that the constitution of identity, through modes of life and thought, and through narratives of self, occurs within communities of persons and social institutions which have specific commitments to ways of acting and ways of thinking, I am proposing an activity that is partisan rather than neutral. In this sense the constitution of self is inevitably a political activity.

2.   In proposing that modes of life and thought, and self-narratives, are constitutive of life, I am arguing that these have specific and real effects in the shaping of persons' actions, and specific and real effects on the lives of others. On this score, the constitution of identity is inevitably a political activity in the micro-world of relational politics.

3.   And in proposing that, in the constitution of self, certain ways of acting and thinking are privileged over other ways of acting and thinking, some of which are marginalised or disqualified, then I am also proposing an account of the personal that is world-shaping.

A frequent critique of the post-foundationalist perspective is that it proposes an "anything goes" moral relativism, and that it deprives persons of a ground for critical judgement and a basis for action in the social world. I believe that the above considerations belie this critique, and suggest the opposite to be the case.

As well, in depriving us of truths about the nature of persons and about the nature of the world to which we might refer in order to justify our actions, the constitutionalist perspective confronts us ever more significantly with the ethical and moral implications of, and responsibility for, the real effects of the ways that we live and the ways that we think.

The Constitutionalist Perspective and Men's Lives

Challenging the essentialist project

The constitutionalist perspective has the potential to free the present-day men's movement from many of the negative real effects of the essentialist project by:

- mitigating against the fabrication of unitary and global "truths" about men's nature, against the privileging of particular so-called "authentic" or "real" masculine ways of being that we must learn from other men;
- opening space for the introduction of rival observations and knowledges from the outside, thus challenging the perpetuation of an inner sanctum and the isolation that is associated with this;
- making it possible for us to refuse the standard classifications and categorisations that are so totalising of men's lives, and to resist the incitement to police our lives, bodies and souls in the pursuit of "authentic" masculinity;
- enabling us to break free of the paralysing nostalgia for those forms of relationship between men that never were, and, at the same time, to challenge the fabrication of those notions of men's needs that are so disempowering of mothers and capturing of men;
- encouraging us to expose those myths that are referred to in order to justify and glorify patriarchal culture as those myths which have shaped patriarchal culture;
- confronting us with our complicity in the maintenance of structures that preserve men's privilege and the domination and the abuse of others, and with the moral and ethical implications of our ways of life - of what we think, and of what we do;
- discouraging us from engaging in the sort of mental gymnastics that spur theories of the "power of the powerless", and from justifications of our behaviour that are informed by notions of the fragile self and of threats to this self;
- rendering visible to us the processes of power associated with disembodied speech forms, and the extent to which these ways of speaking are informed by our positions in the social structures that we inhabit;
- freeing us from the sort of projects of self that give rise to isolated and impoverished individualities;
- introducing political and historical considerations that enable us to face and take responsibility for what we have done to others, and for the predicament in which we now find ourselves;
- enabling us to counteract the blurring of the distinct social domains of gender, and, in preserving the relevant distinctions, acknowledging women's social analysis of their position rather than co-opting this analysis;

- provoking us to dismantle the juxtaposition of men's and women's natures, thus dissolving the imperative for men to separate from women, and openly acknowledging and embracing those significant contributions that women have made to our lives;
- inspiring us to challenge the dominance of phallocentrism in our intimate contact with others;
- requiring that we acknowledge the structures of privilege and power that have ensured men's dominance, and, in so doing, making it possible for us to respect and honour, as protest, the struggle that women have initiated against these structures, and to join them in this.

Alternative ways of being for men

The constitutionalist perspective proposes more than just a challenge to the essentialist project and to its negative real effects. And it is provocative of more than a determination to separate our lives from the problematic aspects of the dominant men's culture.

It also provokes a determination to engage in processes that generate and/or resurrect alternative knowledges and practices of men's ways of being, and that lead to the development and the performance of alternative narratives of self that have preferred real effects. What might be the starting point for such a project?

The renegotiation of subjectivities. I have argued that identity is multi-sited, and that it is a product of the ongoing negotiation of multiple subjectivities. In emphasising the dilemmatic nature of identity, I have also argued for a dynamic account of identity - one that is ever available to contestation, renegotiation, and to change.

Although many of the subjectivities that make up a person's experience of the self will be informed by the same dominant discourses, some will not be. In that some of these other subjectivities will be juxtaposed to those that are more informed by the dominant modes of life and of thought of the men's culture, it will be possible to consider some of these other subjectivities as meeting the criterion of "alternative subjectivities".

These alternative subjectivities, these alternative experiences of self, can be considered to be sites of resistance and can provide a point of entry to the articulation and performance of alternative knowledges and practices of men's ways of being - and, of course, to the renegotiation of identity.

Alternative narratives of self. I have also argued that a sense of identity is achieved through the structuring of experience into self-narrative, and that this requires (a) the management of contingencies, (b) the filling of gaps that relate to ambiguity and uncertainty that feature in all stories about life, and (c) the resolution of inconsistency and contradiction. However, success at this task will always be of a limited nature; narrative coherence is always partial.

Many of the contingencies that confront persons in their daily lives defy interpretation according to their dominant narratives of self. As well, some of the ambiguity and uncertainty, and many of the inconsistencies and contradictions that are associated with these dominant narratives cannot be satisfactorily resolved. In order to facilitate the interpretation of these contingencies, and to resolve this ambiguity, this uncertainty, these inconsistencies and these contradictions, persons engage in the performance of various "sub-narratives" of their lives. In this sense, persons' identities are not single-storied, but multi-storied. Many of these sub-narratives will complement the dominant narratives, but there will be those that will not, and some of these can be assumed to be "alternative narratives of self".

However, not even the multi-storied nature of identity will be sufficient to the task of the ascription of meaning to experience. There will still be many aspects of experience that defy interpretation, negotiation and resolution; there will always be a stock of lived experience that will be neglected - lived experience that cannot be managed by, and that appears to exhaust, the available frames of intelligibility.

Just as alternative subjectivities can provide a point of entry to alternative modes of life and thought for men, so can the alternative sub-narratives of our lives and those neglected aspects of lived experience that have defied interpretation. The exercises detailed in the latter part of this paper provide one account of how this might be done.

Before providing details of these exercises, I will make further comment on the extent to which the constitutionalist perspective brings together the personal and the political, and then discuss some special considerations to our task of generating and or/resurrecting alternative knowledges and practices of men's ways of being.

Resistance and freedom. In that the constitutionalist perspective is provocative of a determination to engage in the generation and/or resurrection of alternative ways of being and thinking for men, it brings together the personal and the political in yet another sense - through the very act of alternative self-formation, it suggests the possibility of resistance to the dominant knowledges and practices of men's ways of being.

There is an intimate connection between the possibility of resistance and the generation and/or resurrection of alternative ways of being and thinking for men. This is a possibility of resistance that does not arise in a vacuum; it is a possibility of resistance that is not the outcome of sheer negation of particular modes of life and thought, but a resistance that is founded upon and made possible by conceptions of a life for men that might be otherwise.

It is through the articulation of preferred knowledges and practices of men's ways of being, those that are associated with alternative subjectivities and narratives of self, that resistance to the dominant ways in which we have been classified and identified as men can be determined, honoured and further articulated. And it is through a commitment to perform these alternative knowledges and practices of life that the dominant men's culture of the present day will be dismantled.

Inasmuch as this notion of resistance is often associated with the connotation of freedom, this should not be construed as a freedom "to become who we truly are", but:

(a)   the freedom to observe the links between certain modes of life and thought and their real effects in the constitution of lives and relationships;

(b)   the freedom to locate particular modes of life and thought within the structures and processes that have legitimated them, and that have excluded or disqualified other modes of life and of thought;

(c)   the freedom to expose the paradox that is associated with all essentialist notions of masculinity;

(d)   the freedom to refuse to be who we do not have to be;

(e)   the freedom to acknowledge the moral and ethical responsibilities associated with living our lives in the way that we do;

(f)   the freedom derived from experiencing some choice about those modes of life and thought by which we might live;

(g)   the freedom to embrace some of the unique and positive developments in our own lives as we go about the process of renegotiating our identities.

Some considerations. Despite our very best efforts to challenge the dominant men's culture, and to develop and to enter our lives into alternative modes of life and thought, and thus alternative identities, it is only reasonable for us to expect that we will be prone to inadvertently reproducing problematic aspects of this very culture. This does not add up to failure. It is not tenable for us to assume that we can achieve a vantage point from the outside of men's culture from which to address men's culture. By accepting that we are prone to reproducing some of the problematic aspects of men's culture, and by expecting that we will carry this proneness into the future, we can be more open to others who might be in a better position to challenge the reproduction of that which we might not be aware of.

On the other hand, if we assume that we are getting it right, and that the risk that we might be reproducing problematic aspects of the dominant men's culture is minimal, then we will be defensive over, distressed about, and closed to feedback. Furthermore we will find it virtually impossible to take responsibility for the real effects of the "alternative" knowledges and practices of men's ways of being that we are championing. And this is entirely problematic, for just as a critique of the established men's culture is dependent on a historical reflection on its real effects, so does a critique of alternative knowledges and practices of men's ways of being depend on a reflection on the real effects of these.

This consideration behoves us to make it our business to take up every opportunity that avails itself to us to render visible those taken-for-granted men's responses that, in ordinary circumstances, we are so familiar with and close to that we cannot perceive. The adoption of this posture signifies a recognition of the insidious and pervasive nature of many of the attitudes and practices of men's culture, and makes us more responsive to the concerns of others, regardless of the form through which they are expressed. And in our efforts to step into alternative knowledges and practices of men's ways of being, this posture commits us to the solicitation of feedback, of both formal and informal nature, from those who are most subject to the real effects of the dominant men's culture - that is women, children, men of other races, and other marginalised groups. Formal feedback can be achieved through the establishment of systems of accountability, and I would refer readers to the work of the Family Centre of Lower Hutt, Aotearoa/ New Zealand, for further discussion of this (Waldegrave 1991; Tamasese & Waldegrave this volume).

Exercises

I will here present a sample of some exercises that I developed in reference to the constitutionalist perspective. The feedback that I have received from those who have engaged in these exercises suggests that many men have found them useful. The first three exercises provide some examples of processes that utilise alternative subjectivities, alternative narratives of self, and neglected aspects of lived experience as gateways to alternative knowledges and practices of men's ways of being with women, children and other men.

The fourth exercise encourages men to further explore alternative knowledges and practices of men's ways of being that are already firmly established in their lives. The fifth focuses on the *direct* deconstruction of essential notions of masculinity. I emphasise the word direct here, as I believe that all of the exercises described contribute significantly to the deconstruction of the modes of life and thought of the dominant men's culture. These exercises also bring the personal together with the political - the renegotiation of identity with attention to the real effects of this, and a commitment to action in the social world.

The exercises, which are structured around specific questions, can be done in small groups, with one person electing to undertake the role of interviewer and another (a man) volunteering to be interviewed. Alternatively, group members can interview each other in a more general way, exchanging experiences as they work through the exercises. It is important that there are at least two women present in each group who are prepared to provide feedback about the exercise. Such feedback will assist the men to determine whether or not they are reproducing problematic aspects of the dominant men's culture or alternative ways of being and thinking that have preferred outcomes.[11] This feedback is best given at the end of the exercise, and the women who undertake to provide this have a choice as to whether or not they engage in dialogue with the other group members about this feedback.

Prior to commencing the exercises, the groups can discuss the questions for the purposes of clarification, and the complexity of some can be reduced by breaking them into parts. These questions should not be asked in a barrage-like fashion, but will serve as a guide - each question asked in this process should be attuned to the responses of the man being interviewed. Men often find these exercises powerfully evocative of other images of who they might be, and surprisingly emotive.

The exercises are structured around a process of questions which represent a progression, and which contribute to men's articulation of, and men's engagement in, alternative landscapes of their lives. Elsewhere, following J. Bruner (1986), I have referred to these as *landscapes of action* and *landscapes of consciousness* (White 1989, 1991). For those readers who wish to refer to other examples of this sort of process, or who would like a framework for designing their own versions of these exercises, I would refer you to "Deconstruction and Therapy" (White 1991).

Exercise A

Introduction

Your sense of who you are as a man is something that seems to carry across different contexts of your life, whether it be at home, at work, at play etc. This is usually a relatively well defined, familiar, settled and certain sense of who you are and what it means to be a man. You usually experience the transition between these contexts as relatively unproblematic, even smooth perhaps.

However, at times you have found yourself in contexts where this familiar sense is not available to you, or where it becomes shrouded in doubt. You probably experienced the transition to these other contexts as somewhat problematic, with your familiar ways of being less available to you, your usual sense of who you are as a man almost suspended. You might even have felt "out of sorts" for a period, at times your discomfort being such that you took flight for more familiar contexts. However, on those occasions when you have not taken flight, after struggling with the sense of the unfamiliar and the awkwardness that is associated with this, you will have experienced some different ways of being and thinking, and will have achieved an altered sense of who you are and what it means to be a man.

Questions

Recall one such occasion when you achieved such an altered sense of who you are as a man, when this seemed to bring with it some new and positive possibilities for your way of life, and what appeared to be preferred real effects in your relationships with others. Consider that this recall could provide the opportunity to identify and to explore alternative and preferred ways of being and thinking as a man, and address yourself to the following questions:

Please describe the context and the different sense of self that accompanied this. From which dominant taken-for-granted ways of being as a man, that you were recruited into as a member of men's culture, did you experience a degree of separation at this time?

Was there some initial discomfort associated with being separated from a more familiar sense of who you were, a more familiar sense of self? How did you manage to resist taking flight from this context? Did you nearly turn back? What did you depend upon to see you through this discomfort? Were there other developments taking place in your life leading up to this that helped to prepare you for it?

What stories could be told about you, from earlier times in your life, that would help others to understand the foundations for this resistance? Which persons would have been in the best position to tell these stories? What do these stories say about what you have wanted for your life?

Could you describe and give a name to the alternative ways of being and of thinking that were associated with this different sense of self? In what ways were these shaping of your interactions with others? How did you know that these alternative ways of being a man suited you? Do you understand what it is about you that attracted you to these other ways of being and of thinking?

At this time, did you have the opportunity to receive feedback about yourself from others who were not wholly invested in the dominant men's culture? If so, what did they witness you doing, and what qualities do you think they were experiencing in you at this time? What do you think this told them about what you value highly in your relationships with others?

Do you have any thoughts about the steps that you might take to explore more fully and to extend these preferred ways of being and of thinking? Let us assume that these other knowledges about what you want for your life, about the ways of life that you are attracted to, and about the values that are important to you, are to become more influential. What further effects would this have on your life and on your interactions with others?

In stepping more fully into these alternative ways of being and thinking, how would this be likely to affect the picture that you have of yourself as a man? And how would this affect your stance on those dominant men's ways of being and thinking that are subjugating of others, and on your commitment to engage with other men in challenging the structures that make possible the domination and abuse of others?

Exercise B

Introduction

There are many situations in life that throw up contradictory requirements about how men should act, and about how men should think. These engage men in different senses of, or images, of their self. At those points at which these contradictory requirements are in greatest conflict, men usually experience strong encouragement to resolve the associated dilemmas in favour of those ways of acting and thinking that are privileged in the dominant men's culture.

However, this is not always the case. There are many occasions upon which the resolution of these dilemmas is delayed despite the conflict that is experienced by the men concerned. And there are occasions upon which, at least for a time, that side of the dilemma which is not supported by the dominant men's culture is favoured.

Questions

Consider these to be occasions upon which men stand apart from the dominant men's culture. As such they are worthy of a more thorough examination to determine what they might reveal about alternative ways of being and of thinking for men. Now address the following questions:

Identify and reflect on an occasion when you took the step of delaying the resolution of such a dilemma, or when you took the step of resolving such a dilemma in favour of the side that was more antagonistic to the dominant men's culture. Describe this by providing details about the event, the scene, and the players.

What was it that led up to this step? How did you prepare yourself for it? What other developments were taking place in your life around this time that might be in some way related to this step?

How did you approach this dilemma? In the first place, were you tempted to resolve this in favour of the ways of life and thought of the dominant men's culture? What helped to see you through this? Who else contributed to this? Did you get to a point when you realised that you had achieved something significant? If so, how did you know that this was significant?

What did this achievement tell you about how you wanted your life to be, and about the beliefs that are most precious to you? Could you describe the different sense of self that was available to you at this time? What does this different sense of self reflect about the ways of being as a man that are preferred by you? Are these ways of being also preferred by others? If so, how do you imagine news of this achievement did (or could) effect the perspective that others have about who you are?

Thinking back, can you recall any other dilemmas, perhaps in other situations of life, around which you might have achieved a similar result, and experienced this different sense of self? What might I have witnessed you doing or thinking at an earlier time that could have given me the hint that, at a later point in life, you might handle such a dilemma in this way? Could you tell me anything else that would help me to grasp the foundations upon which this development depended?

If I had witnessed these earlier events in your life, what might they have said to me about the values that were to become more important to you in your relationships with women, children and other men? How did these earlier events effect your beliefs about what being a man was all about? Whose responses to these events helped most to clarify the importance of these values and beliefs for you?

Is there the space available in your life for the further development of this alternative sense of self? If so, and if you were determined for this sense of self to play a more central role in your life, what further steps are available to you? What effects do you think these steps would be likely to have on your day-to-day interactions with others? And how do you think they might influence your responses to the day-to-day dilemmas that you are confronted with around sexism, inequality, and the many demands for complicity in men's abusive attitudes and actions in relation to women, children and other men?

If it turned out that you were correct in these predictions, what would this convey, to your loved ones, your friends and acquaintances, about what you are committed to?

Exercise C

Introduction

When we relate the stories of our lives they usually come out much the same - the recitation is familiar. We depend on these familiar stories to achieve a sense of meaning and coherence in our lives; to organise our experiences of the events of our pasts, and to organise our lives in the present. And these stories also carry us forward - they are a basis for action in that they enable us to determine what will be our next steps in life.

The interpretation of experiences of the events of our lives - the attribution of meaning to these experiences - requires that we find a way of incorporating them into the central and unfolding themes (or plots) of the stories of our lives. And this also requires that we find a way of fitting these experiences into what we know of ourselves in other ways as well: into the regular accounts that we have of our preferences, desires, motives, goals, values and so on. The storying of our lives in this way usually proceeds relatively unproblematically.

However, from time to time we have experiences of events in life that appear to over-stretch the interpretive resources of these frames that we call stories. These experiences defy a straightforward interpretation; they are not so easily rendered sensible. In response, we find ourselves looking for other interpretive frames, other stories about our lives, that might assist us to ascribe meaning to these experiences.

At these times we can become separated from the dominant stories of our lives, and suddenly find ourselves relating to different accounts of what our lives are about, and to different accounts of our preferences, desires, motives, goals, values etc. Sometimes these alternative accounts significantly contradict the dominant accounts of our lives: those that are informed by the familiar private stories of our lives as well as the dominant stories of our culture into which, as men, we are recruited.

Questions

These alternative accounts can be more fully articulated, and can provide a basis for the exploration of alternative and preferred ways of being and of thinking for men. With this aim in mind, consider the following questions:

Recall an experience of your life that was initially difficult for you to make sense of, and one that didn't fit at all well with the story that you had been recruited into about who you are as a man. Describe this experience as well as its circumstances.

In your attempts to make sense of this experience, did it have you rethinking who you were as a man? Did it trigger a different image of who you might be? Was this image one that was attractive to you? Was it one that might have significant appeal to others? Was it an image that bore the promise of preferred real effects in your own life and on your relationships with others? If so, in what ways?

At this time, did you become aware of any other experiences in the history of your life that might resonate with this alternative image of who you might be? Describe these experiences. Speculate about how these other experiences might connect to the experience that you described at the outset of this exercise.

Upon undertaking this review, what other threads or themes of your life are becoming apparent to you? How would you name these threads or themes? How do you think other persons who know you well would name these threads or themes?

What is the history of these alternative themes of your life? Of all those persons who knew you well at a younger age, who would be best placed to tell me a story about you that would reflect these themes? What story would they recount? What do you think the events that are related in this story said to others about your personal qualities and about your motives?

As you reflect on your responses to these questions, what do you get in touch with about what might be your preferred ways of going about your life; about what you intended for your life, about what you believed to be important in regard to your relationships with others, and so on?

Review some of the realisations that are available to you in the undertaking of this exercise. Do these realisations have you reconsidering some of the conclusions that you had previously made about your life? Perhaps you might like to consider some historical events that, at one time, you took to reflect personal failure to achieve manhood, or to express masculinity? In the light of these realisations, how might you reinterpret these events? Might these events now reflect resistance to the requirements of the dominant men's culture?

How would you describe the alternative ways of being and of thinking that accompany this alternative account of who you are? In what ways have these alternative and preferred ways of being and of thinking shaped your life and your relationships with others?

How have these alternative ways of being and thinking had you speaking about yourself and about others differently? How do you think speaking about yourself and others in this way has influenced what you do?

Assume that these alternative ways of being and thinking will become more available to you in the guidance of your life and of your relationships. What further steps would you expect to witness yourself taking in challenging the negative real effects, on others, of the dominant men's culture?

Exercise D

Introduction

It is one thing for a man to have some thoughts about other versions of who he might be, of other ways of being in relation to women, children, and other men. It is another thing to have the know-how or the practices of life that are required to put these thoughts into being. In view of the extent to which alternative ways of being for men have been disqualified and marginalised by men's culture, orient yourself to the very existence of these thoughts and practices in your own life as one might orient oneself to a mystery.

Questions

Now consider the following questions:

Recall when you first entertained thoughts about ways of being a man that were outside of the dominant and taken-for-granted ideas about men's lives. What experiences provoked these thoughts? And what were these thoughts about?

Could you help me to understand how it was that you were able to entertain these ideas as possibilities for your life at this time? Were there specific persons who played an important role in calling attention to these possibilities for your life?

If there were such persons, how did they contribute? Did these persons provide you with some examples of alternative ways of being as a man in relation to women, children and other men that you judged to be preferred? And/or did these persons respond to you in a way that acknowledged something about you that was apart from what usually gets acknowledged in boys or other men?

At what point in your life did you step further into this alternative way of being? How did you develop the know-how that was required to achieve this? Did you achieve this largely by imagination and processes of trial and error? If so, who provided the necessary feedback to you in this process?

Or were you fortunate enough to be able to take a leaf out of someone else's book? If so, how did you enter into these practices and make them work in your own life and your own relationships? In so doing, how were these practices transformed? And in what way were they transformative of your relationship with yourself and with others?

Just imagine that those persons who made important contributions to your development of these alternative ways of being were present right at this minute, listening to this interview. How do you think they would respond to this interview? What would you say to them about what they have contributed to your life? And what do you think they would say to you about how you have contributed to their life?

Would the sort of interview that you are presently engaged in encourage you to more fully explore, step further into and more completely embrace alternative and preferred ways of being? If so, what would you predict to be the real effects of this on your life, and on your relationships with others? What sort of action do you think this could lead you to in relation the various oppressive men's practices that you witness daily in your world? How would this challenge you further to confront the techniques of power that men rely upon to preserve their position of privilege?

Exercise E

Introduction

There are many notions that have been manufactured by men in their attempts to define what is the essence of masculinity. It is not possible to consider such "essences" without accompanying descriptions of how they manifest themselves in men's lives and in their relationships with others. And these descriptions are not neutral in their effects on men's actions. They constitute specific accounts of men's ways of being that are considered to be "authentic", accounts that men are incited to enter their lives into, and accounts that are actually shaping of men's lives and of their relationships.

Take one notion that represents what you believe or once believed to be a description of what is essential to masculinity; a term that is considered to represent the truth of what it means to be a man, one that provides a keyhole to authenticity.

Questions

Now consider the following questions:

What practices of life and ways of thinking stand behind this word? What ways of living or what lifestyle does this word represent or conjure up?

What sort of operations on your life, on your body, and on your soul does/did this way of thinking and this way of living require you to engage in? How do/did these ways of thinking and living have you relating to yourself? How do/did they shape your life?

What are/were the real effects of this way of thinking and living on your relationships with others? How do/did others experience this way of living and thinking, and how does/did it shape their interactions with you?

If you were to step/had stepped further into the particular way of being that is associated with this notion, what do you imagine this would require/would have required you to do to your life into the future? What other real effects of this way of being do you think you would witness/would have witnessed?

From what other positions or perspectives might you evaluate the effects of this way of being?

From these positions or perspectives, which of these effects might be judged to be preferred effects, and which of these effects might be judged not to be preferred?

At what point in history do you think this essential notion emerged? What do you know about the use to which this notion has been put over time? What does it appear that this notion has made possible, and what have been its limitations?

Can you identify and describe the specific processes by which you were recruited into the practices of life and ways of thinking that are associated with this notion?

By what processes has this notion, in providing the grounds for an authentic way of life, been privileged over other notions, which provide different claims about such grounds?

Conclusion

In this paper I have argued that, in the history of the dominant men's culture, the essentialist project has been central to the maintenance of gender inequality. I have also argued that the adoption of, and the attempts to adapt, this project by a significant section of the men's movement puts those men involved at risk of reproducing problematic aspects of the dominant men's culture - often, those very aspects that these men were so concerned about in the first place.

I have proposed an alternative frame of reference for men's attempts to transform the dominant men's culture, one that I have referred to as the constitutionalist perspective. I believe that this perspective makes it possible for us to face and to come to terms with our history, and frees us to do something that is very difficult - that is, to take the courage and to find the wherewithal to act against our own culture. It is a perspective that draws together the personal and the political at several levels.

The constitutionalist perspective mitigates against the determination of an alternative global and unitary knowledge of men's ways of being. But it does invite us to (a) engage in processes that contribute to the identification, resurrection and generation of alternative and preferred "local" knowledges of men's ways of being, and to (b) embrace the unique and positive developments in our lives and our relationships as we do so. In embracing these unique developments, we will not be assuming that they reflect an original nature, but will be aware that we are acknowledging that which we are originating as we renegotiate the dilemmas that are thrown up by our different experiences of self, and as we transform our personal narratives.

Notes

1. I accept that this is a generalisation, and acknowledge that there exist groups of men who relate themselves to the men's movement, for whom these observations are inaccurate.

2. In Australia the term "suffragette" does not have any of the negative connotations it sometimes has in the US.

3. Here, I emphasise the word 'some' for several reasons. First, because there exist alternative versions of what is essential to being a man which may bring about preferred

real effects in the lives and in the relationships of those men who step into these versions. Second, because this particular 'some' is an entirely significant some, which brings with it far-reaching negative real effects. Third, because there are many other real effects of the essentialist project that warrant critical appraisal.

4. For example, bodily postures, ways of speaking, attitudes towards women, children and other men, relational tactics of power and control, valued pursuits and so on.

5. Contrary to the commonly held idea that the mentoring of younger men by their seniors is a requirement for the transformation of younger men's lives, I often find in my work with men that the reverse seems to be the case. What so often appears transformative is the development of an account of the contribution that these men made or might have made to their father's life. This account can be developed in response to questions like:

In what ways do you think that your father's life might have been all the richer for having known you as a child and adolescent?, or

If your father had been less blind to what there was to appreciate about you as a child and adolescent, and if he had been truly interested in acknowledging and experiencing this in you, what effect do you think this would have had on his quality of life?, or

If you had yourself for a son, what potential would your interaction with this son have for enriching your life?, and so on.

Many men are initially stunned by these questions. These are clearly the more difficult questions, probably because they contradict the usual one-way requirements of men's culture; that is for men to pay homage to their elders. It is so often a deeply moving experience to witness men's struggle with questions of this sort, and to be privy to the conclusions that they begin to arrive at and to the positive effects of these conclusions on their sense of self.

6. In an attempt to review this claim, I have done a little research - I have made it my business to ask men about their relationships with their fathers. Sure enough, many of those men whose fathers ran out on their families wished that their fathers had not done so. However, many other men whose fathers had run out on their families were pleased and relieved that their fathers had done so. I also interviewed men whose fathers had stayed. Many of those men whose fathers hadn't run out on their families were glad that their fathers hadn't. However, there were many men whose fathers hadn't run out on their families who wished that their fathers had done so.

7. I would refer readers to Silverstein & Rashbaum's book (1994) that is devoted to, among other things, the deconstruction of those myths that provide the foundation for patriarchal culture.

8. For example, although many boys do learn to exhibit contempt for their mothers, it is clearly apparent that, by and large, children fear their fathers much more than they fear their mothers.

9. These language practices introduce ways of speaking that are considered to be rational, neutral and respectable, emphasising notions of the authoritative account and the impersonal expert view - ways of speaking that are designed to elevate the opinions of

men over the opinions of others, and ways of speaking that are marginalising or disqualifying of other ways of speaking. These practices disembody the perspective and the opinions of the speaker. The presentation of the knowledges of the speaker is devoid of information that might give the respondent information about the conditions of the production of the expert view. Without this critical information, respondents experience a certain "suspension" - they do not have the information necessary to determine how they might "take" the views that are expressed, and this dramatically reduces the range of possible responses available to them.

10. This isn't to suggest that a very great number of us men haven't had terrible experiences of men's culture - for example, the institutionalised violence of war, the various public rituals of degradation and humiliation, and so on. But it is to suggest that we develop our own language of description and analysis of our experience of men's culture instead of robbing women of theirs.

11. This feedback does not take the form of a judgement about the experiences that are related by the man, nor about his responses to these experiences. Rather, it takes the form of speculation about, and an appraisal of, the real effects that might accompany the alternative ways of being and thinking which are being articulated and performed in the exercise.

12

A Feminist Journeying
through Masculinity
Elizabeth Biff Ward

The Masculinity Project

because we live in a
world of war & mayhem,

deconstruction of what
it means to be a man

is actually as imperative
as remembering to breathe

even when events quite
take your breath away

(© Elizabeth Biff Ward, 1995)

In my twenty-four years of feminist journeying, I have moved from eager enthusiasm, a puppy with a wildly wagging tail, for us to work together, through turning right away from men, and back again, to my present position, of knowing there are some men who want sexism to end (almost) as passionately as I do. And that for it truly to end, men have to be involved in profound change.

The Beginning

It began for me in 1970 at a Vietnam Anti-war Conference where an afternoon had been put aside for the women to talk about Women's Liberation. I was actually outraged and incensed at this - Women's Liberation had just begun to appear in the newspapers; it was the American stuff: all bra-burning myths, "women's libbers", put-downs and making fun. My outrage was that the people of Vietnam needed all of our energy, so I took the position that this women's stuff was self-indulgent crap, ridiculous. I went to the meeting prepared to be angry, but it was run in a way that I'd never seen a meeting run before, so straight away I was confronted by change and I started to shift.

It was chaired by one woman with five other women up the front, and an audience of probably 50 to 60. The chairwoman said, "Well, the way we're going to run this meeting is that I'm chairing it, but I won't be saying very much because the other five here are each going to speak for 10 minutes about why they are in Women's Liberation". I'd just had a very intense five years of constant male left-wing meetings; the main topic in Sydney and Canberra for that whole period of the anti-war movement was the ideological battle between the Trotskyist group I was part of and the Communist Party. I knew all the arguments inside out - including the analyses of the Russian and Chinese revolutions and all sorts of ideological exotica. So the fact that people got up and spoke personally was amazing. There was also a different quality to the listening that afternoon: a lack of point-scoring.

I only really remember the second speaker. She talked about how she had been brought up in a family that told her she was as good as the boys and she was the equal of anyone. She'd played sport and gone surfing, she'd done well at school, she went to university, and she was going into market research; she could compete with anyone and she was just on the verge of getting a good job. When she went to parties she talked politics with the men and she didn't want to be in the kitchen with the women who talked about babies, or dresses - she was as good as a man in every way. And then she had read Franz Fanon's book in which he talked about the experience of Algerians who thought they were as good as the French and were thus 'colonised' in that they identified with the oppressor and believed that, in so doing, they were different from their own people.

As she said that, I had an epiphany: it was like being hit in my solar plexus with a sledge hammer - I just went "hohhh". She finished the sentence saying, "I realised that meant I hated my own people, I hated who I was, I hated being a woman". In that instant, I joined the Women's Liberation Movement. I was converted, I thought: "I've done that, that's who I am. I've wanted to be seen as good as a man, and this means I hate myself", and I was profoundly shocked to realise it.

In the discussion that day, we had talked particularly about the anti-war scene and how the men did the speeches and the discussion, and we did all the work of organising and getting the coffee. In my relationship I did 100% of the housework, shopping, cooking, washing up, everything; and I also did 95% of organising demonstrations - I was a brilliant organiser - and then we'd get there and the men would get up and speak. They got all the glory. And so we began a discussion that went on for years - it still does - about why and how men speak the most, and women are silent or silenced.

Take-Off

Canberra Women's Liberation met as an open group every Wednesday night for six years, starting in 1970. Virtually everyone in that first group was heterosexual, "happily married", and nothing about those relationships had ever been questioned or politicised. Of course, as we started our talking, suddenly aspects of these relationships were up for examination - such as struggling to get this wonderful compassionate caring lefty man to do the washing up.

Those early meetings were extraordinary. Because we'd mostly been such activists, many of us did have a history of going to meetings with our husbands, with child-care, for The Cause, The Revolution - but this was suddenly for us and the men had to stay home on Wednesday nights. Often we wouldn't get home till 11pm - we'd drop each other off and sit in the car and just talk. I can remember even ringing each other up after we'd got home because there was something else we'd meant to say, and talking for another hour on the phone. The energy and excitement of the ideas was incredible, because every idea was new to us. We now know it had all been thought of before, but to us it was new and we were creating it. It was permeating our lives - our political commitments, the anti-war movement, but also in our homes, affecting everything around us.

The men with whom we lived showed this effect in different ways. The night we talked about Freud - a paper called "The Haves & Have-Nots: A story of the penisless people", my best friend's husband rang several times, crying, and begging her to come home. Another night, when we'd been talking about marriage, he threw crockery at the plate glass windows when she got home.

We used to laugh about his eccentricity. We could not see that what we were doing was threatening the very fabric of his existence. He used to say, "they're planning to end all our marriages" - and we'd laugh some more, in disbelief. Yet he was right, of course - nearly all our marriages did end.

Brick Walls

My husband responded differently. He tried to join me. Only later would it be clear that it was the same fear that motivated him - a desperate desire to control this alien force that had lobbed into his life. He called the first men's meeting in Canberra in 1972. Six men gathered together, and they met almost weekly, copying the women's format.

The group disintegrated after about six months - the outward form was because one man in it played a joke, a very elaborate practical joke, on one of the others. He posed as a visiting American journalist and rang the other man and said, "I've heard that you've got this men's group here, and I'm really interested in that, and would you let me interview you about the men's group and your marriage and sex?", and so on. He did the interview over the phone, and the other man fell for it completely. The one the joke was played on reported to the group in an excited fashion about how he'd been interviewed, and then the joker told them what he'd done. But for the group all trust was gone, of course.

With hindsight, I think that there was no way they could have survived so early on. As soon as they started to look at sexism, they were confronted by guilt. It seemed it was all their fault - the oppressor role was so large and there seemed no way out of that. They were living within all the things that are part of men's socialisation, like the competition and that joke, putting each other down, and terrible difficulties in getting really close, and they didn't have an analysis around those issues. At that stage, too, it was hard for men to see that there was anything in it for them, that anti-sexism projects would benefit them.

I believed that women's liberation was about human liberation, that you couldn't liberate women without changing life profoundly for men and children too. It seemed to me that this struggle against sexism was the way to *really* change society. Sexism was made up of what had happened to men and what had happened to women, and it was like the yin and yang symbol, except out of balance because of the power factor. But it was two halves, and I was very keen on the men working out their half of it.

But the men's group fell apart, and my relationship also fell apart. All through this time our (women's) analysis of marriage and the family as institutions of female entrapment and human stultification were proceeding apace. The catalyst, in my case, was particular to the baggage carried by me and my partner, but I felt fuelled by a sense of inevitability and even rectitude.

Looking back, I realise I denied my feelings as hard as I could. I cried for months, even so, and felt very lost.

It was an enormous rift in my life. The effect of this rupture and the manner of its happening was devastating - especially for my children, then 11 and (twins) 5. Twenty years later, we are still living with the aftershocks. I wrote a poem at that time that said far more than I knew:

Brick Walls
Straight up and down,
the image right:
well-organized
1960s female:
good at her job,
fair to average mother
(children mostly planned),
could do a hostess turn,
domineering enough
to at least be seen
beside her man -
in other words,
making it.

Then some human beings
who were merely women
turned into a coven of witches,
introduced each other
and I discovered
the beginnings of myself.
Friends became sisters
and together
we demolished walls.
Square edged bricks,
straight up and down
splintery beams
and iron girders
crumbled at our touch
and there before us
lay a garden
with winding paths
of soft green leaves
and endless possibilities.

But the men in our lives,
who had not helped
in this demolition,
were left lonely,
said
How can you live without me?
But it was
   hard
     to
        hear
through the laughter
under the trees.

Empowerment

In 1979 I stopped teaching, and became a worker in a feminist women's shelter. In 1978 I'd been date-raped, and part of my response to that was that I wasn't able to be sexual with anyone. But increasingly I was having friendships with lesbian women, and in my feminist life mixing with women-only circles. The refuge had decided that they were losing touch with their feminist politics and they were looking for someone with a strong feminist commitment. I got that position, so I was really encouraged to bring my feminism into the refuge. It meant that now my working life was all women, as well as most of my social and political life.

I also remember my brother and sister-in-law asking me about my lack of relationships from that period, and my saying, "Well, when I do have a relationship again, my guess is, because I'm now working with all women, I'll probably have a relationship with a woman". And I did. For me it was never a case of "this is my true identity", although for a lot of women that I'm close to, it was. I didn't deal with it very well; I didn't even recognise that it would be traumatic for my kids. But I increasingly became part of that women-only scene, and that became how I lived my life.

Without ever making a conscious decision to be a separatist, I moved into a way of being that looked separatist to everyone else. I worked with women, I mixed socially almost exclusively with women, and in that same four-year period that I worked in the refuge, I wrote my book on the sexual abuse of girls, and was part of the whole discovery of that phenomenon within Australia. So I was working in the refuge, dealing only with domestic violence, and writing and researching the clinical literature on sexual abuse of girls. I was being outraged by what I found at a time when the dominant culture had no knowledge of the existence of this phenomenon. So my anger was very high. My grief about what was happening to the girls and women, the battering and rape, and so on, were the stuff of my working life and most of my friends' lives. The anger was shared.

It seemed that the only way we could address this situation was on our own, that men were hopeless and backward; they were, after all, the rapists and batterers - or else they were too slow, and you couldn't rely on them ever to be completely okay, to change enough, to change fast enough.

Through this time, I had a couple of male friends who really mattered to me, but increasingly they felt frozen out by my friends, even though I delighted in them coming to my house. One stuck through everything ... and then he died. I still miss him.

Somehow I know I never lost sight of The Question - which was, *why do men do these things*? I found the complete despair of some separatist statements (men are mutants, dead men don't rape) frightening. I abhorred the feeling of hatred it engendered, and I disagreed with its nihilism, the fact that it led nowhere. Seeing men as unchangeable is biological determinism; it leads to the most literally conservative point of view.

Somewhere I always maintained the knowledge that human beings are infinitely changeable. After all, we women in that vanguard were changing at an unbelievable pace!

At the end of 1982, I moved to Alice Springs, in the middle of Australia, a very long way from any large feminist centre, inside a whole world of Aboriginal concerns and desert.

I was centrally involved in organising the big women's peace camp at Pine Gap in November 1983 - nearly all my first year in Alice Springs was obsessed with this project. It was an amazingly successful event in terms of putting Pine Gap on the map in Australia, and increasing the level and type of discussion about gender politics and war and peace. We were the Australian version of Greenham Common. Within Alice Springs, it was a very hard thing to be a feminist or a lesbian or both during that period. We were ridiculed every week, even three times a week, in the local newspaper, and often on radio - vicious cartoons and jokes.

However, one of the things I enjoyed about living in Alice Springs was that the community was so different, and the lesbian feminist group was so tiny, I was able to be friends with some men, and I enjoyed that. It was hard though - there was great pressure from the women to keep separate. I found out from a man, just when I was leaving Alice Springs, that my house was known as "the women's house" - which meant that even these men who liked me wouldn't drop in at my house; the separatist ambience began at the kerb.

So while some of the separatist experience was problematic for me, it was also amazingly empowering. I absolutely know that women could run the whole world: build the bridges, feed the millions, make the decisions - all those things that are kept so far away from us now. I have been in so many situations where women have done everything that I know we can do anything. I have lived years of my life knowing and feeling I needed nothing from men, having no expectations of them. To reject patriarchy in this sense of how daily life is lived is a great freedom - but exhausting in that it requires constant vigilance as well as carrying the oppression of the extremely marginalised.

Answers

As already mentioned, I always wanted to understand the yin and yang of sexism, to know the other half - what the socialisation into sexism was really like for men.

In 1987 I was a speaker at the annual "Reclaim the Night" march, and I spoke about how we, the activists around the rape issue, had done an enormous amount of work and clarified for the entire community, for the entire society, what rape was like for women, why it was an outrage, and why it had to stop. We had also put services and systems in place to try to deal with the worst excesses of that, and we were constantly pushing at the boundaries and trying to improve them.

I spoke about wanting to go a step further than that, and that my next step was to demand that men begin to work out how it was that they got socialised into the behaviours of abuse and sexual violence. The example that I gave on that occasion was a very specific one that had happened to a friend. She was walking home at dusk and a man drove past her and a block or two further on he had parked his car and was standing in a hedge and flashing at her.

I said I wanted to understand exactly how male socialisation could lead that man to end up behaving in this precise way, to really understand the sort of sexual acting-out and the specificity of the so-called perversions and abusive behaviour that we were trying to deal with, that keep women in terror and leading limited lives. And so I put it to this crowd in 1987 that I thought we were at the stage where we could say, we want to go further, we want to understand exactly how this happens so that we can really start to address the business of stopping it. At the time, nobody responded to what I said, no-one referred to it. I presumed they were outraged that I talked about men at all. But I didn't forget it.

And over the last few years, in the context of the new energy of the small men's movement that became particularly obvious at the beginning of the 1990s, I've heard some of the men's stories, and heard some theories, and I feel as if I have now got the beginnings of an answer to that question. I have also, years later, had women talk to me about what I said in 1987 and discovered that they found it useful and have been doing this thinking too.

As I understand it, there are three cornerstones of male socialisation. The first is to be unfeeling - don't cry if you are hurting or if you are seeing your best friend being hurt. Three-year-olds learn this. The reason for this is the second cornerstone - be unfeeling because you might one day have to be a soldier/killer. We'll dress it up as a warrior/hero, but the facts are the same: you may have to kill other human beings who are identical to yourself.

Having established the first two, we position the third cornerstone. Having been set up to compete, fight, not trust each other, and certainly not to expect human warmth and compassion from each other, and since they can't be friends with women because that's wimpy and reduces their status, and children aren't even in the picture - men are given one place, one situation in which they're allowed to be close (very briefly) to another human. That place is (heterosexual) sex. And so cornerstone three is sex obsession.

In the context of presenting gender awareness training courses, I have run this theoretical framework past scores of men now, and none have disagreed with its central tenets. Indeed, many proceed then to tell about their terror around the warrior expectations, or their exhaustion and frustration at the tenacity of the sex obsession. Some men figure they think of sex 90% of their waking hours. Such ways of being are clearly obsessional, irrational - and the outcomes, as we know, can be horrendous.

More recently, men have started speaking in my training groups, of sexual abuse and rapes they endured as boys. Some also speak of the fear they live with nowadays around their own children, because any touch feels like it can be misconstrued in a society that is in a state of hyper-awareness around child sexual abuse. It seems to me that men speaking of these things is a new step, a beginning to the unlocking of their secrets.

I am especially interested in this part of the male cultural experience because I am an anti-war activist. I keep returning, again and again, to the peace/antimilitarist movement as the site of my political activity. I believe absolutely in human beings being able to find solutions to conflict other than war. It seems to me that this training into soldierhood - in being ready to come if your country calls - is at the core of how men become the rapists and batterers and murderers. If you train half of humanity to be potential killers, then some of it is going to spill over.

I have been asked if I have compassion for men, and I say I have this kind of grief and horror (which may be what compassion actually is), about how savage the socialisation is on men. I think that to be socialised not to feel, so as to be prepared to kill people, to be a soldier, is unbelievably savage. We have a mass system of desensitisation - that's what our society holds out to little boys - this is what masculinity is.

The Current Point of Arrival/Movement

I keep coming back to that core of wanting to understand and change the sexist socialisation received by both women and men. It's not the same point, because I am so changed by these 24 years of exploration. When I reflect on what I've done, let alone what thousands of other women have done, what we have done with our own lives, with our own bodies, and the changes we have wrought in ourselves and in society, I'm quite overwhelmed by the amount of wisdom we have acquired.

To have been engaged in this struggle to change this thing called sexism is like having lived right at the front line, it feels like a place of fire, like forging new ways of being. I'm not suggesting for a moment that where I am now or where anyone else is now the end point - the journey is still going on, and it will go on long after I'm gone. It is the most enormous social upheaval, as far as I can see, since the Industrial Revolution.

I now want to have relationships with men and get on well with men. I no longer have that marginalised self-concept that I had. I expect now to live, to socialise, to operate politically, wherever I choose to be. I greatly enjoy reconnecting with the human beings in the other 49% of society.

Many separatists consider that giving attention to men or to masculinity is nurturing them, because the imperative to nurture the world is seen as yet another one of the ways in which women are oppressed. But I am now choosing to hear men's stories, and to use my emotional energy on this, because I'm fascinated. I'm fascinated because I want to undo the whole package, I want to understand the whole issue. I don't want to hear whining stories of how the women's movement has been hard for men, although humorous stories are okay - what I do want to hear is those real stories, what life has *really* been like for men - and I feel privileged when I do.

One of the things I have learnt from men, and about men, is to have some appreciation of the degree of alienation that they have, from other human beings. Masculinity sets men up to be ultimately alone. It's a very complex exercise to undo this male half of sexism, because the place where a lot of men are looking for an escape from the horror of it is in bonding with other men, and that is often exactly where they are perpetrating the horrors of the misuse of power. For example, pack rape is really about male bonding, but it's acted out around absolute subjection and oppression and humiliation of another being. Other male bonding - the spurious feeling of not being alone - happens at the points of systematic oppression of other people, like going to war, or buying some land and stripping it, being pioneers, making money, or imperialist ventures and taking another country and killing a lot of people. Those things have been called history and end up being remembered as great events.

We are at that point in history where some men are beginning to take up this challenge, beginning to address the brick walls as they see them.

What I want is a men's movement that has an anti-sexist ideology at its heart; it's that simple. However they organise around that is their business, and it'll be done in men's ways, the same as the women's movement has been done in women's ways. But even those "ways" of operating that the men choose must counteract sexism; the means is the same as the end-point, the goal. Any part of the men's movement that isn't constructed around anti-sexism at its heart is not going to help me and all the other women end sexism.

I want to say: "I need you to be my complete ally in anti-sexism. Are you doing that?" And, of course, men will only do that when they see it is for themselves as much as for women, and see that they will benefit absolutely when we are free of these limiting shackles of masculinity and femininity. It would just feel magnificent to have real allies from across the divide in this anti-sexism revolution. The intimations of it that are beginning to come in are like a dream.

I was recently driving interstate with my daughter (aged 31), her male partner (aged 34), and my half-sister (aged 17). My daughter was driving and she remarked that each truck and semi-trailer that was slowing us down pulled over, one after the other. Her partner, my son-outlaw, said, "With three feminists in this car, they can feel the future coming". It was a gentle, reflective remark - we laughed because it was funny too - but I know that all three of us sat straighter and felt acknowledged in this difficult work we do in confronting sexism. (We also know he works to change men's attitudes and behaviours.)

The women's movement is the leading edge and that won't change no matter how big the men's movement gets. At the recent "Reclaim the Night", when I gave a speech, it was very different from six years ago: I was listing our achievements to the 500 of us - it was huge, it was very celebratory - and one of the things I listed was MASA (Men Against Sexual Assault). I said, it's great that organisation exists, but let's remember it would not even have thought of existing if not for us - that is the true relationship.

The part of the men's movement that has an anti-sexism agenda will, by definition, be struggling with the issue of accountability to women. They will be working out ways of challenging their own sexism as well as systemic sexism - and also ways of being open to listen to criticism and to explain their current best thinking.

I am happy, indeed delighted, to work with men who are engaged in the struggle to end sexism. When I reflect that it is 24 years since my epiphanous moment of perceiving the deep, internal damage done to me as a female, I am struck both by how far we have come, and also by how far we have to go. A measure of how far we have yet to go is to imagine as many men being desperately anxious to be perceived as non-sexist, as there are people nowadays who are anxious to be perceived as non-racist.

I want anti-sexist men to work on other men and to be my ally. As we say in the management training field on Equal Opportunity issues, "Ask: Listen: Act". This process is at the core of accountability structures, and at the core of being an ally.

I am looking forward to the future of men supporting the women who are leading the world out of sexism, and the resultant dominant male paradigm that is so damaging for the planet.

13

Adopting the Principle of Pro-Feminism

Ian Law

(This paper was originally presented on 7th April 1994 at a public meeting organised by the Adelaide Men Against Sexual Assault.)

When I was first asked to speak at this seminar on the issue of "pro-feminism", I was hesitant. I was unsure if I, as a man, should be talking about what it might mean to be pro-feminist. I discussed it first with a number of people close to me, particularly women, to get their advice on the matter before making the decision.

When I reflect on this, it struck me how different my response would have been in the not-too-distant past. I would have confidently accepted, sure in the knowledge that the right to make that decision in isolation was mine, confident that I, as a man, could assert what being pro-feminist was and was not. I had, after all, been claiming my support of feminism as an ideology since my early adolescence. I would engage in political debate and action in support of feminist causes.

Yet, when I look back on that time, I am ashamed to recognise my own sexism and perpetuation of male dominance through my lifestyle, in relationships, and in how I conducted myself in my daily life. In retrospect, the contradiction between what I did and what I said I supported seems embarrassingly clear. However, at the time I was completely blind to it.

Gradually, over time, I have had pointed out to me the way in which I have been caught out by the ways of thinking and acting of dominant male culture, and have come to recognise some of these ways and challenge them in myself.

Some of the ways of thinking and acting that I, like so many other men, have challenged, involve:

- dominating airspace, making sure it is my voice and views that get heard;
- feeling a responsibility to come up with a solution, to problem-solve rather

than listen and understand;

- keeping control of decision-making, seeing co-operation as a loss of control;
- not being able to accept responsibility for perpetuating injustice, either deliberately or unwittingly;
- not being able to apologise, to say that I was sorry;
- assuming that another person's or group's silence meant that they had forgotten about my wrongdoing and that I could carry on my relationship with them without doing anything to redress the injustice;
- searching for a woman's opinion that supported my own opinion, rather than listening to women's opinions which were different;
- dividing women from each other by quoting or representing a woman's view that supported my own, to other women who had a different view;
- undermining or silencing women's challenges of my behaviours by labelling them "hard-line" or over-critical;
- dismissing issues raised by women because they were not raised in what I believed to be the right manner or context.

Now, I have not said much so far about how I can act in a pro-feminist way, but I think it can be suggested that acting in the ways I have just outlined would fit more with acting in a sexist way than in a pro-feminist way.

I have to say that the recognition of my part in the perpetuation of these practices was not through self-reflective, introspective insight. Nor was it through the challenges of other men. It was (and continues to be) the challenges of those women who experienced the effects of these actions, that is, those women who cared for me and valued, as I did and still do, their relationship with me. The female members of my family, my female friends and colleagues. They have, in fact, been in the role of educating me about my part in the oppression of women. And women certainly know more about the oppression of women by men than we as men do, because it is women who experience the effects of our sexist practices, not men, just as any marginalised group understands the oppressive practices of the dominant culture better than any members of the dominant group, whether it be classism, racism, or heterosexual dominance.

So when I look back in my life I can see that, although I believed that I was acting in a pro-feminist way, I was at the same time blind to my own sexism. It is clear that I was a poor judge of whether I was acting in a pro-feminist way or not.

I could clearly not rely on myself to hold myself accountable. I could not rely on other men to hold me accountable for my sexism when they were blind to these practices, not only in me but also in themselves. It is clear that it was women, those persons who experienced the effects of my sexism, who were in the best position to judge whether I was acting in a pro-feminist way or in a sexist way. I have to say, of course, that when I look back on this current period in my life, from some future point, there will be aspects of my perpetuation of sexist practices that I am at present blind to that will become embarrassingly clear through the ongoing efforts of women to challenge me.

However, if I as a man leave it to women to take on the responsibility to educate me in my sexism, is that not shirking my responsibility to take action against the abuses of power perpetuated by my gender?

Yet, if I take on this responsibility as a man, or with my gender in isolation, how can I know I am challenging and not perpetuating our abuse of male privilege?

Such questions have been responded to by the men and women of different cultures at The Family Centre, a therapy service in New Zealand (Tamasese & Waldegrave this volume), and more recently written about by Rob Hall (1994). They, and others, have developed a process of gender accountability that involves men and women, not in hierarchical accountability where one is answerable to and supervised by another, but in a process of horizontal accountability where one is accountable in a partnership.

To return to the beginning of my talk, I spoke of how I consulted women on their views of my speaking on the issue of pro-feminism and their views of what needed to be said. A better process might have been to apply such a partnership accountability process. Such a process could have been:

- gathering a group of men to discuss what it might mean to adopt a principle of pro-feminism;
- having a group of women observe this discussion and, following this, have a discussion amongst themselves about their responses to what the men said;
- the men would be an audience to their responses and would, in turn, discuss amongst themselves their responses to the women's experience of their initial discussion;
- finally, observers who had witnessed the entire proceedings could be called upon to reflect upon the whole process.

Such a process of partnership accountability with men and women, in a context of respect, trust, partnership, and openness to critical analysis, can lead to men taking the responsibility for taking action against the abuse of male culture whilst gaining access to the knowledge and partnership of women.

To quote Rob Hall: "It would appear that there is value in establishing a basic structure for men to access the wisdom of women without patronising them or giving them the responsibility for monitoring men." (1994)

Unfortunately, time constraints mean that my redescription of the process of accountability is brief, but those who are interested may like to read Rob Hall's paper (1994; see also Tamasese & Waldegrave this volume).

This seminar is about the adoption of certain principles by the organisation, Men Against Sexual Assault. If MASA is to adopt a principle of pro-feminism then I suggest that, as an organisation, it needs to be mindful of its part in the reproduction of the dominant culture of masculinity and the ways of being that perpetuate the oppression of women through sexist practices, some of which I outlined at the beginning of this paper (by no means an exhaustive or comprehensive list). If these practices are identified as occurring, then it would mitigate against it being seen as a pro-feminist organisation. The best judges of whether these practices are occurring are not men, but the women who experience the effects of these practices; and the knowledge, wisdom, and partnership of women can be achieved through structured processes of accountability.

14

Partnership Accountability
Rob Hall

This chapter proposes a way of operating, in the arena of gender relations, which continues the process of challenging patriarchal practices and ways of thinking. It is a proposal referred to by others in this book and is derived from the problems those articles address. The process is referred to as "partnership accountability", to stress the spirit of equity which it entails and to separate this concept from older, often hierarchical, ideas about accountability. It also explores my own experiments and experiences with partnership accountability which have been developing for a number of years.

The Story Begins

Some twelve months ago, a South Australian judge caused a nation-wide furore over comments he made in a rape-in-marriage case. The judge in question made the following remarks: "There is of course, nothing wrong with a husband faced with his wife's initial refusal to engage in intercourse, in attempting, in an acceptable way, to persuade her to change her mind, and that may involve a measure of rougher than usual handling." (*The Advertiser*, 12th January 1993, p.5)

Some months later I attended a public meeting where Kathleen Mahoney explained that, in Canada, not only did judges acknowledge the need for education on matters of gender to prevent bias in judicial decision-making, but that they had undertaken a number of training courses which they had found informative, relevant and worthwhile. At this meeting, women made up the majority of the audience. A male member of the audience made a statement which basically put forward the view that women were asking to be raped. I was embarrassed, as a man, that he should voice such a view, and I wanted to silence him, offer a different view, and give evidence that not all men thought the same way about women as he did. But I sat in silence, looking down at my feet - not wanting to be there any more, not wanting to be associated with his views, but also not wanting to take up the meeting's time engaging in a male competition about rightness or grandstanding about being more ideologically sound than he was. My friend prodded me and encouraged me to speak out but I remained silent, and I regretted my silence.

Later, this same friend asked me to consider what it meant for women that the only view offered by a man at that meeting was one in support of gender bias. She then invited me to consider this question further in a structured accountability group meeting - a meeting run according to a model developed by workers at The Family Centre in Wellington, New Zealand.

The Family Centre Accountability Model

The model which The Family Centre proposes goes beyond a simple concept to a practical tool. The purpose of the process must be a sincere desire by a dominant group (or an individual member of a dominant group) to move their attitudes and practices towards a position of equity with a dominated group, not in a way that denies the power differential between them, but in a way which promotes the acceptance of responsibility for their dominating practices.

Essentially, the model is built on the understanding that the dominant group on any issue, be it race, sex or social position, are accountable to the least powerful. On any issue, the group considered less powerful has the right to caucus in order to consider both the issue in question and the way they will raise their concerns with the dominant group. The more powerful group has the responsibility of hearing the concerns of the least powerful and to working towards finding a mutually acceptable way of resolving the issue.

A Structure

Broadly outlined, this form of accountability (in its application to the issue of gender) involves groups of women and groups of men meeting, separately and together, to discuss concerns, to develop effective ways of raising these concerns with the other group, and to develop mutually satisfying resolutions. If the issues of concern involved ethnicity, for example, then the groups would be divided on those grounds. Generally it is the people who are not of the dominant culture who meet as a group in order to discuss the concerns, then raise them with the dominant group, with the objective of establishing room for a resolution of the concerns. It may take several meetings of the oppressed group before they are ready to meet with the dominant group.

The model requires that the dominant group, in the interests of real communication, privileges the view of the group of lesser power and works to re-examine their own practices and attitudes with a view to resolving the concern. The group of the dominant culture may also need to meet separately on several occasions before they are ready to move to resolution.

In practice, it has usually been the least powerful group which has met, caucused and raised the concerns, and the dominant group which has responded. There is no set formula, but the example above is given as an illustration. Another common experience is that the dominant group meet at the same time as the oppressed group and take on the task of considering what the concerns, experience and feelings of the oppressed group might be. In this way the work of the dominant group immediately contributes to a climate of trust, understanding and empathy, and a genuine desire to move to real communication about the concerns and resolution of the issue.

Vital to this process is a metaphor of partnership in which both parties desire to work toward an equitable relationship. Fundamental to the process is the dominant group's acceptance that they cannot presume to know when their actions are being experienced as oppressive by the less dominant group but must seek information from, or be informed by, the less dominant group. On the issue in question, the dominant group then choose to put themselves into a position of being accountable to, and in partnership with, the less powerful.

Outcomes from Use of the Model

I have been using the accountability model in a number of ways: in group training, in therapy with abusive men, in examining my own practices, and in collaborating with colleagues, largely around the issue of gender. What has become clearly apparent from my experiences is that the process opens up space to challenge dominant and oppressive ways of thinking. It is a healing process, but it also generates ways to dismantle dominant ways of being, fostering instead a climate of equity and justice. It does this in a number of ways:

- By observing the links between certain modes of life and thought and the real effects these have on lives and relationships;
- By identifying the structures and processes which have legitimated these modes of life and thought and which have excluded or disqualified other modes. This is achieved through the dominant group hearing the experiences of members of the oppressed group and reflecting on the impact of the dominant culture on persons in the oppressed group.
- By exposing the paradox associated with all essentialist notions of masculinity (as outlined by Greg Smith, 1992). As dialogue and problem resolution between both groups are facilitated by the partnership accountability process, the very dichotomies proposed by masculinity are challenged and exposed.
- Through feedback about the real impact of oppressive practices, and steps to

resolve them, the options and choices to discontinue oppressive practices expand.

- Through feedback, the moral and ethical nature of our attitudes and practices becomes more obvious and available for consideration.
- Through experiencing some choice about the modes of life and thought by which we might live, the options for problem resolution through partnership accountability open real options for informed choice.
- The partnership formed by the process of accountability opens a larger, more understanding audience for the positive developments in our lives as we go about the process of renegotiating our identities.

Background

The issue of accountability and gender has become more topical and more clearly pressing now that issues of men's violence toward women are being examined at a broader social level. Men who work with men who are abusive in their families have been increasingly asked to be accountable to women for their work. Workers at The Family Centre (Wellington, New Zealand), early in the development of their agency's work with abusive men, agreed that: "men working with those who abuse should make their therapy accountable in a direct way to women workers in the agency" (Waldegrave 1990, p.32).

In Australia the reaction to The Family Centre's proposal, from some men who work with men who abuse, is one of mistrust and a conviction that such a proposal is unworkable and ludicrous. If we consider Greg Smith's (1992) article, this response from men is not surprising even from therapists. I suspect that these men's notion of "accountability" is a hierarchical one which understandably brings about considerable concern that their work will be open to intense scrutiny by people whose views may be diametrically opposed to theirs, and that their ways of working will be modified by these people. As a result, they fear they will lose control and responsibility for their work practices and may be forced to work in ways that they consider unhelpful or even unethical.

Many organisations regard accountability as hierarchical in nature. For example, in therapeutic organisations workers and therapists are held accountable to a superior, in either an administrative capacity or a professional one, for the quality or nature of their work. This notion is clearly one of power-over, of being answerable to a superior, and hence is one of threat. In this example the superior becomes the person who has access to "true" information and thus would be regarded as the "expert". In this way of thinking, the views of the person being held accountable hold less status and the concept of accountability is one of judgement. In some senses, to be accountable means to willingly accept judgement and punishment. Uhr (1993) noted that "Accountability is usually discussed as an obligation owed by agents to their principles, the ultimate power-holders" (p.2). These hierarchical notions of accountability are in direct contrast to the notion of partnership accountability being proposed here.

Challenge to Patriarchal and Power-Over Ways of Thinking

Many organisations and individuals are working hard to challenge the practices, policies and frameworks which work to oppress people who are not members of the dominant culture, race or way of thinking. Some organisations, for which these objectives are fundamental, have been made up of people who would generally be considered members of the privileged group. Some examples of organisations and people in this position would be men-only organisations formed to stop men's violence, male counsellors who have focused their work on challenging those practices which work to dominate women, and white people who have joined Aboriginal groups. Yet such groups and people can unwittingly contribute to and collude with the very oppression that they believe they are trying to challenge.

Tamasese & Waldegrave (1993) acknowledge this trend, and have gone on to ask:

> How do workers, women and men and people of different cultures in an agency
> or institution, protect against gender and cultural bias in their work on a day-to-
> day basis? Furthermore, how do they do this in societies where sexist and racist
> assumptions are an integral part of the upbringing and way of life, as they are in
> most modern industrial states? (p.29)

Organisations that wish to challenge the dominant outlook sometimes employ personnel of the background they feel is being overlooked. However, unless more is done, this person can be left to carry the burden of the agency's response in the most fraught and neglected area, or be left as a "token" worker while the agency's practices continue unchanged. The problem of agencies finding constructive and creative ways of challenging such integral bias is further compounded by the response that a lot of men or members of the dominant culture have to receiving feedback.

The Problem of Feedback

The reluctance of men to accept feedback about their work has been noted by Tamasese and Waldegrave (1993), and they document the range and complexity of response when issues relating to oppression are raised between the oppressed and oppressive groups:

> Most therapists have experienced the situation where a group which has been unjustly treated in society begins to raise subtle and not so subtle experiences of discrimination which they discern among their colleagues and in their workplace. When such discussions centre on issues of culture and gender, feelings can run very high. In our experience, therapists who are usually very concerned to facilitate resolution in the conflicts of others, tend to be very slow to address these issues among themselves. Instead, people on both sides of the conflict retire hurt, and are left to carry a mixture of feelings of fear, outrage and distrust. (pp.30-31)

In Adelaide in 1992 a series of articles appeared in a men's magazine that were perceived by many women and some men as sexist and inappropriate, and attempts were made to get the magazine to exclude such material in future. Positions were formed around this issue, and two opposing camps emerged. There was confusion right from the start, as it was difficult even to reach agreement on what the central issue was. To the women it seemed clear that a group of men, who were doing good work in opposing sexism, were unwittingly replicating the very behaviour they had previously opposed. They experienced the men's response to their concerns as hostile and dismissive. The men, on the other hand, were genuinely hurt by what they experienced as unfair and unjustified attacks, particularly as some of them had not been aware of the real attempts women had been making to communicate with them. The inability to resolve this issue quickly and effectively caused a great deal of pain and suffering for people on both sides.

Finding a process which enables the exploration and critique of work practices, yet does not invite a defensive reaction, is something The Family Centre believe they have achieved through the process they describe as accountability. I have found this defensive reaction to be present even in issues relating to gender where men are aware of the patriarchal nature of society. The Family Centre's model of accountability may be seen to be taking control away from men which, in Greg Smith's view, would be challenging the very core of the patriarchal view of masculinity. He believes that the metaphor for men of "being in control" (Smith, 1992, p.18), is a central metaphor which strikes in many ways to the core of maleness. Being in control is linked with 'rationality', the need to hold a universal truth, to be hierarchically superior and to be individual and not connected.

It should therefore not be a surprise that some men, in their attempt to make discoveries of new ways of being which are more sensitive to the needs and wishes of others, have largely isolated themselves from women. Some men have believed that it was necessary for men to achieve their own understanding of "maleness" and that it would be inappropriate for men to look to women for such a description. In a sense they practiced what many men have done in the past - they met as men, and organised functions as men only.

A number of incidents alerted me to the possible value of the partnership accountability model. Two colleagues, who work with the utmost integrity and in the interests of challenging exploitative practices, found they had behaved in ways that were inconsistent with their objective. Initially they did not accept the criticism that resulted from their behaviour, but saw it as ill-informed and working against the longer term goals of challenging inequity. Their first response was to find others who would support them. Initial steps taken to address the issue tended confuse the issue and to be seen by others as avoiding facing the inappropriateness of what they had done. In each of these cases the men have gone on to look further into the issues and to work to resolve the hurt and confusion produced by their initial response.

An alternative approach (possibly informed by the concept of partnership accountability) could have been: to listen to the critique, to welcome the interest of the women, to recognise the trouble the women had gone to to express an opinion, to seek a range of women's views on other matters related to their work, and to consider instituting ways to access the feedback of women in an ongoing way so that such mistakes did not recur. The outcome of such a more responsive and less defensive approach, would, I suggest, have fitted the goals of each person and furthered the longer term goal of promoting equity.

It would appear that there is value in establishing a basic structure for men to access the wisdom of women without patronising them or giving them the responsibility for monitoring men. In the field of domestic violence, where the imbalance of power is such a dominant theme (and fundamental to treatment), the need for a workable format to deal with issues between male and female workers becomes imperative.

The New Understanding

The new understanding of accountability proposed by The Family Centre goes some way to providing such a structure and format which makes a defensive response by men less likely. The basis of understanding for this form of accountability is expressed by Tamasese & Waldegrave (1993) thus: "In our view, the best judges of injustice are the groups that have been unjustly treated. Thus, the women are accorded the role of guardians of gender equity, and the Maori and Pacific Island sections the guardians of cultural equity at The Family Centre." (p.34)

This model originally evolved in a context in which cultural notions of horizontal rather than hierarchical accountability were readily available, since in Samoan and Maori cultures an individual is accountable to his or her brothers and sisters, cousins, aunts and uncles. The Family Centre's model of accountability takes the following shape:

The approach attempts to reverse the societal bias against women and the dominated cultural groups ... Within our overall collective at The Family Centre, the Maori and Pacific Island sections are self-determining. The Pakeha (white) section, because it is the dominant culture, runs its own affairs, but is accountable to the other two sections ... Likewise, the women and the men caucus separately at times to address their own issues. As with the cultural work, we have found it helpful to agree to creative forms of accountability and monitoring that address our gendered histories and consequent biases. The women's work is self-determining. The men manage their affairs and responsibilities, but are accountable to the women. (p.33)

The Family Centre workers make the point that the unique aspect of their approach is the reversal of the usual modes of accountability. Management and decision-making is commonly exercised by men or white people, and so patriarchal and racist assumptions in society generally also permeate the therapeutic community. Their reversal requires full recognition of dominated groups to be self-determining, and dominant groups to check key aspects of their orientation and projects with other groups.

Cultural caucuses have now been institutionalised as cultural sections. With regard to gender, we have formalised groupings of men and groupings of women into separate caucuses. The women's caucus call the men's caucus to a meeting when an issue of injustice is felt in staff relationships, models or practice. Issues are laid out, and a convergence of meanings is sought about the incidents. This may take one or several meetings depending on the complexity of the issues. Meetings can also be called where a group wishes to put forward innovative ideas for discussion. (Tamasese & Waldegrave 1993, pp.33-4)

The process described appears a simple one, but it must be realised that a number of conditions, personal understandings and commitments apply to make this process effective. The two sides on an issue have ideas and contributions to make, but the responsibilities of each is somewhat different:

We set clear boundaries to ensure the caucuses carry out their responsibilities. For those associated with injustice, their primary responsibility is to collectively transform attitudes, values, structures and forms of relationships that dominate. The responsibility of the subjugated groups is to identify their pain, recover their untold stories and articulate their direction in relation to others who share the same pain. (Tamasese & Waldegrave 1993, p.34)

The group associated with the injustice is then committed to listen as openly as possible and authenticate the complaint in whichever aspects they can, with integrity, agree ... After clarification of any misunderstandings and points of fact, we usually discover substance in the concerns that have been brought forward. (p.35)

Through the accepting of responsibility and the working through of the issues, the process takes effect: "The authentication from the group associated with the injustice enables a converging of meaning between the two parties." (p.36)

The process of accountability is one that is necessarily emotional and engaging. In The Family Centre's experience, where this process occurs authentically, it is very painful. Through this process anti-sexist and anti-racist learnings take root in an organisation. The outcome at a personal level is a sense of greater shared purpose and organisationally clearer and more consistent goals and working practice. The overall outcome of such a process is:

- a genuine monitoring of discriminatory behaviours and processes;
- building of trust between the cultural groups and between the genders;
- creative and equitable arrangements between the cultures and the genders;
- a commitment to actions which will make a difference to the lives of those who suffer;
- an open dialogue where hidden and exposed meanings are both addressed;
- a calling forth of humility, respect, sacredness, reciprocity and love from all parties;
- the building of trust with the group with whom trust has been broken;
- an ethical structure to move towards true equity and healing between the cultural groups and genders.

The Spirit of the Process

The spirit of partnership entered into in this model has a number of important components:

* *Goodwill*: entering into the encounter with respect for the views of others and a commitment to seek ethical solutions which promote social justice.
* *Critical self-appraisal*: a recognition that we are a product of our society and that in order to avoid inadvertently reproducing problematic aspects of our culture, we need to open ourselves to critiques from others who have traditionally experienced the real effects of those problematic ways of being.
* *Responsibility*: an understanding that to accept responsibility for our actions gives an opportunity to explore new understandings and try new approaches, a preparedness to work at appreciating the real impact on others of the practices and attitudes we adopt, and an opportunity to explore others' experience through sensitivity to their understandings.

When these components are incorporated into the process of accountability, a genuine partnership between both groups is fostered. Such a partnership accountability provides a direct challenge to dominant and hierarchical ways of thinking and behaving. It provides the dominant group with the opportunity to take up the freedom offered by resistance to dominant cultural approaches and outlooks. It releases the creativity to arrive at new and responsible solutions to problems between the oppressed and the unwitting oppressor. It fosters real partnership as the experiences, understandings and solutions become known and shared by both groups. It promotes ethical personal and political work practices as each issue is tackled in the context of vulnerability - of exposing oneself to criticism with the humility to acknowledge that solutions can only be found through partnership.

Experience with Partnership Accountability

In essence accountability is about building trust with the group with whom trust has been broken. Therefore accountability in such a process is not about a simple reversal of roles in the hierarchical sense. It is an offering of vulnerability in trust to each other, so that the pain of injustice can be transformed. (Tamasese & Waldegrave 1993, p.42)

What follows is a description of my experiences of the process of partnership accountability - not only the format and structure - but in particular the many personal and essential components which make such an approach successful, and what this success has meant to people who have experienced the process. The description will use summaries from an interview with the two women who initiated my first experience of partnership accountability (following my attendance at the meeting on judicial reform), and extracts from a workshop developed to train people in the use of partnership accountability.

The Story Continues

In that public meeting I felt confused and convinced that no matter what I did in response to the oppressive views put forward, I would have been contributing to the problem. A sense of being stuck overwhelmed me. Doing nothing seemed the only option, despite knowing that even that could be problematical. I did not know how to make it clear that I opposed the views being put without buying into traditional masculine styles of confrontation. Cheryl asked me if I would like to participate in a meeting to look at what it meant for some women to experience men's silence on these issues of gender. The invitation was irresistible since it offered me an opportunity to look at my non-behaviour in the public meeting.

The Meeting

Cheryl White and Maggie Carey had invited a number of people to the meeting and had explained its purpose to each of us who would be present, and outlined the proposed structure of the meeting. A lot of preparation had been done before we entered the room, and an observer had been appointed to note and give feedback on the process.

We were all aware that we were breaking new ground and were concerned to ensure that the issues did not get lost in the process of caring, but also that the process did not get lost in the issues. On reflection, the role of the observer was underestimated, and so that role was later included in the training workshop. At this accountability meeting we all discussed the process fully, and agreed to a final structure for meeting. The role of observers was also discussed in full, especially with the observer.

The process began with Maggie interviewing Cheryl about her experience of men and their silence at a time when articles which many women found to be sexist appeared in a magazine which aimed to promote equity and social justice. The interview was conducted in front of a group of five men, some of whom had been the focus of the petition. In Maggie and Cheryl's presence, we (the men) then spoke about what it meant for each of us personally to hear of the women's experience, and to have participated in the silence. We also discussed what we as men felt about the women's experience of men's silence generally on many matters of male dominance and abuse of women.

Next, Cheryl and Maggie reflected, in the men's presence, on their own experience of the men's discussion. The observers commented on the process of the whole meeting and gave feedback on what they observed of the flow of ideas and the process of caring. Finally, we all informally commented on the experience as a whole.

I was astonished at the impact the meeting had on me. I felt honored and privileged to have heard Maggie's and Cheryl's story, and although I had guessed at the impact on them, I was very moved at the depth of their experience, and my reaction was heartfelt. The most surprising aspect was hearing Cheryl and Maggie's response to our discussion. They found that our response went some way to healing the experience of men's silence. I felt a sense of sharing and understanding across the gender divide, going beyond just talk and sympathy to real understanding and joining in practical, workable steps to resolution. It was an experience of a true partnership against the oppressive practices of patriarchy.

Cheryl and Maggie, after the success with this meeting, later went on to look at the issue of heterosexual dominance. They, along with other heterosexual women, began a process of accountability to a group of lesbian women in order to examine the oppressive practices in which they as heterosexual women had engaged.

On the other hand, I became preoccupied with my experience of that meeting and began to look at the meaning of partnership within the model of accountability I had just experienced. I saw that for a member of the dominant group the process offered so much. It meant that I had been faced with a fuller understanding of the hurt brought about by my inaction and inattention. At times I was moved to tears and the pain I felt did not - and does not - stop at the end of the meeting. I believe it was only through the intensity of the experience, facilitated by this accountability process, that I was able to gain access to a more complete perspective of what I had done.

Further, from this understanding, some directions and options for action occurred to me. It was also a liberating experience. I had a chance to talk the issues over with other men, and hear from them about the dilemmas we had faced and the debilitating experience of uncertainty. What also grew out of the meeting was a sense of joining to defeat the uncertainty of whether there were people from whom I could get genuine support. I feel convinced that when next I am faced with a public meeting where I want to speak out against oppression there will be support for the stand I take, but also real feedback on my words and actions, and whether the outcome of my speaking will have worked toward reducing oppression or will have added to the problem. I feel that I am linked in partnership with a range of women and men who will aid me in my endeavors to stand against the silence.

The recognition of what such a partnership was offering me as a member of the dominant culture was clear. However I was left uncertain about exactly what the oppressed group might gain and how they felt as the group who made themselves so vulnerable, through offering their story of the pain they had experienced. To learn more, I went on to interview Maggie and Cheryl, about their experience of a number of accountability sessions, but with the focus on the concept of partnership.

Summary of an Interview

Cheryl and Maggie informed me that they believed the strength of the partnership metaphor rests on wanting to build on a long-term relationship. Irrespective of the issue, both parties to the discussion had made a commitment to each other and to their respective groups to persist no matter how difficult the discussion got, and no matter how long the process eventually took.

Clearly the partnership they sought is one which has a number of important personal, professional and political commitments. One of the most important aspects was mutual understanding about the objectives of the process and the end goal. For example, in the first meeting, Cheryl and Maggie wanted an experience of men hearing about women's experience of men's silence - an experience of being heard, which is different from being angry or challenging current behaviour. They needed an audience for what had happened to them, and validation from men about men's responsibility, even if it couldn't be from the men who had actually participated in their original experience of not being heard.

In conversation with Maggie and Cheryl it was apparent that before they felt able to meet with the men they needed to prepare and plan, to be clear about what they wanted to discuss at the meeting, and what they wanted to get out of it. There was also a feeling that they wanted to be able to raise the issue in a way that would be heard - a respectful, non-punitive and non-shaming way - one which would eliminate a defensive response. These preparations are the essence of caucusing.

Cheryl and Maggie introduced some of the important and relevant aspects of partnership accountability to the group, and explained that they had definite expectations as to how the men were going to approach the process. Tamasese & Waldegrave (1993) put the men's role in this way: "Men in the agency, for example, are seen to be responsible not just for themselves, but for each other. The unenviable task of honing new sensitivities among men is not just left to women" (p.37).

Cheryl and Maggie felt that the process had contributed to healing the pain and rift they had felt from their experience of men's silence. It was a very positive experience for them. There was no sense of being frightened, but a sense of confidence in the men's intentions and desire to build trust and they appreciated that the men were working to understand.

It was also important for them to observe the men join in kindliness towards each other as they talked, and to feel the honesty of their emotions, in solidarity with theirs. Witnessing the women's experience fostered warmth and compassion between the men. Clearly the men hearing the women's experience as a group was very different from men hearing it individually. Hearing the women's story as a group is perhaps a structural process which more easily enables men to think collectively.

However, dialogue in itself is not sufficient to mean that the partnership accountability has substance. Cheryl drew on the conversation with one of the lesbian women to point out that there needed to be a commitment to follow through with action - that although the oppressed group might be prepared to expose their vulnerability and speak from a position of hurt and pain a number of times, eventually they would be unwilling to continue the dialogue unless evidence of action for change on the part of the heterosexual women became apparent. Eventually one needs to look at who continuing the conversation is for

- it is not for the education of the dominant group, but to promote real equity which would lead to changes in workplace practices and in personal practices and understandings. With the men's group, it was the measure of their taking on new understandings of her experience which mattered. Indeed, Tamasese and Waldegrave (1993) point out that "these new strengths are not driven by reaction, but by the deep commitment to honour each other" (p.37).

Partnership Accountability is a Structure

In extolling the value of the accountability group concept, it must be remembered that there were specific boundaries placed on the discussion. Through the interview with Maggie and Cheryl, I realised that we were dealing with an issue which grew from the power differential between the genders in our society, and we were seeking the discovery of a process which facilitated its constructive resolution. We were not in the process of creating an intimate group which felt the need to expose itself on all matters or to form an ongoing network of close friends. The project was clear and the role of each person was kept clear. The role of the dominant group is to develop and learn a sensitivity to the experience of the oppressed group which is not normally accessible to them. The oppressed group must have confidence that the dominant group is trustworthy, will hear their pain respectfully and will take responsibility for their part in the oppression which the dominated group have experienced.

The structure under which this process takes place need not be fixed but must adapt to take account of the real goal of forming a safe and workable forum that will work to resolve sometimes complex and emotional issues in the spirit of partnership. It would seem clear that, in situations where the partnership accountability process is new, then the oppressed group will want some form of evidence that the dominating group can exercise a sufficient degree of sensitivity to listen respectfully and with empathy to the stories the oppressed group feel they need to tell.

For this reason, the dominant group should present first on their understanding of what it might be like to be in the shoes of the oppressed group. This approach gives an indication not only of sensitivity and empathy, but also of the dominant group's preparedness to take up the responsibility for their attitudes and practices. This approach is not unusual. In the work I have done with men who have been abusive, where the man has moved to a full acceptance of responsibility for his abuse and there are steps towards a reconciliation, then the perpetrator is invited to present to his victim his understanding of her experience of the abuse he has perpetrated. His evidence of understanding and sensitivity is essential before the relationship can move to a stage where he can start earning trust in his relationship with her. In recognition of the power imbalance, control of the process in the spirit of partnership must stay in the hands of the oppressed group.

A further consideration is the level of relationship to be worked toward in the partnership. Maggie and Cheryl chose very carefully which information to share with the men. They did not want simply to express their emotional distress and have that responded to. There needs to be quite a separate source which provides emotional support - this is not an expectation which should be filled by the accountability group.

My interview with Maggie and Cheryl taught me that each element in the process of partnership accountability plays a crucial role. Each person who comes to the process needs to have a thorough understanding of the process and its boundaries, each group and caucus has responsibilities which are particular to it and separate from the other. Then there is the process of communication and feedback between the two groups, which has a powerful impact both collectively and individually. Each part facilitates the other and the role of observer and facilitator is to assist in keeping the various roles and functions working effectively.

The Partnership Accountability Workshop - Discoveries in Preparation

It was with the above information and experience in mind that I joined with my long term friend and colleague Dallas Colley to design a workshop to both explore and teach these aspects of partnership accountability with practitioners who counsel in the field domestic violence.

We were aware that, although there is now general recognition that the issue of domestic violence is related to gender, practitioners, however well meaning, often fail to appreciate the subtle continuation of patriarchal values which their approaches entail. We believed the concept of partnership accountability applied to this issue would provide a constructive and continual feedback loop to such practitioners. We hoped that through teaching the model of partnership accountability we might facilitate much needed communication across the gender gap in a way which acknowledged and addressed the power imbalance inherent in that relationship.

The workshop was limited to considering the role of partnership accountability for counsellors and organisations offering counselling in the field of spouse abuse. We believe however that the framework of the workshop and the significant components of partnership accountability apply wherever there is an issue stemming from positions of dominance and power imbalance. In many areas of our society - Aboriginal affairs, the treatment and general life access of the disabled, the rights of children and the role of women in all spheres of life, and in the church and the judiciary - the more powerful are beginning to acknowledge that their position of privilege holds commensurate responsibilities to people in less powerful positions.

In the preparation of the workshop - now titled "Communication Between the Genders: Domestic Violence - An Issue to Join On", I made a number of personal discoveries. I found that I was able to remember the many occasions when my colleague Dallas has pointed out things to me that helped to address my training and therapeutic work more sensitively and appropriately. I found I gained a new understanding of her question, "Now why did you do that Rob?" Dallas had been prepared to critique my work - not to hold up my fragile ego but to offer a real and genuine criticism. In acknowledging this I saw the valuable role she had played in making my work "accountable" and that this had been done in an environment of trust, and, when uncertainty was present, with complete faith that we would in time arrive at a mutually suitable resolution. There now seemed to be a title for the way we have worked through many difficult issues together: partnership accountability.

We also realised that there were probably many other people who, in their working relationships, already worked through many issues in a type of partnership accountability process. If people were to examine their work and their working relationships they would find many clear examples of partnership accountability in action, but the process of labelling and formalising the process makes it more accessible. We decided that the role of the workshop would be to highlight the value of this process and give people a framework in which to access the process around the issues of gender and spouse abuse.

The Workshop

The aim of the workshop was to foster dialogue between the genders, with the issue of domestic violence being one which could help focus such dialogue in ways which are clear and helpful and urgently needed.

The first exercises were designed to familiarise participants with their own understanding of what contributes to an environment of trust. Other exercises followed which invited participants to consider the impact of gender-ascribed messages on their lives. Participants in gender-specific groups told stories of their experience of growing up and the influence of the gender messages on them. The purpose and outcome of the gender-specific groups was to allow unfettered talking, but also to emphasise the different influences of the gender messages. Further, the conversations were not recorded in full, a summary of the messages each group discovered being reported to the combined group.

The process of partnership accountability was introduced to participants in these terms:

As counsellors and trainers we carry a certain status and power, so recognising your power and the power of your position is important. It is an ideal in some circles that counselling be approached with a detached professionalism - that there are strategies, or "tricks" of their profession which they use impartially, and that if they become emotionally involved with a client's experiences, then they have "lost it" professionally. We worry that the day we are impartial and fail to appreciate the experience of a person or the significance of what a person has done, then we have lost touch. Power and self are central to working in the area of domestic violence, and responsibility and blame are key words. Violence, power and gender are linked and many men have tried creative ways to deal with this. In some ways it's like sexual difficulties counselling. The men are out to help their partner reach sexual fulfillment without appreciating that they are still setting the agenda. The workshop is about linking back to women around gender issues and what it would mean to do this.

Responsibility in Partnership Accountability

We then explained that, in partnership accountability, responsibility is about taking responsibility for what we do and what we say. It is not about adopting a position of devil's advocate or having a session of dumping. We emphasised the following aspects:

- *Respect* for each person's value positions and experiences. We each have something to say about the issue and the experience of the process. Not every issue will be able to be resolved or worked through, and some things will not be said. This is appropriate and respecting of all views and experiences.
- *Trust*: You would choose people with whom you want to work through the issue because of the trust which already exists, and you would show respect for that trust. The objective is to acknowledge that trust and help to build on it.
- *Partnership* means being there for however long it takes to sort out the issue, and having a commitment to helping the other person see the issue and come to his or her own way of resolving it. Partnership also means really trying to see the issue from the other's point of view and to work toward resolving it so that the result satisfies the other.
- *Critical Analysis*: The person you select will be able to critique the practices and ideas you are exploring around a specific issue.

After this introduction to the workshop, a significant question was raised: how to ensure that the oppressed group, who call the dominant group to account, do not take responsibility for the monitoring and resolution of problems. Could a practice of accountability possibly work against the objective of helping men step into the shoes of women, be more sensitive to their needs, or anticipate what is likely to be experienced as oppressive?

Dallas and I set out another exercise to introduce the concept of accountability and to begin the experience of what this process could offer. We asked the group to divide on gender lines and to consider the following questions:

If this was an ideal process and it was working effectively - as women, we would like you to consider what would be the advantages of this accountability process? How could you ensure that women did not end up taking the responsibility for the issue?

As men, we ask that you consider the following question: What would be the advantage for men if this process of accountability was to work? How could you ensure that women do not take responsibility for the issues?

The following responses were written by the recorders of gender-specific groups and are summaries of what was said by each group to the other in the workshop.

The Men's Response

In the men's group the men worked hard at ensuring that each idea was heard, and imagining how the ideas they came up with would be received in the women's group. There was a consistent striving to find words which were not "loaded" or able to easily carry a mistaken meaning. Words like "wrong" were replaced with "unhelpful"; however, it was acknowledged that recognising when something was actually wrong was also very important. The sorting out of ideas and how they would be communicated through the reporter, although two different processes, were sometimes melded into one - a process which aided the men in considering the impact of their thoughts and actions on women. The men recognised that, as men, they had all grown up within dominant men's culture. Despite their best intentions and efforts to stand apart from that culture, they knew that they would not always be successful.

The men thought that accountability structures could provide:

- a space where men could acknowledge their continued participation in the dominant male culture, and hear women's experience of men's actions;
- a place where men can examine their own behaviour and make decisions about taking action to change it;
- a way of combining theory and action as part of a process of liberation;
- a general enrichment of relationships;
- a release from the dominant masculine expectation of being "right all the time". Men have grown up with the expectation that they must have the answers to any problem which confronts them, and if they don't, they should pretend that they do. This was generally experienced by the men's caucus as an intolerable burden, which would be considerably lightened by accountability structures;
- a context where trust could be established, so that men could work at

understanding their participation in dominant male culture and hear feedback from women without the fear of "getting it wrong" and being judged negatively;

- a way of demonstrating that acting on women's concerns does not mean reversing positions of power, with men becoming subordinate and women dominant. Rather it provides a way of moving away from relationships based on power to ones based on reciprocity and partnership.

It was interesting and important that, at every reporting back, the people who made up the two gender groups would return to their original seating, which made the context for the feedback a single group of mixed sexes, although the message that they were hearing was that of a particular gender. Dallas and I came to believe that this process of uniting the gender groups between caucusing sessions was vital to the sense of collectivity and to the whole group owning the results of each gender's considerations.

The Women's Response

The women, on hearing the men's comments, were impressed by the similarity of the responses to their own, and felt heartened that the men had been prepared not only to open themselves up to what the process could offer, but also to open themselves up to telling the women what they had thought. They believed accountability partnership structures provided the following advantages:

- A lot less energy would need to be spent on analysis of situations. Finding time/place/ways to be heard and looking after the hearer would no longer be required.
- A greater sense of being valued, of having a bigger voice, of taking up more space. This would be shown by the commitment of the men and by their respectful listening.
- The workplace would be an exciting place to be, with equity and joy part of each day's experience. There would no longer be a constant sense of struggle to be heard.
- Checking concerns with others would help remove self-doubt and validate experiences.
- There would be no sense of wanting to "be on top" or "pay out".
- Men meeting and being proactive as a group is a powerful statement, and an example of men taking responsibility for other men.
- The process would be transformative of women's communication. Respectful listening breeds respectful responses and ways of raising issues.
- The quality of service would be transformed, with greater sense of accountability to clients, and greater energy and joy.

Responsibility

The concern expressed in the workshop that the model of partnership accountability might encourage women to take responsibility for men's behaviour was addressed as an adjunct to the first question.

The women believed that claiming their space, their power, and their experience was not hard work and is theirs to do - it is powerful for women to initiate process/discussion. To raise and identify concerns is taking appropriate responsibility. Warning signs that women may be taking responsibility for men's behaviour may be a flagging energy level. If they feel drained, then they may be doing all the work. Awareness and care for others, with consequent filtering and censoring at the expense of the content, may mean that they have been trapped again. They felt that the process could not work without community and commitment to equity and justice. There may therefore be major difficulties if there is a problem with trust.

The men felt that when women are asked for feedback, it should be made clear that if they did not want to deal with a particular matter immediately, this would be an acceptable response and that men should go back and work on it more among themselves. Men should try to put themselves in women's shoes, attempt to empathise with women's experience and try to think about how their actions or decisions as men might be seen by women before asking for women's feedback. Men also have experienced the effects of abusive power, and can use this experience to work among themselves in order to learn how to use power well. They can be alert to unhelpful practices in themselves and in other, men and challenge those practices, without leaving this to women. When attempting to go beyond dominant male patterns, it is helpful to have a clear view of the goal, and a realisation that effort needs to be put into developing such a vision and seeking out other men who share such a vision.

Working on Direct Concerns in the Workshop

The next phase of the workshop enabled participants to look at an actual issue of a direct concern which would have relevance for all women and men in the workshop and was related to the issues which Dallas and I had raised. Women were asked to consider what their concerns were about men working with men who are violent. The men were asked to consider what women's concerns might be and produced the following list:

- Men might reinforce abusive behaviour by the process used to work with men who are violent, i.e. not what is said, but how it is said.
- If a person has power they can make those with less power think what they want them to think. In teaching "non-violence", there is a danger that what is actually being taught is the superior power of the teacher.

- Men have been trained to respond to violence with violence and to meet force with force. Using this model in working with domestic violence would be entirely inappropriate. What is needed is for men to work in ways which change the whole model. Simply being policemen over the actions of violent men removes the possibility of men taking responsibility for themselves.
- There could be a concern that violent or abusive men would simply be learning how to play the system much more effectively.
- If men are taught the "correct" language about violence and sexism they might simply become more subtle in their harassment. The concept that "knowledge is power" was discussed, and it was said that any kind of teaching which resulted in violent men being able to play the system better was like "giving a gun to a child".
- Male therapists might desire to be a "buddy" to the men they are working with, and put the best possible interpretation on a man's actions. This could outweigh concerns about the safety of those affected by the man's violence. This desire for a "buddy" relationship could undermine the therapist's willingness to take a strong moral stand against the offender's actions. The opinion was expressed that in some circumstances a strong sense of "righteous indignation" was useful and necessary, and that men might be more lacking in this than women.
- There could also be a danger that male workers might unconsciously agree with the perpetrator. They might have some degree of empathy for an offender's anger against women, due to their own socialisation or life experiences.
- A concern was also expressed about the tendency of men's work to be regarded as mysterious and special. If the work being done with violent men was not entirely open and accountable then it could become another area of "men's business" and used as a way of excluding women.

The Women's Concerns About Men Working with Violent Men

The men decided not to comment on the women's concerns as each point was brought up, but to allow the women to present their concerns to the men without interruption.

The women first of all wanted the men to know that they were really glad the men were doing this work. They believed that it is men's responsibility to take on this work, and they were asking that men do it. It was important to the women that these men knew that they were willing to offer partnership and solidarity over the issue. They were concerned that the work that women have done in dealing with the outcomes and the effects of violence be acknowledged; that the work done by women in the shelters and crisis centres not be diminished by men taking on working with violent men and thus being seen as heroes in this work.

The women felt good about men taking on the responsibility of this work and were concerned at the pressure this puts on the small number of men who work in the field. They acknowledged how complicated it is for men to embark on this work with other men. Men have been trained to be separate, and they are being asked to join and work with men against their socialisation. They were concerned that because of men's particular socialisation they may find it hard to talk about their work and to ask for help in this work, and they may not have personal supports in place. Their male socialisation may prevent them from expressing vulnerability and uncertainty regarding their work.

The women were also concerned at the abuse men may perpetrate on each other when they feel that other men "have not got it right"- a disregarding of the perpetrator's experience, or an "out-powering" by the therapist. There was also worry that some men's need to "get it right" would put them under excessive pressure as workers in this area. Men may feel surrounded by these issues even when they come out of the counselling room, and the women wondered what this might mean in terms of burnout. They also wondered whether the socialisation men have undergone to separate theory and practice might lead to a sense of an "artificial remove" - that men might theorise rather than reflect back to their personal experience and this might not be helpful in this work.

The women had some concerns that men who work with men who are violent might "dump" on the perpetrators from the morally high ground. They also expressed concern over the use of humour for joining in a "blokey"[1] way, in that this colludes with the dominant male mode and there is dishonesty or manipulation in it. They nevertheless believed that there are respectful ways of men joining and using humour. They wondered at what happens in the agency as a whole when this work is being done, and whether respectfulness is carried over to other workers, e.g. reception staff.

The Men's Response to Women's Concerns about Men Working with Violent Men

On hearing the women's concerns, the men were truly shocked. They were surprised and moved by the strong expression of appreciation and affirmation. It felt like a true sharing, and there was a feeling of awe at men's responsibilities in working in this area. The men were also very moved by the concern expressed over their wellbeing, and by the recognition of how few men are doing this work. Some men felt moved to tears of joy. It had not occurred to them that women would be concerned at their welfare, and they asked themselves what this said about their expectations of criticism and scepticism. There was a strong sense of relief, and a recognition of how much fear they had felt at times about not being appreciated by women. There was a feeling of happiness, and the women's expression of appreciation took away some of the feeling of isolation that men often experience when standing outside of and against the dominant male culture.

The men were impressed by the overall positive tone of what the women said, and appreciated both the expression of support and the non-judgmental expression of concerns. This felt like a very new experience. There was a sense of safety and of being trusted, but also a nice sense of vulnerability. The men felt they could be more open about the vulnerability they were experiencing in working in this area and that this would be respected. There was also a sense that the men would be prepared to take a few more risks in their work. They recognised the concerns expressed about the possibility of male therapists "out-powering" the men they were working with and this coincided with some of the discussion in the men's caucus.

The women's concerns about "bloke humour"[2] left the men feeling somewhat perplexed. They felt that they had no clear idea of how to get inside the women's experience of what is and is not "bloke humour". However, a common point was the recognition of how important it is to hear women's experience of men's humour. The men were struck by the women's point about the need to recognise the range of women working in the domestic violence area and their concerns for the safety of support staff. They also recognised and appreciated their concern that men working in this area might be seen as heroes and be set up as the "goodies" against the "baddies" with whom they are working.

In discussing the benefits of the workshop, there was no dispute about the fact that the process had worked and that the women and men who had participated felt they had had their concerns heard in new and significant ways. They felt more appreciated by the other gender than before, and obviously closer to new joint understandings of ways of working together. There was also an increased appreciation of ways of working which were separate, yet still took into account the concerns of the other. The men felt they were being left to come up with their own ways of working and their own appreciations - yet not in isolation or separate from, but with a new sensitivity to, women's understandings and women's experience.

Conclusions

Dallas and I had made a number of important discoveries, but also had been confirmed in some of our decisions about the process. It was indeed possible to take people of goodwill but limited understanding and introduce them to partnership accountability. It was possible to have them work around a specific worthwhile issue and introduce an understanding of partnership which was genuine and productive but which did not necessarily mean engaging in a full expose of personal beliefs. We believe this approach could be used in a number of environments.

The process experienced by Cheryl and Maggie where the men spoke in front of the women was most appropriate for the group they were dealing with and helped face the issues they wanted dealt with. However, for the participants in the workshop, it was important for the genders not to engage in group discussion of the issues in front of each other. For a closer knit group however, this could be helpful. Having someone to monitor the process through the role of chairperson, and also having a recorder in each group is important. The questions asked and the frame in which the feedback is offered can add to the sense of partnership and the sense of resolution rather than of "dumping". The energy which people derived from the process appeared to encourage further communication between the genders and a new resolve to work together, to consider the views of the other in their work, and to seek out partnership and what it could offer, rather than continue to work in isolation or in fear of criticism.

My experiences thus far with partnership accountability suggest the model does offer a challenge to the tendency to reproduce dominant cultures, and it certainly offers hope that real partnership across the divide of the powerful and the less powerful can be achieved.

Postscript

The writing of this paper has been a process of regular consultation with as many of the people referred to in the article as possible. Tamasese & Waldegrave (in personal communication) appreciated the content of the paper and the way the article furthered the concept of accountability first developed by The Family Centre. They encouraged me to refer to the process of writing the document as a further example of the equity process. In addition, Cheryl White, as editor of the Dulwich Centre Newsletter, already had in place an editorial policy that facilitates this process in all material they publish:

> Where people's actions are under discussion in the literature without their permission - no matter who they are and what is being said - these people are at the mercy of the writer's descriptions about their behaviour. Rather than being active in the story, they are rendered passive bystanders - their experience is appropriated by the writer. This constitutes an act of power over others. (White & Kamsler 1990, p.23)

It was realised, from the beginning, that reading this paper and seeing it in print was likely to be a painful process for some people. The events which prompted Cheryl and Maggie to call the first meeting were difficult enough at the time, and there was a danger of seeming to be opening old wounds for those people who had not been involved in the ongoing accountability process.

However, despite some trepidation, copies of the paper, from first-draft stage, were sent to as many people as possible who had been involved in the events discussed, and the resulting consultations actually led to a reopening of dialogue that was gratifying and somewhat surprising to all involved.

I feel compelled to end the article with an anecdote. At the end of a day's presentation in Canada on the concepts of responsibility and partnership accountability, I decided to finish the presentation with an exercise. Everyone was willing and the exercise was meant to go like this: the men in the room were to sit out the front in a circle and to discuss what using the concept of partnership accountability might mean to women. Once we sat down I, as leader, was asked to clarify the question for discussion and I changed it to an easier question and that was: what would it mean to the men if they were to adopt practices that worked in a partnership accountable way. The men spent time answering the second question. We left the room for the women to caucus in privacy so as to prepare to give us feedback. On returning to the room the women criticised the change in question and I immediately realised my mistake. Some of the women felt cheated that the question had been changed in a direction that made it more self-centred and easier for the men to answer - and they had been genuinely interested in hearing the men answer the first question.

On reflection I see that both questions are worthwhile, but the original one had been set for the very purposes that the women identified, and was central to the whole concept of partnership accountability. Men are generally quite capable of thinking about the benefits to themselves of any particular situation, but much less able to put themselves in women's position. It is crucial to keep in mind that partnership accountability is primarily about redressing the effects of oppression, and the silencing of less powerful voices that this entails. The ease with which we, as men, shifted away from women's experience, and back to our own, was itself a powerful demonstration of the need for these accountability structures. As it turned out, the participants generally felt the process successfully allowed this to be addressed - the women had the opportunity to let me and the men know of their disappointment and to help sensitise us to the true and significant meaning of the change that could have been seen as trivial to the dominant group.

Editorial Comment

The primary purpose of accountability structures, as outlined in this paper, is to allow structurally less powerful groups to have their voices listened to, understood, and responded to. There are also concrete benefits for the dominant group which Rob Hall's article explores in some depth. However, it is important to not lose sight of the reason for accountability structures - the need to shift our attention away from the concerns and viewpoints of the dominant group to make space for those who have historically been silenced.

To explore these issues and to consider the outcomes now that 12 months had passed, I approached Maggie Carey and Cheryl White, who were central in calling one of the gender-accountability meetings discussed by Rob Hall in his paper. I asked them about what they wanted from the meeting and about their experience of the process. I was interested to know whether their hopes were realised, whether they had felt any concerns about what might happen in the meeting, and what had made it possible for them to feel safe enough to go ahead with the process.

As outlined by Rob, Maggie and Cheryl had been involved in trying to raise concerns about a series of letters, which they and many others considered to be sexist, which had been published in an otherwise pro-feminist newsletter, that women's experience of raising gender issues with men individually can often be problematic and, in this case, it was hoped that the accountability process might be able to provide an opportunity to really be heard by men *as a group*.

Maggie and Cheryl were clear that their concerns were not simply the result of individual, personal experiences, but were part of women's shared experience of attempting to speak out in a male-dominated culture. They were not looking for an opportunity to simply share feelings, and did not want the men to respond primarily to the emotional content of what was said, but to really look at the gender issues involved. They wanted the men to look at their own actions, and were certainly not going to them out of a need for help, or to be rescued.

Thus, the issue was clear. What was wanted was to experience being heard and understood by a group of men. They wanted evidence that this was possible by hearing their collective experience as women being reflected back to them in a way that demonstrated men's collective capacity for empathy, and a willingness to acknowledge mistakes and difficulties. Most of all, it was important that the men demonstrate a willingness to take action on the basis of what they heard.

Both Maggie and Cheryl had heard about the accountability process at The Family Centre in New Zealand (see Tamasese & Waldegrave 1993). They had been most impressed by it and were keen to try it out for themselves. Their willingness to call a meeting and present their experience to a group of men was due, largely, to a confidence in the process itself. They believed that it actually enabled groups from different positions of power to treat each other respectfully and to gain an insight into each other's experience. Added to this was their trust in each other. Acting as a group (even if it was only a group of two!) allowed a strength and confidence that would not have been available to an individual.

There was certainly also a trust in the men's openness and desire to make the process work, but it was not a case of simply choosing men with whom they felt completely safe. The men had taken a variety of positions at the time of the published letters, and Cheryl and Maggie were not in a position to feel absolutely sure about how all of the men would respond.

As it turned out, Maggie and Cheryl found the experience healing to an extent that was quite unexpected. They observed the men genuinely grappling with the issues that had been raised, and relating them to their own lives. It was important to see this happening collectively, as the men shared their fears and mistakes, and demonstrated a genuine commitment to dealing with what were often quite painful realisations. It was a truly significant experience to participate in a meeting that generated a high level of intimacy, while remaining firmly focussed on the central issues. While this process worked very effectively in this instance, it is important to point out that in most cases the members of the dominant group should initially process their responses separately. Doing this in the presence of the marginalised group can often be counter-productive, as members of the dominant group generally have not spent much time or effort really thinking through the issues, and are likely to make unconsidered comments, which are likely to polarise relationships between the two groups. (See Callie, 1994)

Finally, it is important to emphasise here that the accountability process does not stop with the meeting itself. Action on the part of the dominant group must result, or it becomes a "feel-good" exercise for those with power, and a painful experience of wasted self-revelation for those without. In this case, 12 months down the track both Maggie and Cheryl feel that what they wanted has occurred - the men have demonstrated a greater readiness to take action publicly, to challenge men's sexist behaviour, and have shown a real energy and willingness to work in solidarity with women in doing so.

CMcL

Notes

1. Male manner, often with sexist overtones.
2. Male humour, often with sexist overtones.

References

Atkinson, B. & Heath, A. 1987. "Beyond Objectivism & Relativism: Implications for Family Therapy Research." *Journal of Strategic & Systemic Therapies*, 6(1):8-18.

Apple, M. 1992. "Educational Reform and Educational Crisis." *Journal of Research in Science Training*, 29(8):779-789.

Australian Bureau of Statistics 1993. *Women in Australia*, Canberra.

Belenky M.T., Clinchy, B.M., Goldberger, N.R. & Tarule, J.M. 1986. *Women's Ways of Knowing: The Development of Self, Voice and Mind*. New York: Basic Books.

Berg, R. 1990. "Sexuality: Why Do Women Come Off Second Best?" in Grieve, N. & Burns, A., eds, *Australian Women: New Feminist Perspectives*. Pp.155-170. Melbourne: Oxford University Press.

Billig, M., Condors, S., Edwards, D., Gane, M., Middleton, D. & Radley, A. 1988. *Ideological Dilemmas: A Social Psychology of Everyday Thinking*. London: Sage.

Bird, J. 1992. "Are You Interested In Men? The Impact of Gender Socialisation on Our Work With Men." Workshop at the 2nd Australian & New Zealand Family Therapy Conference, Melbourne.

Bly, R. 1990. *Iron John*. New York: Vantage Books, Random House Inc.

Bly, R. 1991. *Iron John*. Longmead, Dorset: Element Books.

Bly, R. 1992. *Iron John*. New York: Vantage Books.

Bowen, M. 1978. *Family Therapy in Clinical Practice*. New York: Jason Aronson.

Boyd-Franklin, N. 1989. *Black Families in Therapy: A Multisystems Approach*. New York: Guilford.

Brod, H., ed, 1987. *The Making of Masculinities: The New Men's Studies*. Cambridge, MA: Unwin Hyman.

Bruner, E. 1986. "Ethnography as Narrative", in Turner, V. & Bruner, E., eds, *The Anthropology of Experience*. Chicago: University of Illinois Press.

Bruner, J. 1986. *Actual Minds, Possible Worlds*. Cambridge, Mass: Harvard University Press.

Bruner, J. 1990. *Acts of Meaning*. Cambridge, Mass: Harvard University Press.

Butler, J. 1989. "Gendering the Body: Beauvoir's Philosophical Contribution", in Garry, A. & Pearsall, M., eds, *Women, Knowledge, and Reality*. Boston: Unwin Hyman.

Callie, A. 1994. "Pain, Hope and Heterosexual Dominance." *Dulwich Centre Newsletter*, Nos.2&3.

Caputi, J. & MacKenzie, G.O. 1992. "Pumping Iron John", in Hagan, K.L. ed, *Women Respond to the Men's Movement*. San Francisco: Harper.

Carrigan, T., Connell, R.W. & Lee, J. 1987. "Towards a New Sociology of Masculinity", in Brod, H., ed, *The Making of Masculinities: The New Men's Studies*. USA: Allen & Unwin.

Chodorow, N. 1978. *The Reproduction of Mothering: Psychoanalysis and the Sociology of Gender*. Berkeley: University of California Press.

Clark, M. 1989. *The Great Divide: Gender in the Primary School*. Victoria, Australia: Curriculum Corporation.

Connell, R.W. 1987. *Gender and Power: Society, the Person and Sexual Politics*. Australia: Allen & Unwin.

_____ . 1989. "Cool Guys, Swots and Wimps: The Interplay of Masculinity and Education", *Oxford Review of Education*, 15(3):291-303.

_____ . 1991. "Live Fast and Die Young: The Construction of Masculinity Among Young Working-Class Men on the Margin of the Labour Market", *Australian & New Zealand Journal of Family Therapy*, No 2, August, pp.141-171.

_____ . 1992. "Drumming up the Wrong Tree." Tikkun, Feb/March.

_____ . 1993. "The Big Picture: Masculinities in Recent World History." Theory and Society, 22:597-623.

_____ . 1994. "Knowing About Masculinity: Teaching Boys and Men." Paper for Pacific Sociological Association Conference, San Diego, April.

Connell, R.W., Ashendon, D.J., Kessler, S. & Dowsett, G.W. 1982. *Making the Difference: Schools, Families and Social Division*. Sydney: Allen & Unwin.

Crawford, J. et al 1992. *Emotion and Gender: Constructing Meaning From Memory*. London: Sage.

Davies, B. 1993. *Shards of Glass*. Sydney: Allen & Unwin.

Davies, B. & Banks, C. 1993. "Zum Mann Werden", In Psychologie & Gesellschaftskritik, 17(3/4):5-24.

Durie, M.H. 1986. *Maori Health: Contemporary Issues and Responses*. Mental Health Foundation of New Zealand.

Ehrenreich, B. 1983. *The Hearts of Men*. Great Britain: Pluto Press.

Falenaoti, M.T. 1992. *Sina e Saili*. In press.

Farrell, W. 1975. *The Liberated Man*. New York: Bantam Books.

_____ . 1994. *The Myth of Male Power*. Sydney: Random House.

Fitzclarence, L. 1993. "Violence in Schools." *Education Links*, 46, Spring, pp.16-18.

Fletcher, R. 1994. *Boys Education Strategy 1995?* Discipline of Paediatrics, Uni. of Newcastle, NSW.

Foucault, M. 1973. *The Birth of The Clinic: An Archaeology of Medical Perception*. London: Tavistock.

Foucault, M. 1979. *Discipline & Punish: The Birth of the Prison.* Middlesex: Peregrine Books.

———. 1980. *Power/Knowledge: Selected Interviews and Other Writings.* New York: Pantheon Books.

———. 1984. *The History of Sexuality.* Great Britain: Peregrine Books.

———. 1988. "The Political Technology of Individuals", In Martin, L.H., Gutman, H. & Hutton, P.H., eds, *Technologies of the Self: A Seminar With Michele Foucault.* Amherst: University of Massachusetts Press.

Frank, B. 1993. "Straight/Strait Jackets for Nasculinity: Educating for "Real" Men." *Atlantis*, 18(1&2):47-59.

French, M. 1991. *Beyond Power: On Women, Men and Morals.* London: Cardinal.

Freud, S. 1925. "1933 New Introductory Lectures", In *Some Psychical Consequences of the Anatomical Distinction Between the Sexes.* Standard Edition of the Complete Psychological Works. London: Hogarth Press & Institute of Psycho-Analysis.

Gatens, M. 1986. "Feminism, Philosophy and Riddles Without Answers", in Pateman, C. & Gross, E., eds, *Feminist Challenges: Social and Political Theory.* Sydney: Allen & Unwin, pp.13-29.

Geertz, C. 1983. *Local Knowledge: Further Essays in Interpretive Anthropology.* New York: Basic Books.

———. 1988. *Works & Lives: The Anthropologist as Author.* Stanford CA: Stanford University Press.

Gilligan, C. 1982. *In A Different Voice: Psychological Theory & Women's Development.* Cambridge, MA: Harvard University Press.

Gilmore, D. 1990. *Manhood in the Making: Cultural Concepts of Masculinity.* Birmingham, NY: Vail-Ballov Press.

Goldner, V. 1985. "Feminism and Family Therapy." *Family Process*, 24:31-47.

———. 1992. "Making Room For Both/And." *The Family Therapy Networker*, 16:2.

Grieve, N. & Burns, A., eds, 1990. *Australian Women: New Feminist Perspectives.* Melbourne: Oxford University Press.

Gurnoe, S. & Nelson, J. 1989. "Two Perspectives on Working with American Indian Families: A Constructivist-Systemic Approach", in Gonzales-Santin, E., ed, *Collaboration: The Key.* Arizona State University School of Social Work: Tempe.

Hagan, K.L., ed, 1992. *Women Respond to the Men's Movement.* San Francisco: Harper.

Hall, R. 1994. "Partnership Accountability." *Dulwich Centre Newsletter*, Nos.2&3.

Harre Hindmarsh, J. 1987 [formerly Pilalis, J.]. "Letting Gender Secrets Out of the Bag." *Australian & New Zealand Jnl. of Fam. Therapy*, 8(4):205-211.

House of Representatives Standing Committee on Legal and Constitutional

Affairs, 1992. *Half Way to Equal: Report of the Inquiry Into Equal Opportunity and Status For Women in Australia.* Canberra: AGPS.

Hughes, A. 1992. "If we are a movement." *XY Magazine*, Autumn.

Hunter, A. 1992. "Same Door, Different Closet: A Heterosexual Sissy's Coming-Out Party." *Feminism & Psychology*, 2(3):367-385.

Jenkins, A. 1990. *Invitations to Responsibility: The Therapeutic Engagement of Men Who Are Violent and Abusive.* Adelaide: Dulwich Centre Publications.

Kamsler, A. 1990. "Her-Story in the Making: Therapy With Women Who Were Sexually Abused in Childhood", in White, C. & Durrant, M., eds, *Ideas for Therapy with Sexual Abuse.* Adelaide: Dulwich Centre Publications.

Karp, S. 1994. "The politics of education: An Interview with Herbert Kohl." *Z Magazine*, April, pp.19-24.

Keen, S. 1992. *Fire in the Belly: On Being a Man.* New York: Bantam Books.

Kenway, J. 1990. *Gender and Education Policy: A Call For New Directions.* Geelong: Deakin University Press.

Kenway, J. 1994. "Presentation to the NSW Government Advisory Committee Inquiry", in Lemaire, J., ed, *Girls, Boys and Equity.* Sydney: NSW Teachers Federation Centre for Teaching and Learning.

Kimmel, M.S., ed, 1987a. "The Contemporary Crisis of Masculinity in Historical Perspective", in Brod, H., ed, *The Making of Masculinities: The New Men's Studies.* Pp121-153. Cambridge MA: Allen & Unwin.

Kimmel, M.S., ed, 1987b. *Changing Men: New Dimensions in Research on Men and Masculinity.* Newbury Pk, CA: Sage.

Kohlberg, L. 1963. "The Development of Children's Orientations Toward Moral Order: I. Sequence in the Development of Moral Thought." *Vita Humana*, 6:11-33.

Lakoff, J. & Johnson, M. 1980. *Metaphors We Live By.* Chicago: University of Chicago Press.

Lewis, P.M. 1991. "Mummy, Matron and the Maids: Feminine Presence and Absence in Male Institutions, 1934-63", in Roper, M. & Tosh, J., eds, *Manful Assertions: Masculinities in Britain since 1800.* Pp.168-189. London: Routledge.

Luepnitz, D.A. 1988 *The Family Interpreted.* New York: Basic Books.

Martin, R. 1993. "Violence in Australian sschools." Paper presented at Second National Conference on Violence, 15-18 June, Canberra.

Maslow, A.H. 1968. *Toward a Psychology of Being.* New York: Van Nostrand.

Maturana, H. & Varela, F. 1988. *The Tree of Knowledge.* New Science Library: Shambhala.

McCann, T. 1992. "In a Passionate Voice." *XY Magazine*, Autumn.

McClintock, A. 1993. "Gonad the Barbarian and the Venus Flytrap: Portraying the Male and Female Orgasm", in Segal, L. & McIntosh, M., eds, *Sex Exposed: Sexuality and the Pornography Debate.* Pp.111-131. New Brunswick, NJ: Rutgers University Press.

McGoldrick, M., Pearce, J.K. & Giordano, J. 1982. *Ethnicity and Family Therapy*. New York: Guilford.

McKinnon, L. & Miller, D. 1987. "The New Epistemology and the Milan Approach: Feminist and Sociopolitical Considerations." *Journal of Marital & Family Therapy*, 13(2):139-155.

Middleton, P. 1992. *The Inward Gaze: Masculinity and Subjectivity in Modern Culture*. London: Routledge.

Miles, R. 1991. *The Rites of Man: Love, Sex and Death in the Making of the Male*. London: Grafton.

Nelson, J. 1992. *Male Sexuality, Masculine Spirituality*. London: SPCK. (First published 1988, Philadelphia: Westminster Press.)

New South Wales Standing Committee on Social Issues, 1993. Youth Violence Issues Paper No.1, September.

Nichols, J. 1975. *Men's Liberation: A New Definition of Masculinity*. Middlesex, UK: Harmondsworth.

Parker, I. & Shotter, J., eds, 1990. *Deconstructing Social Psychology*. London: Routledge.

Pleck, J.H. 1987. "The Theory of Male Sex-Role Identity: Its Rise and Fall, 1936 to the Present", in Brod, H., ed, *The Making of Masculinities: The new men's studies*. Pp21-38. Cambridge MA: Allen & Unwin.

Prescott, J.W. 1975. "Body Pleasure and the Origins of Violence." *The Futurist*, 9(2):64-74.

Roper, M. & Tosh, J., eds, 1991. *Manful Assertions: Masculinities in Britain Since 1800*. London: Routledge.

Sarbin, T.R., ed, 1986. *Narrative Psychology: The Storied Nature of Human Conduct*. New York: Praeger.

Sawicki, J. 1991. *Disciplining Foucault: Feminism, Power, and the Body*. New York: Routledge.

Segal, L. 1990. *Slow Motion: Changing Masculinities, Changing Men*. London: Virago.

Segal, L. 1993. "Sweet Sorrows, Painful Pleasures: Pornography and the Perils of Heterosexual Desire", in Segal, L. & McIntosh, M., eds, *Sex Exposed: Sexuality and the Pornography Debate*. Pp.65-91. New Brunswick, NJ: Rutgers University Press.

Segal, L. & McIntosh, M., eds, 1993. *Sex Exposed: Sexuality and the Pornography Debate*. New Brunswick, NJ: Rutgers University Press.

Silverstein, O. & Rashbaum, B. 1994. *The Courage to Raise Good Men*. New York: Viking.

Smith, G. 1992. "Dichotomies in the Making of Men." *Dulwich Centre Newsletter*, Nos.3&4, pp.9-23.

Somerville, J. 1989. "The Sexuality of Men and the Sociology of Gender." *The Sociological Review*, 37(2):pp.277-307.

Spender, D. 1980. *Man Made Language*. London: Routledge & Kegan Paul.

Spretnak, C. 1992. "Treating the Symptoms, Ignoring the Cause", in Hagan, K.L., ed, Women Respond to the Men's Movement. San Francisco: Harper.

Stoltenberg, J. 1989. *Refusing To Be A Man*. London: Fontana.

_____ . 1990. *Refusing To Be A Man*. Glasgow: Fontana.

Stone, L. 1992. "Dry Heat, Cool Reason: Historians Under Siege in England and France." *Times Literary Supplement*, Jan 31, p.3.

Tacey, D. 1991. "How New is the New Male?" *Australian Society*, June.

Tamasese, K. & Waldegrave, C. 1993. "Cultural and Gender Accountability in the 'Just Therapy' Approach." Journal of Feminist Family Therapy, 5(2):29-45. Republished 1994 in Dulwich Centre Newsletter, 2&3:55-67.

The Advertiser, 1993. Adelaide, South Australia. 12th January.

The Gen, 1994. "What about the boys?" March, Commonwealth Department of Employment, Education and Training, ACT.

Tiefer, L. 1987. "In Pursuit of the Perfect Penis: The Medicalization of Male Sexuality", in Kimmel, M.S., ed, *Changing Men: New dimensions in research on men and masculinity,* Pp165-184. Newbury Pk, CA: Sage.

Tomm, W. 1987. "Myths, Attitudes & Social Realities: Woman's Nature". One day workshop presented in Adelaide, South Australia.

Townsend, H. 1994. *Real Men*, Sydney: Harper Collins.

Uhr, J. 1993. "Redesigning Accountability." *Australian Quarterly*, Winter, Pp.1-16.

Vance, C.S. 1984. "Pleasure and Danger: Toward a Politics of Sexuality", in Vance, C.S., ed, *Pleasure and Danger: Exploring Female Sexuality*. Pp.1-27. Boston, MA: Routledge.

Waldegrave, C.T. 1986. "Mono-Cultural, Mono-Class, and So-Called Non-Political Family Therapy." *Australian & New Zealand Journal of Family Therapy*, 6(4):197-200.

_____ . 1989."Weaving Threads of Meaning and Distinguishing Preferable Patterns." Plenary, 1st Australia & New Zealand family therapy conference.

_____ . 1990. "Just Therapy." *Dulwich Centre Newsletter*, No.1, pp.5-46.

Waldegrave, C. & Tamasase, K. 1992. "Social Justice." Plenary address to the Australian & New Zealand Family Therapy Conference, Melbourne.

Walker, K. 1994. "Men, Women, and Friendship: What They Say and What They Do." *Gender & Society*, 8(2):246-265.

Walters, M. 1993. "Co-Dependent Cinderella and Iron John." *Family Therapy Networker*, March/April, Pp.60-65.

Walters, M., Carter, B., Papp, P. & Silverstein, O. 1988. *The Invisible Web*. New York: Guilford.

Warren, M.A. 1990. "The Social Construction of Sexuality", in Grieve, N. & Burns, A., eds, *Australian Women: New Feminist Perspectives*, Pp.142-154. Melbourne: Oxford University Press.

Wendt, A. 1991. *Ola*. Penguin.

West, P. 1994a. "The SON also must RISE." *Sydney Morning Herald*, 22 July,
    p.12.

_____. 1994b. "It's Time to Talk." *Sydney Morning Herald*, 18 March,
    p.15.

Wexler, P. 1992. *Becoming Somebody: Toward a Social Psychology of School*.
    London: Falmer Press.

White, C. & Kamsler, A. 1990. "An Open Invitation to Formulate Policies
    Around Publishing." *Dulwich Centre Newsletter*, No.3, pp.22-24.

White, K. 1993. *The First Sexual Revolution: The Emergence of Male
    Heterosexuality in Modern America*. New York: New York University Press.

White, M. 1988. "Saying Hullo Again: The Incorporation of the Lost
    Relationship in the Resolution of Grief." *Dulwich Centre Newsletter*.
    Republished 1989 in White, M., Selected Papers. Adelaide: Dulwich Centre
    Publications.

_____. 1989. "Family Therapy Training and Supervision in a World of
    Experience and Narrative." *Dulwich Centre Newsletter*. Republished 1992 in
    Epston, D. & White, M., Experience, Contradiction, Narrative &
    Imagination. Adelaide: Dulwich Centre Publications.

_____. 1991. "Deconstruction and Therapy." *Dulwich Centre Newsletter*,
    No.3. Republished 1992 in Epston, D. & White, M., Experience,
    Contradiction, Narrative & Imagination. Adelaide: Dulwich Centre
    Publications.

_____. 1992. "Men's Culture, the Men's Movement, and the Constitution
    of Men's Lives." *Dulwich Centre Newsletter*, Nos.3&4.

_____. 1993. One Week Intensive Training Workshop, at Dulwich Centre,
    Adelaide, South Australia.

White, M. & Epston, D. 1990. *Narrative Means to Therapeutic Ends*. New
    York: W.W.Norton.

Wittgenstein, L. 1953. *Philosophical Investigations*. Oxford: Basil Blackwell.

Zinsmeister, K. 1993. "The Need for Fathers." *IPA Review*, 46(1):43-46.

About the Editors and Contributors

Maggie Carey works as a family therapist, and divides her time between an inner-city agency in Adelaide, an outer-suburban health service, and a community centre for Aboriginal people. Her approach to therapy challenges individualised constructions of problems in people's lives, particularly with those people who have been disempowered by social and political systems. Her concern with exploring issues of masculinity arose out of intense personal, political and professional involvement in this area.

Laurence Carter, a counsellor and educator at the Bouverie Family Therapy Centre in Melbourne, has been working in the areas of HIV and sexuality. More recently he has been particularly interested in an analysis of sexuality issues based on concepts of heterosexual dominance.

David Denborough is involved in working with men and boys in a variety of contexts: he has participated in the National Gender and Violence Project, organised by the Australian Department of Employment, Education and Training; he works as an educator in a maximum security prison; runs anti-violence workshops in New South Wales' secondary schools; and is a member of Sydney Men Against Sexual Assault. He is currently involved in a research project investigating ways of challenging and changing the culture of masculinity in schools.

Rob Hall has been providing and developing services for men who are abusive since he began his work in a crisis organisation in 1981. He has always sought to make his work responsive to those who have experienced abuse. He formed a multi-agency reference group that became a model for the initiation and co-ordination of many preventative programs throughout South Australia. Recently Rob Hall and Alan Jenkins, along with 3 others, formed a privately funded organisation called "Nada". Nada's services focus on respectful gender-based intervention, prevention and training in the fields of family abuse, school and work-based harassment.

Alan Jenkins is a clinical psychologist with 15 years of experience in working in the area of violence and abuse within families. He has developed models of working with men and boys who have been physically or sexually abusive which have been adopted by domestic violence and sexual abuse treatment and prevention services in many parts of Australia, North America and New Zealand. He is particularly concerned with developing ways of being accountable in this work to victims of abuse and to the wider community. His therapeutic approach is detailed in his book *Invitations to Responsibility: The Therapeutic Engagement of Men Who are Violent and Abusive* (1990). Alan regularly conducts workshops and training presentations, and consults to a variety of organisations, throughout USA, Canada, United Kingdom, and New Zealand.

Ian Law lives and works in Adelaide, South Australia, and works as a counsellor and training-provider, both in independent practice and for the Adelaide Central Mission. As an alternative to pathological construction of problems, Ian applies a competency based approach to his work in such areas as problem gambling, substitute care, child abuse, male violence, parenting, and problems of childhood, relationships and mental health.

Peter Lee lives in Adelaide, South Australia, and has been involved in men's groups since the mid 1970s. He was one of the founders of the Adelaide Men's Contact and Resource Centre, the first men's centre in Australia. He has been a lecturer in law at the University of South Australia since 1979, where he has chosen to work 3/4 time, initially so that he could share household responsibilities and the parenting of his two children, and more recently so that he could maintain some balance in his life and leave some time for himself.

Christopher McLean is currently completing his PhD researching the social construction of middle-class masculinity in Australia, and is on the editorial board of Dulwich Centre Publications. He has worked as a secondary teacher, and has a special interest in issues concerning children's rights. His involvement with gender issues was initially stimulated by the experience of being a single parent of a daughter.

Gregory Smith is a psychologist and a co-director of Dulwich Centre. He is involved in a wide range of counselling, and is joint co-ordinator of the Graduate Diploma of Narrative Therapy offered at Dulwich Centre. He has been extensively involved in teaching and consulting about work with adolescents and their families, and is currently pursuing interests around the social construction of emotions and the relationship between dialogue, empowerment and possibility.

Kiwi Tamasese is a Samoan woman and co-ordinator of the Pacific Island Section of The Family Centre in New Zealand. She is a cultural consultant to the family therapists at the Centre; a Pacific Island community development worker; a social policy analyst; and has published a number of papers on social policy and family therapy subjects. Kiwi is contracted regularly to run workshops in Australia, Africa, North America, the Pacific, and Europe, in the fields of family therapy, community development, and social policy analysis.

Charles Waldegrave is a family therapist and a social policy consultant at The Family Centre in New Zealand. He has published extensively in the fields of social policy and family therapy, and has co-authored a book: *Poor New Zealand: An Open Letter on Poverty*. He also heads the Social Policy Research Unit at The Family Centre. Charles is an Anglican priest and a psychologist, and regularly runs workshops in Australia, Africa, North America, the Pacific, and Europe, in the fields of family therapy, community development and social policy analysis.

Elizabeth Biff Ward is a feminist, or, more accurately (as Biff says), a proponent of one or more of the possible feminisms at any given moment. She has been an activist, especially around sexual violence and anti-militarist issues, since she was seventeen, and is now a member of the Australian Non-Violence Network. She is also an educator, trainer, writer and mother of three grown children.

Cheryl White is the editor of Dulwich Centre Publications.

Michael White is a co-director of Dulwich Centre in Adelaide, where he works both as a therapist and a lecturer in a post-graduate training course in Narrative Therapy. He has been actively involved in developing the narrative approach to therapy, and his work has been widely published in a number of languages around the world. He has been particularly interested in exploring the ways in which therapeutic approaches may inadvertently reproduce unhelpful or oppressive aspects of dominant culture. Michael is regularly invited to give presentations in the United States, Europe, Scandinavia, South America, Asia, and Africa.

About the Book

This book addresses many of the crucial questions confronting gender studies. The readings included here have emerged from the experiences of men and women struggling to make sense of the impact of the men's movement on their individual lives and on their communities.

Blending theory and practice and informed largely by postmodern and social contructionist perspectives, the chapters bring together personal issues and political concerns against a background of therapeutic and political approaches to change. The overall tone is hopeful, providing practical ways to move forward. However, issues of structured power, inequality, and oppression are firmly faced. Balancing these issues is the clearly empathetic understanding of the predicaments faced by men in their everyday lives. The editors are careful to offer an even-handed analysis of men's concerns without compromising women's struggle for gender justice.

Index